To Cal Stault,

For your interest in
and support of other
cultural and other
languages.

Dick Williamson
8 March 1988

About the Northeast Conference

Established in 1954 as an outgrowth of the Yale-Barnard Conference on the Teaching of French, the Conference has focused on effective learning of languages, all those commonly taught in this country, ancient and modern, including English to Speakers of Other Languages.

In preparation for each annual Conference, the Chairman, with the approval of the Board of Directors, chooses a theme and appoints a team of authors to research and write on different facets of the theme. These essays comprise the Northeast Conference *Reports* which serve as the basis for the Conference, keynote speech, workshops, and panels. The *Reports* are mailed to preregistrants one month in advance of the Conference.

In addition to the concurrent and general sessions, there are preconference workshops, film and video showings, and exhibits of textbooks and other teaching aids. The Conference is supported by hundreds of schools, colleges, and educational associations. Representatives of these institutional members form the Advisory Council, whose members meet at the end of each Conference to elect new Directors.

Over the years the Conference has become the largest and most influential gathering of foreign language educators in the country. Some 3,000 teachers, chairmen, and supervisors from across the nation and many foreign countries now attend each annual meeting. The Northeast Conference has encouraged and aided the formation of other similar regional associations: the Southern Conference on Language Teaching in 1965 and the Central States Conference on the Teaching of Foreign Languages in 1968.

The Conference has numerous awards: among them are the annual Stephen A. Freemen Award for a published article on teaching techniques, the Foreign Language Advocate Award for contribution to the profession by an outsider, and the Northeast Conference Award for Distinguished Service and Leadership in the Profession presented in memory of Nelson H. Brooks.

The Northeast Conference is an organizational member of the American Council on the Teaching of Foreign Languages, the Joint National Committee for Languages, and the National Federation of Modern Language Teachers Associations.

NORTHEAST CONFERENCE ON THE TEACHING OF FOREIGN LANGUAGES

TOWARD A NEW INTEGRATION OF LANGUAGE AND CULTURE

Alan J. Singerman, Editor
Richard C. Williamson, Chairman
1988

Additional copies of the Northeast Conference *Reports*
for the years since 1954 may be
purchased from:

Northeast Conference
Box 623
Middlebury, VT 05753

Write for a current listing.

Library of Congress Catalogue Card Number 55-34379
ISBN 0-915432-88-9

3

Contents

Preface

Almost thirty years ago, just when the audio-lingual movement was spreading across the United States, Edward T. Hall stated in his groundbreaking work, *The Silent Language:* "Culture is communication and communication is culture." Because foreign language teachers had engaged themselves energetically in the search for authentic oral language practices, we did not pay much attention to Hall's tautological statement; it seemed fairly obvious anyway. Nor did we concern ourselves too greatly with Hall's "silent" language; our goal, after all, was to make our students communicate in "loud" language.

Today, as we begin to understand more clearly the very nature of "proficiency" in language skills and are developing effective tests to measure it, we need to re-explore the complex role of culture in our foreign language classes. Is it possible for one to learn a language without learning about its cultural aspects? What is the essential relationship of language and culture? How can we integrate the two in our teaching, to foster a more genuine understanding and command of the foreign speech act? And is it not crucial for our students at all levels to learn *how* to learn about a new culture, even if they intend to complete only a two-year sequence of language study?

Indeed, many questions need to be posed. Both in this volume of the *Reports* and at the 1988 Northeast Conference itself, colleagues with rich insights into culture and language will assist us in formulating the types of questions we must ask if we hope to effect the new integration evoked in the Conference theme. We know how a properly phrased question can lead us to answers, or can help us focus more clearly on a problem. The Northeast Conference exists precisely to create a forum in which foreign language professionals can ask pertinent questions, seek answers, and discuss concerns. I am confident that this volume and the 1988 Conference workshops will add much to our understanding of culturo-linguistic relationships. The Board of Directors and I take this opportunity to thank and commend the scholars who have generously contributed their time and expertise to this challenging and enriching venture.

Richard C. Williamson, *1988 Conference Chairman*
Bates College

Introduction

One fact has become abundantly clear in the last few decades: cultural study is no longer the exclusive province of the professional ethnographers; small "c" culture has found a second home in the foreign language classroom. Foreign language specialists are learning that we too can be competent and effective teachers of the social customs, cultural values, and indigenous idiosyncracies which inform and illuminate our target languages. Some would say "must be," for few doubt today the cultural nature of language. A consensus has gradually formed around the notion that our students can achieve authentic communicative competence in a foreign language only if they learn to understand the target culture at the same time; that is, if they learn the language in its cultural dimensions. This basic premise is both the inspiration for and unifying principle of the 1988 *Northeast Conference Reports*.

The question of teaching language as a cultural phenomenon cannot be "covered" in a single, or even several, volumes. We have only endeavored to approach the problem, in both its practical and theoretical dimensions — with the understanding that theory and practice are eminently complementary and equally essential to the understanding and evolution of effective foreign language teaching. We have not attempted, in each chapter, to assure the equal representation of all commonly-taught foreign languages and cultures; each author brings to the *Reports* his or her personal expertise, based largely on extensive professional experience in one particular foreign arena. Specific examples and exercises should be perceived, by and large, as models and paradigms. Finally, the chapters included in this collection are not mutually exclusive: there is considerable crossover from one chapter to the next, whether the orientation be theoretical or practical. And this is to be expected, for whatever the philosophic perspective adopted, whatever the pedagogical bias, the object is the same: language in culture, culture in language.

In the introductory chapter of the present volume, Peter Patrikis issues a challenge to the profession, inviting us to reflect together on the very concept of culture in Western civilization, as well as on the place of culture in foreign language education, the current problematics of teaching language and culture, and the ultimate purposes and goals of the teacher. In a second theoretically oriented offering, Angela Moorjani and Thomas Field survey the contributions of semiotics and sociolinguistics to the effective teaching of foreign languages, bringing emphasis to bear on the study of cultural signs and the nature of the communicative act — without neglecting practical strategies for the introduction of semiotic and sociolinguistic approaches into high school and undergraduate curricula.

In the third chapter, Robert Lafayette begins by outlining specific goals in the teaching of culture and proposes basic principles to help both teachers and students develop a "cultural mind-set." In the ensuing pages he offers examples of proficiency-based materials designed to integrate culture into foreign language teaching throughout the curriculum, followed by practical classroom suggestions for lending a cultural dimension to all aspects of language study. Claire Kramsch, focusing on the principal pedagogical tool in the profession, the textbook, devotes the following chapter to an in-depth analysis of the course text as a "culturally coded educational construct." She evokes, further, the complex conditions of production of foreign language textbooks, highlights the thorny problems of choosing appropriate cultural content, and reflects on the problem, endemic to most textbooks, of teaching foreign language without an authentic cultural context.

Chapters five and six, authored by Jean-Pierre Berwald and Seiichi Makino, respectively, treat the topic of teaching language and culture through mass media. Berwald surveys the whole field, offering detailed advice on the pedagogical exploitation of a wide range of media and realia: radio, television, newspapers, magazines, mail-order catalogues, telephone books, films, slides, menus, and more. Makino, on the other hand, focuses on video alone, describing various materials developed for the teaching of Japanese. Emphasizing the principle of cultural contextualization, he discusses, in detail, personal materials created specifically to highlight culture and communicative functions at the elementary level.

Aleidine Moeller and Norman Stokle share the vast area of linguistic and cultural immersion experiences. Moeller, concentrating in the seventh chapter on the younger student (elementary through high school), insists on the rapid progress in both linguistic skills and cultural understanding achieved by participants in well-organized study abroad programs. She cites guidelines for program selection, as well as standards for evaluation, and describes a variety of successful exchange programs, total immersion weekends, and foreign language camps. In the companion chapter, Stokle deals with questions relative to study abroad programs at the college level. Drawing upon many years of personal experience as resident director, he emphasizes the critical importance, for maximizing cultural and linguistic immersion, of such matters as choice of lodgings, avoiding the "ghetto syndrome," and participation in learning opportunities outside the classroom. He stresses at the same time the responsibility of the director in properly orienting students and in developing innovative opportunities to facilitate their integration into the foreign culture.

In the closing chapter, Barbara Lotito and Mireya Pérez-Erdélyi take up the pedagogical challenge offered by the presence of ethnic neighborhoods throughout the United States. After a thought-provoking probe of the traditional obstacles to the integration of local resources into the teaching of language and culture, they outline procedures designed to prepare students for linguistically and culturally fruitful contact with a minority community. Using the *barrio* as an example, Lotito and Pérez-Erdélyi demonstrate how the preparation for a visit, the visit itself, and post-visit activities can all contribute to both an increase in cultural knowledge and a heightened sensitivity to members of the target culture as individuals — not to mention the enhanced motivation to study the foreign language.

Many voices, many perspectives, a few honest disagreements: we do not promise unanimity in pedagogical philosophy, nor unity of method. But all of the foreign language professionals represented in this volume share a simple conviction — the conviction that culture and language are indeed *inseparable*, that both *can* be taught effectively by dedicated and imaginative teachers.

Alan J. Singerman, *1988 Editor*
Davidson College

Peter Patrikis
The Consortium for Language Teaching and Learning

Language and Culture at the Crossroads

Had we but world enough and time. . . .
Andrew Marvell

Introduction

Our topic is "the new integration of language and culture." These words themselves should make us stop short. They should impel us to pose some fundamental questions. Is there an "old integration of language and culture" that we are now supplanting? Is the very effort to integrate the teaching and learning of culture with language new? What do we mean by the words "language" and "culture" when we use them so easily and so casually? The purpose of this essay is to explore some of these questions, to follow them up and down winding ways, and to begin to determine what the questions have to do with the teaching and learning of foreign languages. My assumption is that posing questions, even questions that have no immediate or easy answer, is in itself salutary. Questions teach us how to be self-critical about what we accept about our daily work, our programs, and our goals. And they teach us to challenge assumptions. I want to challenge some assumptions in this essay, but not so that we can wipe the slate clean, begin once again from nothing, and recreate our field. Instead, I want to challenge some assumptions about the commonly held notions about the place of culture in foreign language education, so that we gain some new perspectives, so that we have the opportunity to reflect upon some of our work in the light of developments in other fields.

The invariably complex and puzzling phenomena of language and culture have occupied the attention of some of the best minds. The writings of the many philosophers, linguists, anthropologists, historians, and cultural critics one could cite—Ayer, Boas, Cassirer, Chomsky, Geertz, Husserl, Lévi-Strauss, Quine, Saussure, Steiner, Whorf, to offer but a small sampling of names—would constitute a lifetime of reading. To be frank, if teachers of language were to direct their full attention to the mountain of scholarship underlying the issues we want to broach here, they would have no time to teach. But the point is not for everyone to become a philosopher, a linguist, and an anthropologist; the point is to enrich and to enhance the field of language teaching and learning by asking questions suggested by other disciplines. The questions posed in these other fields, as we shall see, are directly and intimately related to the fundamental problematics of the foreign language classroom.

The Problems of Culture

CULTURE, CULTIVATION, CIVILIZATION

The word "culture" is no easy place to begin, because it is complicated by its etymology, its semantic development in the various European languages, and its elaboration within academic disciplines like anthropology and sociology. Its root is the Latin *cultura,* which in turn derives from the verb *colere,* to cultivate; *cultura* in Latin is husbandry, the "cultivation" of fields or crops or plants and, by extension, of animals. This agricultural sense is retained in English when we refer to the culture of bacteria in a petri dish for a medical experiment or to the culture of plants in our gardens. The step from the literal to the figurative meaning is short and quick; it is a step from the notion of the cultivation of plants to the cultivation of an individual. The biological metaphor of growth, nurturing, and maturity is thus translated into the notion of education — conceived by the Greeks and Romans alike as a process aimed at attaining a recognized standard or ideal. In many quarters today this teleological metaphor still reigns. Indeed, the history of classical or classicizing humanistic education in the West is the history of cultivating the notions of the good (ethics), the true (philosophy), and the beautiful (aesthetics). In the somewhat old-fashioned phrase "He is a man of culture," we recognize the persistence of this metaphor. Referring both to the process and to the product, the words "culture," "cultivation," and "civilization" merge into a general sense that for almost two thousand years has stood as the hallmark of humanistic education. The features of the educational ideal have in the West been the very features of civilization. Thus, the word "culture" takes on another, somewhat narrower, sense in which it subsumes the general qualities of a society. Thus we can speak of the Greek culture of fifth-century Athens or the humanist culture of Quattrocento Florence. I am not, of course, attempting to present a historical account of Greco-Roman education here; instead, I am trying to show how a word like "culture" embodies certain concepts and ideals, regardless of whether or not those ideals were achieved. Be it dream or reality, this notion of education is deeply fixed in the imagination of Western civilization. The content of the ideal differs from period to period, from country to country, and from thinker to thinker. From the rhetorical and ethical works of Cicero to the Renaissance works of Pico della Mirandola or Montaigne, from the notion of sweetness and light in the thought of Matthew Arnold to the insistence on teaching the canon of the best and most significant works of Western civilization from the office of the Secretary of Education, we witness the survival of the words and the ideal. It is fashionable in many quarters to deride and dismiss this two-thousand-year-old legacy of liberal education as outmoded, elitist, or irrelevant, but only a profound and stubborn ignorance of the complex history of these concepts could lead to such a short-sighted and negative valuation. In a reductionist form, this notion of culture becomes mere refinement: a person of culture knows how to distinguish Blavet's flute sonatas from Hotteterre's, Meissen porcelain from Compagnie des Indes, or Bruges lace from Florentine lace. This is an impoverished social ideal where minor aspects of the aesthetic take precedence over the ethical and the philosophical. Related to this reductionist form is a notion of culture that is merely etiquette: cultural knowledge is reduced to what you need to know not to give offense and to please. Protests about

American ignorance of foreign cultures usually assume this form; a diplomat or exchange student fails to remove his shoes before entering a home in Kyoto or uses his left hand to serve food in India or Pakistan.

From the notion of culture/civilization as the standards of a society, we move semantically with little obstacle to the notion of culture as the features of any nation, region, class, or identifiable group. Thus we speak of "Chinese culture," "the culture of the Trobriand Islanders," "the culture of Silicon Valley," "popular culture," "nomadic culture," or even "academic culture."

THE PREDICAMENTS OF THE ANTHROPOLOGISTS

> Without the aid of prejudice and custom, I should not be able to find my way across the room.
>
> William Hazlitt

It is at this point in the unfolding of the meanings of the word "culture" that we begin to enter the realm of anthropology, where there are multiple definitions of the concept of culture. It is not, however, the multiple meanings — the fine tuning by professionals of their own conceptual tools — that is a problem for anthropologists or for us. The predicament of the anthropologists is deeper than definitional debates, as we shall see.

Some three decades ago, it was generally possible to give a standard anthropological definition of culture: the totality of patterns of thought, feeling, and behavior that characterize a group. The patterns that fall into this definition are many in kind and in number: rituals, symbols, material objects, beliefs, ideas, hunting techniques, jokes, kinship relations, and on and on. The breadth and complexity of these data, however, presented little obstacle to the development of the social science of ethnography. Granted a certain simplification on our part for the purposes of this essay, it is fair to state that classical anthropology, which flourished from the 1920's to the 1960's was — and still is for many practitioners — a discipline in which the traditional empirical research involves doing fieldwork among a group of people, observing the full range of their activities, analyzing the data, and producing a monograph. Classical anthropology operated with certain assumptions. It consciously sought to be objective, in the sense that the anthropologist abandoned ethnocentrism.

Ethnocentrism. Ethnocentrism is the bias by which we observe and judge other cultures according to the ethical, philosophical, and aesthetic values of our own culture. An American who is puzzled by the sight of the Japanese bowing to one another fails to understand the phenomenon because he has no basis in his own cultural experience for figuring out what is going on. In the United States, when we are introduced to someone new, we tend almost automatically to ask immediate questions: "How are you?" or "What do you do for a living?" or "Where is your wife?" The first question is common to many cultures. The second question could give offense to a Frenchman, who would not so quickly speak about personal matters. The third question would insult a Moslem. Ethnocentrism is the basis of considerable misunderstanding, and it is frequently the rationale for ethnic jokes. It can be likened to egocentricity elevated to the socio-economic or cultural level.

It is all too common for some writers to pretend that Americans or Westerners are the only people guilty of ethnocentrism. We hear all kinds of stories about culture shock, the Ugly American, and noisy tourists. Americans, however, have no monopoly on ethnocentrism: the ancient Greeks referred to all non-Greeks as *barbaroi* (barbarians); the Israelites of the Old Testament referred to all outsiders as Gentiles; for centuries the Chinese have referred to foreigners as *yi,* and the Japanese to outsiders as *gaijin.* In these cases, the words convey a strong sense of proud identity and a disparaging detachment from outsiders.

Ethnocentrism is the contrary of objective observation and analysis. Objectivity, however, is no easy goal; indeed some philosophers contend that there can be no objectivity, that no one can shed his or her biases. No one is born *tabula rasa,* with a blank slate. Be it by our genetic code or our experiences, we have dispositions and predispositions. When we encounter something new—squid cooked in its ink, a newspaper article on a presidential candidate, or a visitor from an unfamiliar country—we perceive and we make judgments based on our experience and knowledge. For good or for bad, we all have biases. We see things in terms of what we know. Education, however, can turn a bias into a perspective that opens the eyes and allows understanding rather than into a blinder that restricts vision and ensures ignorance. Perhaps it is not possible to be fully and absolutely objective, but awareness of the problem can lead us to a kind of practical objectivity.

Relativism. Several decades ago the quest for objectivity and the rejection of ethnocentrism led to the creation of the anthropological notion of cultural relativism. Cultural relativism is a doctrine that asserts that no culture is superior to any other. Historically it developed as an attempt by anthropologists to destroy the progressivism of earlier anthropologists who situated cultures along hierarchies of development from "primitive" to "highly developed," with urban industrialized literate Western society representing the highest form of development. For a practicing anthropologist today, there are no "primitive tribes," and every group has its own highly developed and complex forms of expression, emotion, thought, and behavior. People who refer to "primitive art" and the like might themselves be considered primitive in their own patterns of thought.

Cultural relativism is not a single formal philosophical position; indeed, it has assumed forms that themselves have generated considerable and heated debate. First, there is moral relativism. Moral relativism holds that each action in another culture is to be judged not by supposed universal ethical standards (or by one's own ethical standards pretending to be universal), but rather by the contextual standards of the culture. In many examples of behavior, moral relativism is innocuous. The custom of giving dowries in the Middle East might offend an American feminist, and the Orthodox manner of crossing oneself might seem aberrant or even sacrilegious to a Roman Catholic, but neither of these actions lies outside recognized boundaries of social behavior. But what then is one to make of a group that would condone the ritual slaughter of all first-born daughters or the killing of weak and sickly elders? Such practices might have their explanation in ecological patterns—say, the need for a large number of male hunters or shortage of resources for the dying—but they remain morally abhorrent to most people in the modern world. A local context can explain, but it cannot justify, a practice. The Nazis had their "context" for the Holocaust, but only a lunatic would maintain that the context was morally appropriate and justifiable. Moral relativism crumbles when confronted by the horrors of human history.

Second, there is rational relativism. Rational relativism holds that within the context of each society all beliefs can be held as valid and reasonable. This form of the doctrine clearly seeks to prevent "rational," "scientific" Westerners from negatively judging beliefs in spirits, ghosts, etc. (what we would be tempted to call superstitions). If witches and cloud spirits hold your world together, and if the lords of the seas and the tree nymphs (or the currently understood laws of quantum physics) hold mine together, then no one, according to the doctrine of rational relativism, has the right to proclaim one system of belief better than the other. Rational relativism is not "rational," that is, based upon reason; it is rationalizing. It is an attempt to recognize the logical, symbolic, poetic, or affective order of another system of thought.

Third and finally, there is cognitive relativism. Cognitive relativism, which is the most radical and challenging form of relativism, holds that no two people perceive the world in the same way. Effectively, each individual has his or her own culture, and that culture cannot be comprehended by anyone else. Cognitive relativism has a long tradition in the West and can be seen as an extension of the various doctrines of skepticism. It is, like the notion of deconstruction, one of those Alexandrian excesses that renders itself meaningless by its own assertion of the impossibility of assigning meaning. If cognitive relativism were absolute, then there neither could nor would be any communication nor any understanding. The only possible logical outcome of cognitive relativism, if taken seriously, is solipsism.

The different forms of relativism seek to free the mind so that it can observe and account for the variability of human societies without assigning *value* to the differences, without maintaining that one group is superior to another. Whatever antidote the various forms of cultural relativism might provide against ethnocentrism, they are by no means universally accepted, and they are fraught with conceptual difficulties. Cultural relativism as a doctrine depends on closed independent systems, but the moment two systems (for example, your culture and my culture) come into proximity they cease to be separate and distinct: they spontaneously impinge on one another. Cultural relativism assumes that all our fundamental concepts, beliefs, ideas, etc., are determined entirely by culture. No one doubts that culture plays an enormous role in forming our ideas, but it cannot be asserted that culture plays the only role. Moreover, if we place the entire burden on culture, then we are maintaining that the individual has no role or responsibility in his or her own development and that the values of humanistic liberal education are illusions. Pioneering research in neurology and psychiatry now suggests a more significant role for the biochemistry of our bodies in shaping how we perceive and interpret the world; many psychiatric symptoms that Freudians would attribute to the problems of bourgeois Western society are now viewed by some neuropsychiatrists as chemical imbalances or neural dysfunctions.

Even if we can never be totally free of our own biases and perspectives, we must profess our belief in the possibility of change. Anthropologists and many other theorists in the human sciences have analyzed in great detail the problems that we human beings have in studying one another. They have identified problems of interpretation, of ethics, and of epistemology at every thought and turn—so many problems that one almost begins to wonder if we are capable of making any true statements. Our concern, however, cannot be the impossibility of teaching and learning. Every teacher and student who steps into unknown territory—be it the jungle habitat of an Amazonian tribe, a foreign city, or a new neighbor's house—has first been puzzled, has posed questions, and has enlarged his or her frame of reference. We live, and we learn.

The anthropologists have their predicaments, as do scholars in all disciplines. What we learn as teachers or students is to recognize problems and to ask questions. The study of culture and the teaching of culture are acts of inquiry. Our primary role as teachers and students is to keep the questions fair and open.

Sins of Commission

Up to this point, this essay has necessarily been abstract, because I have attempted to cover a great deal of material in a short time and space, and because the issues are at once fugitive and pressing. Now I would like to turn to several practical considerations in the discussion of culture and to treat what I call, playfully and seriously, several sins of commission. The sins we shall all readily understand, and we shall probably find ourselves regularly guilty of their commission. They are:

- the sin of the stereotype;
- the sin of triviality;
- the sin of political bias;
- the sin of dangerous incompleteness.

Many, though not all, of these sins are committed unconsciously and with the best of intentions. Each merits some attention.

The sin of the stereotype is familiar to us all. The stereotype can be flattering ("Roman women dress elegantly") or disparaging ("Russian women dress horribly"). Stereotypes are exaggerations that undoubtedly have some basis in truth. Their worst defect is that they free people from observing, reflecting, and coming to their own judgments. As I think back over language textbooks that I had as a student, I recall a parade of stereotypes: worldly, courteous Frenchmen, obliging Spanish maids, jolly Dutchmen, serious Germans, and American students (who are usually blond) who love sports. But there is no need to belabor the error of the stereotype. What we must do is learn to distinguish between *types* (common traits) and *stereotypes* (fixed images), to teach our students to identify types and to recognize the limitations of the types.

The sin of triviality reduces the dizzying variety of cultural elements to the silly, the out-of-date, or the quaint. Ten years ago, I had the opportunity to review proposals requesting federal support for programs in international understanding. I was struck by the number of well-meaning, but naive, programs that envision other cultures almost solely in terms of the two C's, Costumes and Cuisine. Everyone will agree that the way people dress and the diets that they follow are important. Modes of dress and eating patterns are susceptible to complex analysis, and they are replete with meaning. But the very notions of costumes and cuisine are too often restricted in their scope, because they tend to imply that we wear clothing while others wear costumes, that we eat food while others have cuisine. If we make a point of showing students pictures of women in Breton *coiffes,* then we are not making a general illustration about France. Instead, we are showing a minority's tradition and its effort to maintain a separate identity. If we display Italian or Greek folk embroideries, then we are providing examples of a swiftly disappearing past, and we are not showing what one would commonly see in the houses of Milan or Salonika. Individual examples of dress or food that are not placed in a coherent historical tradition are only tokens that lack the meaning provided by their context.

As we all know, the value of studying and teaching about clothing should not be simply to highlight the exotic. Rather, it should be to examine how modes of dress establish an individual's or a group's identity. A three-piece gray pinstripe suit, a silk sari with intricate gold thread work, ragged blue jeans and a tee shirt emblazoned with a protest symbol—all these costumes can variously mark a person's age, social class, job, or ethnic group. In similar fashion, the study of food should serve not to accentuate differences but to illustrate the forces of tradition, economic necessity, ritual, or the marketplace. The phenomenon of using costumes and cuisine to characterize a country is undoubtedly linked to a facile tendency to dwell on the picturesque and the colorful, to assume that quaint or exotic difference is more telling than common features. All of us are given to nostalgia, and we scarcely have need to apologize for it. But we must be especially careful that we do not resurrect dead or dying traditions as living reality, simply because their differences from contemporary practice are stark.

The sin of political bias is committed by conservatives and liberals alike; it is sometimes conscious and often unconscious. Teachers cannot and should not be examples of indifference. Each of us has our own political beliefs, we need not hide them, and we certainly may not impose them. More to the point, we ought not to allow our own political beliefs to distort what we present to our students or how we present it. Do you remember the Spanish textbooks, all of whose characters were well-to-do urban families, their servants, and their merchants? The solution to that particular bias would clearly not be a textbook in which all characters are Marxist guerrillas, impoverished Indians, or liberation theologians.

Such examples of political bias are obvious. We should also be aware of less overt expressions of political bias. These expressions reflect fundamental ways in which we conceive society, the relations between its members and institutions, and the relations of power between groups. I use the word "political" neutrally, without reference to any specific doctrine. If we are going to begin to bring the conscious and careful study of cultural elements into language courses, then we must be aware of the political aspect of our choices. Let us take one telling example. The women's movement is in no sense limited to the United States, and its analogues in Brazil or Germany offer rich material. The question, however, is not whether or not a culture course should portray the lives of contemporary women. The question is, instead, which women the course should portray: committed feminists, their ardent opponents, or those who are indifferent to the issue. This is a political question, since the women's movement will have its supporters and detractors among both men and women, both in this country and abroad.

Curiously, the cultural material that we may wish to develop in a class and the normative requirements of a language course might come into conflict. There are deep relations between language and class, between linguistic register and social status. A Cockney accent at Oxbridge or a provincial accent in Paris is a strong social marker. Regional differences are, of course, not inferior, but they are also not what we tend to teach. Our own democratic impulses will probably succumb to the reigning standards of linguistic norms. Most of us teach Florentine Italian, Parisian French, Leningrad or Moscow Russian, and not the many other regional accents. It can be instructive and enjoyable to discuss geographic differences in language use, but I would question whether we would be willing to encourage in the classroom the linguistic pluralism that is the reality of so many countries.

The fourth and final sin of commission is the sin of dangerous incompleteness. This phenomenon, which I have witnessed in several attempts at "multicultural education," leaves a crucial part of a cultural picture out. It omits, and often for obviously political reasons, what the most careless glance would include. The examples will be obvious enough. In a recent issue of a foreign language journal, I read an account of a course on multicultural awareness that focused on the Middle East and on immigrants to the United States from the Middle East. The course was intended to deal with issues of Arab-Americans in certain urban communities, but it offered, with no disclaimers, a

Middle East that was exclusively Islamic, a Middle East without Jews, without Christians, without Bahai, or without any other minorities. Another example: I once reviewed a film strip on the background of Polish-Americans, a brief historical and cultural summary of life in Poland earlier in this century. Not once did the film strip mention the existence of Jews in Poland. Instead, it offered a vision of a religiously and culturally homogeneous country that has never existed. No country seems to be immune to this kind of masking of its diversity, and we should recall the Japanese prime minister who recently asserted that the trouble with the United States was its pluralistic population, while Japan's privilege was to have a united, culturally uniform population. The protests from the minority populations of Japan — the Ainu, the Chinese, the Koreans — emphasized that sin of dangerous incompleteness.

This brief account of four cultural sins can undoubtedly be expanded. The issues shed a different light on the current discussions regarding the authenticity of materials. Authenticity takes on new force and meaning and itself becomes a category that we must examine and question. Authenticity is no longer, in historical terms, a simple matter of adhering to what really happened, or, in contemporary terms, of telling how things really are. The complexities of representation put new intellectual and moral demands on the teacher and on the student. We must be ready to justify — to support, to verify, and to vindicate — a given picture that we hold up to students. The days of costumes and cuisine are dead. The days of hollow stereotypes are over.

Culture is a puzzle with shifting pieces and patterns. Complexity and change confront us as teachers and students at every point. As we consider the problems of the new integration of language and culture, we are challenged by difficulties that demand reflection, by difficulties that will enrich and deepen our efforts.

The Problems of Language

Let us begin by posing the ostensibly simple question: "What is language?" There is considerable debate in the foreign language profession now about the goals of courses, and it is possible that much of the confusion or division derives from different, though not mutually exclusive, notions of language. It is perhaps helpful to look at four different concepts of language:

- a concept from semiotics;
- a concept from structural linguistics;
- a concept from transformational-generative linguistics;
- a concept from sociolinguistics.

The general semiotic definition — language is signs that convey meaning — is the broadest, encompassing all aspects of communication, gestures, and symbols as well as words. It embraces the "languages" of infants, birds, monkeys, and dolphins, as well as those of teachers, administrators, alumni, and parents. This is a definition that is, for the most part, too wide for our purposes. We should bear in mind, however, that the current attention to the non-verbal aspects of communication (kinesics, for example) stems from semiotics. The shrugs, pauses, tilts of the head, raising of the eyebrows, and the constellation of physical movements and non-verbal sounds that mark someone as belonging to a culture have not often figured in textbooks, but they are now receiving closer attention with the use of audio-visual materials. Authenticity is best not described; it should be witnessed.

The notion of language that is the legacy of the rather long reign of structural linguistics in this country is much narrower than the semiotic definition and restricted to human speech: patterns of sound (phonology), patterns of form (morphology), and patterns of relation (syntax). Grounded in the notions of empiricism and of behavioral psychology, structural linguistics was the basis for the development of the drills and patterns of the Audio-Lingual Method, a method that in its purest form consciously avoided reference to grammatical rules and explanation. Although transformational-generative linguistics gradually has become the preferred form of the discipline for many in the field of linguistics, and although it is often treated as the successor to structural linguistics, it does not offer a point-by-point negation of all aspects of structural linguistics. Instead, transformational-generative linguistics shifts study and analysis to a different domain; with its rationalistic assumption of the deep structure of language and with its positing of the innateness of human language competence, transformational-generative linguistics offers a concept of language as a well-defined system of rules, conditions for the rules, and a lexicon. These rules are not of the simple order, like the agreement of subject and verb ("she goes," instead of "she go"). Rather they are more abstract, "deeper," and encompass phrase structures (e.g., the components of a sentence) and transformations of sentence types (e.g., the relation of active and passive sentences). The various communication-based methods of language teaching were not derived from transformational-generative linguistics, but they have found their theoretical justification in it.

Both structural linguistics and transformational-generative linguistics share a profound common trait: they treat language as an *autonomous* entity. Their analysis of language occurs without reference to the meaning of words and statements in their broader context. They examine language divorced from culture. Sociolinguistics, however, shifts the primary attention away from the study of language as an independent and isolated phenomenon to the study of language in society. If structural linguistics and transformational-generative linguistics conceive of language as a body of relations or rules, sociolinguistics expands the domain by including in its purview language, speech, the speaker, the addressee, etc. It studies language in communication, the production and reception of meaning. Sociolinguistics may never generate a language pedagogy as did structural linguistics, but it will undoubtedly come to play a larger and larger role in teaching. The current push for the *authenticity* of curricular materials and the trend toward the development of instructional materials more firmly grounded in *content* will demand that teachers have at least an elementary knowledge of the field. Moreover, as E. D. Hirsch illustrates in the opening chapters of his latest work (1987), recent cognitive research confirms that the skills of literacy are best acquired within a rich contextual framework and not as the disembodied activities of reading, writing, listening, and speaking.

Language and Culture

Unkraut vergeht nicht.

The issues we have raised and the questions we have posed thus far converge when we seek to treat the relation of language and culture. Many of the problems of that convergence have already surfaced in this discussion—ethnocentrism, relativism, the dilemmas of interpretation, the varying concepts of language—and they appear once

again. The relation of language to culture will always be partial: language falls under
the vaster rubric of culture. Language is one part, and only one part, of culture; oral
and written expression offers but a small set of data in any given society. It is a product
of culture; oral and written expression find their wellsprings in society and the relation
of the individual to society. And it is a condition for culture; you can study language
without culture, but you cannot study culture without language.

Ethnocentrism as it appears in the convergence of language and culture offers fascinating anecdotes and valuable insights into how societies conceive of their own language.
Everyone knows how the French deal with foreigners who mispronounce their language.
The multilingual Dutch and Scandinavians consider their polyglot status second nature
as well as an economic necessity, but they insist that foreigners could not possibly learn
their languages; the Danes treat their glottal stop as a genetic privilege, and the Dutch
usually respond to questions in their language in the native language of the speaker.
More complex still is the notion of irrefrangible difficulty that surrounds the Japanese
language, a notion that has almost achieved the status of myth.

The investigations concerning linguistic relativism have a lengthy, complex, and rich
history, and I shall not pretend to do justice to the topic here. (The most rewarding
and profound account is undoubtedly George Steiner's *After Babel.*) On the one hand,
there are the romantic nationalist traditions that view languages as a unique expression
of the "spirit of the people" (*Volksgeist*). On the other hand, there are related philosophical
traditions that posit the incommensurability of languages. Herder, von Humboldt,
Cassirer, Sapir, and Whorf are some of the major figures in these traditions. Lexical
items are not equivalent from language to language. *Brot* does not equal *pane. Mujer*
is not the same as *vrouw.* The failure of equivalence — what we would more commonly
call the problem of translation — becomes increasingly complicated at the levels of morphology, syntax, and sound.

Much, perhaps too much, has been made, however, of the fact of lexical difference
in language, of anisomorphism (the doctrine that languages distinguish cultures, keeping
them separate one from the other). What does it matter if Zulu has different words
for a red cow, a white cow, a black cow, and a brown cow? Or that Lithuanian has
different words for the color gray, depending on whether hair, geese, horses, or cattle
are gray? Or that Eskimos have many words for snow, depending on what kind of snow
it is, and that the aborigines of Tasmania have no word for tree but different words
for each kind of tree? The fact that the lexica of different languages might not coincide
does not preclude the possibility of comprehension.

One does not have to assume the extreme posture of the relativist to note, examine,
and probe differences and similarities between how language permits us to express
thought, belief, and emotion, how language enables us to commit our knowledge to
reproducible form, how language empowers us to share knowledge with others. The
differences and similarities between languages force back upon us the responsibility of
determining and justifying why we teach and what we teach.

Language and Culture — Teaching and Learning

When we examine the concepts of culture and language it is difficult to say what
counts and what does not count, to determine what should be included and what should
not be included. It might seem that the lessons of anthropology and linguistics tell us

that we must be dumb and not dare say anything, that anything we say will be distorted, incommensurate, or fictive.

Is there a solution out of the dilemmas? It is clear that broad statements about a culture simply will not wash. We cannot get along with maintaining that Latins are passionate, that the French are cynical, that Middle Easterners are shrewd in matters of commerce, or that the Japanese are refined in matters of taste. Yet there is a sense in which each of these statements has some truth. We may not be able to make blanket statements, but we must be able to generalize. I would like to suggest that we may be looking at the problem the wrong way, if we follow solely in the footsteps of anthropologists and critical theorists. From anthropological and critical theory we have become painfully aware of the limits of how we can observe and represent social reality. But we and our students are not anthropologists and critical theorists. We cannot know all the questions, issues, and problems, but we must admit and understand that the questions, issues, and problems exist. On the one hand, we must act as if observation and representation were immediate — without the distorting intermediaries of our experience and pre-conceived notions. On the other hand, we must act as if we were sharply cognizant of the persistent difficulties of interpretation. We must be able to make statements, and we must comprehend the shortcomings of those statements. We must be creative and critical at the same time.

This double position has deep repercussions for teaching. The job of instruction is not simply to pass on information (although we must certainly do that); it is also, and perhaps most importantly so, to teach students how to negotiate meaning and to think about the process of negotiating meaning. Foreign language teaching, perhaps more than many other fields, offers the opportunity to teach students to use a language and how to reflect upon language. Foreign language learning allows a student to acquire knowledge and the opportunity to observe his or her own mind at work. Knowledge of others and self-discovery can go hand in hand as simultaneous and interdependent actions.

When we speak of a new integration of language and culture, we are at the crossroads. We can no longer continue the old well-marked path that continues the legacy of autonomous linguistics, leveling the richness and complexities of words and concepts. At the same time, we cannot take the path that transforms the language classroom into an encyclopedia of cultural facts. The foreign language classroom cannot become the repository of all things foreign; nor can it be a course in anthropology, linguistics, philosophy, sociology, etc. Our search for a new integration of language and culture must compel us to re-examine our fundamental purposes and goals.

We have a sense of what we cannot do. We do not yet know fully what we can do. We can, and must, ask questions. What is it to *learn* a language? What is it to *know* a language? What is it to look at another culture? Do we ever know a culture? Do we want our students to be able to emulate a native speaker? Do we want them to know about how languages work? For many years we have been teaching foreign languages without a clear perception of the goals. But a new integration of language and culture affords us the opportunity to rethink the objectives we have set for ourselves and our students.

At the beginning of the *Metaphysics* Aristotle maintains that knowledge is born of wonder. Wonder is our sense of surprise, of curiosity, of discomfort, and of pleasure of the unknown. It is the primal and primary condition of learning. Foreign language teaching and learning, when it is integrated with the teaching and learning of culture, creates its own occasion for wonder, puzzlement, and surprise. The title of this essay was meant to suggest that language teaching and teaching about culture have been, for the most part, separate paths. The roads are now coming together, and it is our responsibility and our good fortune to make the vital decision where to proceed. We can continue to follow old paths, where the landscape will be the same. We can set out in new directions. The choice is ours.

References

Campbell, J. *Grammatical man: Information, entropy, language, and life.* New York: Simon and Schuster, 1982.

Clifford, J. & Marcus, G. E. *Writing culture: The poetics and politics of ethnography.* Los Angeles: University of California Press, 1986.

Geertz, C. *Local knowledge: Further essays in interpretive anthropology.* New York: Basic Books, 1983.

Harris, Roy. *The language myth.* London: Duckworth, 1981.

Hirsch, E. D. *Cultural literacy: What every American needs to know.* Boston: Houghton Mifflin, 1987.

Hudson, R. A. *Sociolinguistics.* Cambridge: Cambridge University Press, 1980.

Marcus, G. E. & Fischer, M. M. J. *Anthropology as cultural critique: An experimental moment in the human sciences.* Chicago: University of Chicago Press, 1986.

Newmeyer, F. J. *The politics of linguistics.* Chicago: University of Chicago Press, 1986.

Sperber, D. *On anthropological knowledge: Three essays.* Cambridge: Cambridge University Press, 1985. 1985.

Steiner, G. *After Babel: Aspects of language and translation.* Oxford: Oxford University Press, 1975.

Steiner, G. Viewpoint: A new meaning of meaning. *The Times Literary Supplement,* November 8, 1985, 1262 and 1275-76.

Angela Moorjani
Thomas T. Field
University of Maryland Baltimore County Campus

Semiotic and Sociolinguistic Paths to Understanding Culture

Introduction: Culture, Literacy, and Dialogue Across Borders

"Culture" in one form or another has always been a component of American language teaching. A glance at the backfiles of any of the major journals of the profession demonstrates unequivocally the continuing desire on the part of language teachers to renew and expand their approaches to cultural phenomena and to develop ways of educating their students about the world that speakers of the target language inhabit. Even the most orthodox structure-based approaches have explicitly stressed the importance of teaching certain cultural insights. The question facing the language teaching profession has, in fact, never been whether or not to teach culture, but, rather, what sort of teaching will pass on to students our current understanding of the nature of language, communication, and human relations. Thus, there can be no definitive answer to the question of how to integrate culture into language instruction. If we are careful to take into account all that is currently known about signifying practices, however, and if we make the best possible practical use of whatever tools recent scholarship may have put at our command, then we ought to be able to devise effective and satisfying solutions to the problem of teaching culture for our generation.

Linguistics and semiotics, the disciplines that are most directly concerned with the understanding of human communication, have focused throughout most of this century primarily on the structure of the communicative message and, in a very basic way, on the component elements of the communicative act itself. These self-imposed limits restricted to some degree the potential contribution of these fields to research into the teaching of culture. Over the past twenty years, however, there has been a clear shift in focus in both fields, such that large numbers of researchers are now concerned primarily with communication as a social act, the interaction of two or more human subjects in all their complexities, within an intricately structured cultural context. The development of this second major research thrust in linguistics and semiotics has not, of course, made structural considerations irrelevant, but it may have opened the way to new insights that can have direct relevance to the teaching of culture in the language classroom. In this paper we hope to show how an integrated understanding of both structure and function in the communicative act can illuminate intercultural questions for the language instructor and contribute significant new content to the practice of language teaching.

We might do well to examine first, in a general way, what it is that we as teachers of culture are about. In particular, we need to take note of the fact that the process of teaching intercultural communication is itself a communicative act. What might current research on communication have to say that would help us to understand this very peculiar process, the attempt to inform one people, with its particular mindsets and habits, about another people with quite different characteristics? Our task can perhaps best be seen as the weaving together of two rather dissimilar sorts of discourse, each with its own complexities and practical problems: on the one hand, we are concerned with dialogue on an intellectual level between one way of life and another; on the other hand, we are involved in instructional interaction between teacher and student in the classroom. Let us look briefly at each of these communicative acts in turn.

INTERCULTURAL DIALOGUE

The general trend of recent work in sociolinguistics and semiotics (along with literary criticism and the social sciences in general) has been to view the communicative act in terms of its properties as dialogue within a specific cultural context. Hymes (1974) pioneered this approach in linguistics and anthropology in a classic article, first published in 1962, that established the ethnography of communication as a field of research. An important precursor of the dialogic approach has been found in Mikhail Bakhtin, whose work on dialogism and heteroglossia has influenced literary studies and semiotic, linguistic, and anthropological inquiry. Especially significant for the attempt to understand a second culture is recent work in anthropology, notably Tedlock (1983), who has emphasized the futility (and dishonesty) of attempts at presenting the target culture strictly "on its own terms," without reference to the culture of the investigator. Tedlock has thus foregrounded the dialogic nature of the study of a second culture, and the necessity of displaying rather than concealing that interplay between home culture and target culture that is the cradle of eventual intercultural understanding. Closer to home, Brière (1986) has written, similarly, of the misguided attempts of language teachers to present the target culture "isolated as a system which can be described objectively, the teacher or the writer presenting himself [sic] as a kind of detached outside observer belonging to no culture in particular" (p. 204). In other words, the study of a second culture can only be a contrastive process, a dialogue between two ways of living and viewing the world. To take a trivial example, if it is worth saying that Europeans drive fast in cities, then this can only be because they drive faster than some other people, presumably Americans.

This implies that we cannot hope that "authentic materials" alone will allow students to gain cultural understanding through a simple process of induction. In fact, one infrequently discussed liability of authentic materials is that they assume no intercultural dialogue and can only be effective (as far as the teaching of culture is concerned) with the help of an interculturally sophisticated instructor. For this reason, an "anecdotal" book like Laurence Wylie's *Village in the Vaucluse,* whatever its defects, is probably preferable as a model for the presentation of French culture to many sociological-type works published in Paris and based on cultural assumptions that are entirely foreign to our students. For example, one frequently used book on French civilization (Paoletti and Steele, 1983) informs students (p. 10) that twenty-four percent of the French population consists of people for whom material security and prestige are an overwhelming concern. What are they to make of this? Is this percentage higher than what we would find at home? Without intercultural dialogue (which may, indeed, be provided by the teacher) there can be little intercultural understanding.

The term "culture" is, of course, used in many different senses. We shall distinguish (1) high culture, (2) popular culture, and (3) deep culture. While clear distinctions cannot always be made between high culture (Joseph Brodsky and Pierre Boulez) and popular culture (Hildegard Knef and Julio Iglesias), the former is generally more highly elaborated and requires a certain apprenticeship to be fully appreciated. Both aspects are crucial to our teaching, however, for both are in a sense concrete realizations of deep culture. Deep culture is "culture" in the sociological and anthropological sense: more a set of organizing principles that underlie behavior and thought than a collection of curious practices that contrast with our own. Ultimately, we would like to communicate some of these principles to our students. If we were teaching Navajo, we would be lucky enough to have at our disposal Gary Witherspoon's *Language and Art in the Navajo Universe,* a dialogic approach that has as its goal the search for the very foundations of Navajo culture. On the other hand, the technologically advanced societies that are the target of most of the language teaching done in the U.S. do not lend themselves well to an anthropological-guidebook approach, partly because of their relatively greater heterogeneity.

The heterogeneity of these societies is in itself an enormous stumbling block in the teaching of culture, for it imposes upon us a choice that can only be made on ideological grounds: what culture do we teach, or, rather, whose culture do we hold up as a model (see Westphal, 1986)? On a superficial level, one would think that, since we are almost without exception teaching an educated middle class linguistic repertory (how many language teachers are teaching anything else?), we ought, logically, to select for cultural teaching the "prestige" culture that this form of language subtends. But this sort of simplification and idealization, while useful for the teaching of language, is certainly harmful when we are concerned with culture, for it reduces the target world to a one-dimensional caricature. Arizpe and Aguirre (1987), for example, have culled from the pages of current first-year Spanish textbooks a surprisingly large number of objectionable cultural images, many of which occur because the authors seem to have adopted unquestioningly the points of view that characterize certain high-prestige groups in Hispanic culture. Many language teachers today are ill at ease with such a strong bias in favor of one particular social class in the target society, but alternative solutions are hard to find. We would certainly be putting our students in a curious position if we were definitively to shift our cultural focus to a social group that does not speak the forms of language we are teaching. The linguistic understanding of standard and nonstandard may be of help in this dilemma.

American linguistics has always had as one of its most cherished axioms the iconoclastic assertion that "standard" language is no better structurally or expressively than any nonstandard form of speech, that its perceived beauties and advantages are actually an expression of admiration for the classes that use it natively. However, the influence exerted by standard models and their usefulness in heterogeneous societies have always been felt so strongly that the public at large has been hesitant to agree with this point of view. Today linguists are more likely to accept the fact that, although the selection of standard norms in language may be linguistically arbitrary, the socio-political, affective, and practical reasons for the existence of a standard are too strong to be resisted in any categorical way. As a result, we can teach standard language with a good conscience, but we still owe it to our students (even at beginning levels) to point out the reasons for the prestige of standard forms of speech and to suggest the important functions of nonstandard and regional speech forms.

Returning to the problem of culture, we find a very similar situation. Prestige forms of culture have a force and influence that make them crucial to our teaching (this is another reason for not dispensing with high culture). However, we need to help our students understand the fact that none of our target cultures is homogeneous, that each exhibits a constant tension between the culture of the prestigious and the powerful and that of minorities and the dispossessed. The most effective way of teaching culture, in fact, may be a kind of triangulation by which American cultures are allowed to interact with and reflect off both a "prestige" form of the target culture and an alternate (working class, regional, or ethnic minority) culture within the target society. This kind of three-way dialogue allows a richer appreciation of the nature of cultural communities and provides a far more realistic basis for the eventual insertion of the student into the target world.

INSTRUCTIONAL DIALOGUE

The second of the dialogic aspects of the act of teaching culture is the communication between teacher and student. This is, of course, not a dialogue that is of concern only to language teachers, but nowhere are the difficulties of communication between teacher and student more acute than in the area of foreign culture teaching. To begin with, the ideological considerations that guide the teacher's selection of materials, approaches, and goals may be completely foreign (or objectionable) to the student. We cannot expect all of our students to see the value of critical analysis, contrastive cultural insights, or major works of art (assuming that these are among our goals); we can indeed expect some students to object to the humanistic perspective that informs the teaching of most of the profession. These are not differences of opinion to be taken lightly or to be ignored, for they concern the very foundation of our activity in the classroom, and if we expect students to profit from our cultural instruction, we may need to provide clearer justification for our activities and approaches.

In addition, in recent years linguistics, anthropology, and other fields have been noting a shift in Western culture (related to changes in the dominant media) away from the prestige of literate modes of communication, typically characterized by linear classification and analysis, toward a greater reliance, even in "standard" contexts of communication, on nonliterate modes, characterized by a functional conception of knowledge and a strong reliance on shared assumptions (Ong, 1982). It has been argued also that the decline of literate modes of discourse may be leading to a decline in traditional analytic thinking, a connection first suggested by Goody and Watt (1962). We, as teachers of language and culture, are the product of a selection process that used as its main criterion the mastery of literate modes of communication, while our students are part of a generation for which oral strategies of thought and language have become acceptable and even dominant in many areas of human interaction where they were disvalued previously. In other words, an important change in the pragmatics of language use, a shift from literate to oral modes, is taking place in our society; thus, teaching today is, in a sense, already an intercultural activity. At the simplest level, we cannot expect that students who write (as one of ours did) that "people used to use books for entertainment" will grasp quickly the significance of French literary prizes or a literary television show like "Apostrophes." At a deeper level, the ongoing changes in the practice and prestige of literacy may account for student resistance to what seems "abstract" and "impersonal" to them in the study of foreign culture (including history). For all of us, then, except those who teach select, traditionally literate groups, a large part of our task must be to help our students to continue their apprenticeship in literate modes of analysis and understanding. We cannot expect progress in these areas to occur naturally, and we cannot afford simply to rail against the lack of reading in the younger generation. As Greenfield (1984) has pointed out, this attitude has prevented us from taking advantage of the possibilities that new media provide and of the ways of thinking that they may encourage. In any case, students whose cognitive approach is disvalued in the classroom are unlikely to want to meet any of the higher goals we may have in mind for them. We feel very strongly that part of the solution must be to begin where the students are, with cultural phenomena familiar to them (popular culture, visual communication) and with approaches that make sense to them (functional, global-type explanations); from there we ought to try to direct students on toward analytic approaches to concrete examples of cultural production and toward more abstract principles of cultural interaction. Our suggestions for the classroom in a subsequent section will assume the existence of this difficulty and will include some approaches intended to deal with it.

Goals: Preparing Students for Cultural Diversity

Most of the standard materials available for language teaching do not have especially ambitious goals in the area of "culture." It is our feeling that much more can be done with the teaching of culture than is currently the practice, even at beginning levels. We can distinguish five basic sorts of abilities whose growth we would like to encourage through the teaching of culture.

First, the ability to "get along" in the target culture, to be able to communicate effectively with people in the fundamental activities of everyday life. Such an ability includes familiarity with appropriate cultural settings, basic social organization, the pragmatic rules for personal interaction and social occasions. This goal is one that is quite generally recognized and implemented in language teaching. The profession's use of the term "communicative competence" to describe the goal of our courses implies a dedication to the teaching of at least this kind of cultural knowledge.

Second, a certain level of "cultural literacy," that is, familiarity with enough of the facts of culture and tradition to allow informed communication with native speakers. While the study of culture certainly cannot be understood as the acquisition of bits of information, this does not mean that information is not also important. Hirsch (1987) has claimed that American young people are severely lacking in this capacity within their own culture, and similar situations are clearly the rule today in other Western societies as well. What we are seeing is a major change in the makeup of the corpus of elements of cultural literacy that are needed for cultural "citizenship." Without endorsing Hirsch's conclusions, we would agree that we need to begin to show our students at least some of the cultural "baggage" that is *not* in the process of disappearing. At higher levels of proficiency, we can also introduce students to more sophisticated and less commonly mastered aspects of cultural literacy.

Third, the ability to explore, analyze, and appreciate the important cultural productions of the target culture. Many American students find that they appreciate the more elaborate forms of high culture for the first time when they are studying a second language. If we, as teachers, can help this interest to emerge in our students, there is certainly good reason to make this one of the goals of our teaching from the beginning.

Fourth, the ability to understand that there may be good reasons for differences in ways of acting, speaking, and thinking, and that most of these reasons have to do with "culture." Seelye (1974) breaks this point down into four more specific goals: students should understand that (a) people act in accordance with a repertoire of behaviors allowed by their culture; (b) social variables — age, sex, class, etc. — affect the way people communicate; (c) there are specific conventions that rule people's actions in common situations; and (d) cultural connotations play an important role in language use (pp. 38–43).

It is certainly difficult to teach students to *expect* cultural difference, but this is without doubt one of the most valuable of the lessons to be learned from the study of culture. A desire to help students develop this ability is also one of the main reasons for the reappearance of language requirements at the college level in recent years.

Fifth and last, a critical appreciation of conflicting practices and points of view. As Crawford-Lange and Lange (1984) suggest, this means not only learning about the structure of the Spanish system of education, but also gaining the ability "to show how it is carried out in different regions in Spain, analyze its successes and weaknesses, recommend ways in which it could be more successful, and show why it is successful and why it is weak" (p. 156). This is a much more abstract goal, one that requires a lifetime of application, but the development of critical thinking can be a natural outcome of the process in which students, as they are faced with what to them are new cultural practices, continually uncover their own prejudices and presuppositions.

Some teachers of culture may feel that it is not their job to foster the development of all five of these abilities in their students. Certainly, while the first two are crucial to any teaching of language and culture, the others are not the domain of language teachers only, but are part of a broader, more ambitious program that aims to make students well-educated, critical thinkers. We feel very strongly that it is only as we integrate these higher goals into our teaching that we are really educating our students.

Theory: Lessons Learned from Semiotics and Sociolinguistics

If we wish to adopt the more ambitious goals outlined above, the lessons of semiotics and sociolinguistics become crucial input for the development of our programs. We shall thus begin by outlining those aspects of research in both fields that have the greatest potential for contributing to the effective teaching of culture.

WHAT IS SEMIOTICS?

Although definitions of semiotics abound all the way back to the Stoics, we will limit ourselves to a few twentieth-century classics:

- A science that studies the life of signs within society (Saussure [1915], 1959, p. 16).
- Semiotics is concerned with everything that can be *taken* as a sign. A sign is everything which can be taken as significantly substituting for something else (Eco, 1976, p. 7).
- . . . the study of all patterned communication in all modalities, of which linguistics is the most technically advanced (Mead, 1964, p. 275).

- • . . . an inquiry into the communication of all kinds of messages (Jakobson, 1971, p. 698).

What all these definitions have in common is the insistence on signs, messages, and communication, in short, the social production of meaning. In the wake of Saussurian linguistics, this line of inquiry undertook the systematic study of signifying practices, such as gestures, sounds, images, objects, social space, and the media and discourses making use of them: advertising, film, drama, sports, television, visual, musical, and written texts, and so forth.

Some of this work tried too insistently to fit such myriad systems of meanings into the Saussurian structural framework, with disappointing results. Many of the semiotic studies that appeared in the sixties and early seventies on, let's say, kinesics (the study of non-linguistic gestures) or on film or music thus attempted to align these sign systems too closely with language. But non-linguistic signs stubbornly refused to fit in. It was a strange game, somewhat like trying to fit the pieces of one puzzle into a different puzzle's matrix.

SIGNS AND CULTURE

A more useful approach turned out to be the influential classification of signs developed by the American philosopher Charles Sanders Peirce (1839–1914). According to this typology, the two parts of the sign—the signifier (the sign's form, such as the sounds that make up the spoken word *apple*) and the signified (the sign's meaning, such as a particular fruit)—may be related to each other in three different ways. How, for example, does (1) a realistic photograph of an apple differ from (2) the image of an apple standing in for the entire apple industry or the Apple computer company, and (3) an apple signifying health? The photograph is an example of an iconic sign, in which the signifier (form) imitates or echoes the signified (meaning) in some way. To further illustrate this concept we use René Magritte's renowned paintings depicting a very realistic pipe or apple, under or over which appear, respectively, "Ceci n'est pas une pipe" (This is not a pipe) and "Ceci n'est pas une pomme" (This is not an apple). The ironic contrast between the visual semblance of an apple, painted to give as perfect an illusion of the object as possible, and the negative label, draws attention to the status of the image as an iconic sign: this is an icon, not an actual apple to bite into. On the other hand, indexical signs, such as the second apple which stands for an entire industry, privilege a relation of contiguity, such as a causal, temporal, or spatial nearness and part/whole relations. Medical symptoms, clues in detective novels and pointing gestures fall into this category. Examples from film would be a close shot of a facial expression to stand indexically for a corresponding emotion or tension-creating music signifying excitement. And finally, the third apple above, with its cultural association of health, is a symbol, as are likewise most linguistic signs; symbols are the most abstract of the three types, since their meaning and form are related arbitrarily or by cultural convention.

Now it is necessary to add that the three types of signs—icon, index, and symbol—are not so easily categorized as the above paragraph would make it seem. It is interesting to note that Peirce himself preferred those signs that blend the characteristics of all three as equally as possible (Jakobson, 1971, p. 349). Most useful, especially for cultural studies, then, is the concept of the hybrid sign, the cultural icon and the cultural index, combining socially produced meaning with likeness and indexicality. In fact, in reconsidering the categorizations of the above paragraph, it becomes clear that iconic signs such as Magritte's painted apple are best considered cultural icons, since someone unfamiliar with the conventions of Western representative art is unlikely to grasp the meaning of Magritte's painting. And understanding indexical symptoms—clues, gestures, and facial expressions—is closely linked to cultural conventions as well.

Of what use, though, are all these complex classifications for deciphering cultural messages? Most immediately, such analytical categories make possible the crucial distanciation required to work with signs as socially produced (not natural) vehicles of meaning. One of the first major semiotic readings of popular culture, *Mythologies,* the 1957 collection of essays by Roland Barthes, thus bares the layers of social or ideological meaning at work in a large variety of signifying practices, such as the election portrait, detergent ads, popular women's magazines, the *mise en scène* of wrestling matches, and Hollywood film conventions. To take the election portrait as an example, Barthes points out how posture, gestures, facial expression, dress, the inclusion or exclusion of family members, setting, props, all are carefully selected and organized to give the illusion of naturalness to a complex orchestration of hierarchical and political messages. To the receivers, however, who see themselves mirrored in these posed icons reflecting shared middle-class values, such social production of meaning appears "natural" instead of contrived. The function of this type of semiotic reading, then, is to break the pattern of identification, and ultimately to permit the receiver to recognize the cultural icons, indexes, and arbitrary symbols as vehicles of socially constructed meanings whose validity is open to question and doubt.

POETIC/AESTHETIC DISTANCIATION AND CULTURE

Distanciation was also a major concern of the Russian formalists and of the Prague Circle—the former active from 1915 to 1930 roughly, the latter in the 1930s—whose influential theories became inseparable from semiotic inquiry during its structural phase. Such concepts as "defamiliarization" and "foregrounding" or "deautomatization" served to draw attention to deviations from conventional expectations. The unexpected, the formalists stressed, makes the receiver aware of the conventionality of all that is otherwise unheedingly consumed as natural. (Since such unconventional foregrounding is also a clever attention-getting device, modern advertising offers abundant examples. One that comes to mind is the recent series of Grand Marnier ads in which, for instance, a large orange functions as cultural icon of the sun and as cultural index and symbol for the liqueur.)

In addition to the distanciation techniques involved in unconventional or pattern-breaking usage, the formalists paid special heed to what later became known as "textuality," that is, the material elements or signifiers of a work—sounds, colors, lines, etc.—and their cohesive organization in space and time. In the above Grand Marnier ad, along with the foregrounding devices, cohesive patterns of warm colors (orange and browns) and rounded shapes, for example, draw the viewer's attention to the image's design at the expense of the picture content. In the poetic use of language, which is not limited to poetry as such, patterns of repetition and contrast among phonological, lexical, syntactic and rhythmic components render language palpable and often pleasurable in itself.

But is the study of the aesthetic organization of formal elements in time and space, whether in literature, theatre, music, film, or the pictorial arts, related to understanding not only high and popular culture but the "deep" culture of which we spoke in the first section? First of all, in similar fashion to what was described as the distancing function of the cultural sign, the foregrounding of aesthetic forms and processes discourages the automatic consumption of meaning. And secondly, instead of concentrating on a work's theme or subject matter (its "referential/representational content"), focusing on textual organization, the interrelations between a work's material or formal elements (its "aesthetic content") gives us a valuable avenue of access to a culture's "out-of-awareness" organizing principles and values. A culture's preferred aesthetic patterns, visible as they are in artistic practices of all types, are inseparable from other modes of conceptualization, social structuring, and cultural communication. A classic in this line of analysis is Claude Lévi-Strauss's chapter in *Tristes Tropiques* on the social meaning of the pictorial designs the Caduveo of Brazil tattoo or paint on their bodies (pp. 160–80).

FROM STRUCTURE TO FUNCTION

When the members of the Prague Circle turned their attention to the functions fulfilled by various signifying practices in society, they privileged in particular the "poetic" orientation that the previous section describes, that is, the focus on the aesthetic organization of the message. In the wake of an influential 1958 paper delivered by the linguist/semiotician Roman Jakobson, a former member of the Circle, the "poetic" or "aesthetic" function and five other orientations became one of the commonplaces of semiotics. Jakobson identifies six components involved in any speech event: an *addresser* sends a *message* to an *addressee* via a *contact*, defined as a physical channel and a psychological connection, using a *code* (a sign system, such as spoken English) within a shared *context*.

The sender of the message can emphasize any one or more of the foregoing basic elements of the communication event. Foregrounding the message, as we have seen, gives the *poetic* or aesthetic orientation. A focus on the addresser corresponds to the *expressive* or *emotive* function, in which the sender's feelings and attitudes toward each of the other factors involved in the communicative event predominate. Special emphasis on the addressee makes the speech act largely *conative* or directive, whereas the purpose of the *contact* or *phatic* function is to establish and maintain the communication channel. The telephonic "hello" and "you still there?" as well as party talk, store music, and hotel art are examples of phatic communication. The phatic or contact orientation is in turn to be distinguished from the *metalingual* function, where focus is on the code. Based on the distinction made in modern logic between object language and metalanguage, that is, between language used to discuss objects in the world and a language used to refer to itself, the metalingual orientation makes use of language to check reflexively on language itself. Finally, the *referential* orientation draws attention to the context and consists primarily in the transmission of information or content (Jakobson, 1960).

Since of the above six functions, the poetic (which has already been described) and the expressive are perhaps the most controversial, a bit more discussion is in order for the latter. In his analysis of the emotive or expressive orientation, Jakobson (1960) adds the absolutely crucial qualification that the sender's emotive stance could be either "true or feigned" (p. 354). Whether we consider the interaction between two people, an ad, a painting, or a symphony, our understanding of the expressive elements, to be gleaned by paying attention to all types of evaluative features, necessarily wavers between accepting the message as sincere or not. In interpersonal relations in all cultures, for example, politeness rules require the expression of emotions and evaluations that are "feigned." Solidarity takes precedence over "true feelings." In ads, it is the intent to sell a product that obviously excludes truthful evaluation. In literature, film, painting, and music too, of course, the expressive function may serve to transmit fictional, not felt, emotive and evaluative states. Ultimately, it is the ability to contextualize, that is, to identify the relevant social situation, that provides the basis for semiotic interpretation in such cases.

The gusto with which Jakobson's model, which extends the work of language philosophers and theorists of the 1930's, was adapted to both linguistic and nonlinguistic discourse is perhaps largely to be explained by its shift of focus from linguistic structure to the interactive dimension of communication and to the many artistic and social uses to which language is put. This shift away from the "idealized" grammars, i.e., abstracted from social situation, that constitute the object of theoretical linguistics and semiotics, has gathered momentum in the past twenty years or so and has led to renewed attention to context and social variation in the fields of pragmatics, sociolinguistics, the ethnography of communication, and ethnosemiotics. This concentration on the local or situational nature of the production of meaning has to some extent overshadowed the concern with the universal features of language and culture that structuralism emphasized. (Hawkes, 1977, provides a good general introduction to structuralism and semiotics.)

SITUATIONAL AND INTERCULTURAL MEANING

One way of approaching the analysis of situational meaning is to ask what participants need to know in order to understand and produce the multiple semiotic practices available to them as members or prospective members of a culture (Lyons, 1986, p. 573). Such an approach would lead to a definition of what Hymes (1971) called "communicative competence," a term about which much has been made since, and would help circumscribe the concept of "cultural literacy." In this section we will suggest a synthesis of the many approaches linguistic and semiotic theorists have taken in their effort to describe this truly daunting aspect of human communication.

The production of situational meaning includes the following seven broad areas of understanding:

Knowledge of conversational principles. Participants must have an understanding of certain general principles of interaction, such as (1) the cooperative principle, which posits the purposeful nature of cultural communication and "conversational implicature," (2) politeness principles, and (3) conventions of playfulness and their different applications in each culture. Leech (1983) contains a particularly useful discussion of how the cooperative and politeness principles may clash one with the other (pp. 79–151).

Anchoring in the participants' perspective. Senders and receivers must be able to reconstruct each other's personal and spatio-temporal perspectives by means of the indexical or shifting terms of discourse. This is accomplished, for example, by means of first- and second-person pronouns, each "I" implying a "you" and vice versa, and such spatio-temporal expressions as "here" and "now" signaling proximity to speaker and "there" and "then," expressing distance from the speaker. Pointing gestures also fall into this category. The ways in which different cultures anchor in the spatio-temporal and personal perspective of interlocutors is a crucial piece of the puzzle of intercultural communication.

Awareness of social positioning. Participants must take into account one another's (1) social characteristics, (2) social roles, and (3) status. This includes, under (1), age, sex, class, ethnic group, geographical origin, education; under (2), roles such as parent-to-child, student-to-teacher, clerk-to-customer, or lover-to-lover; under (3), relative social standing and positions of power and authority, which are in turn closely intertwined with social characteristics and roles. On the basis of this knowledge, participants must be able to adjust their positions appropriately in discourse. This too requires a constant shift of signifying positions, but unlike the personal shift from "I" to "you" indicated above ("personal deixis"), and the conceptual/cultural dialogics described below ("world-sharing deixis"), this positioning depends on social factors ("social deixis"). (For in-depth discussions of the concept of "deixis," that is, shifters, see Fillmore, 1975; and Lyons, 1986, pp. 636–724.)

We are, of course, all familiar with the complex negotiations—and the frequent discomfort—associated with the adjustments in signifying behavior required because of the foregoing variables within our own culture. Are we or do we consider ourselves the social equals of the other participants? Are we or our interlocutors in a position of authority? How close do we consider ourselves personally to the others? Depending on the answers to these questions—the first two concerned with the dimension of hierarchy and power, the third with interpersonal ties—our selection of dialect, terms of address, phonological, lexical, and syntactic forms, tone of voice, posture, dress, gestures, physical proximity and touch, turn-taking privileges, and so forth, will vary accordingly. (Useful references on this topic include Joos, 1967; Henley, 1977; and Gumperz, 1982.)

Considering the complex production of social meaning outlined above for our own culture, it need hardly be said that the careful consideration of similar parameters for societies other than our own is of utmost importance to intercultural communication. How does a culture relate social characteristics (age, sex, class, ethnicity, geographical origin, etc.) and social roles (parent, doctor, judge, teacher, and so forth) to status and authority? How are hierarchical differences expressed in language, dress, gestures, use of time and space, and so forth? When relations are taken as equal, who is properly addressed in intimate, casual, consultative, and formal terms (Joos, 1967)? That the lines between informality and formality, for instance, are drawn differently in different cultures and subcultures is obvious from the frequent misunderstandings concerning what others judge to be the excessive familiarity of Americans, while many Americans feel disoriented by what they consider to be the excessive formality of other cultures.

Shared cultural knowledge. Understanding situational meaning implies an awareness of the cultural horizon shared by participants. In intercultural communication, this is surely the most difficult area in which to acquire literacy. If we take the case of lexical items, each word, in addition to its polysemic possibilities related to semantic and situational variables, is charged with multiple cultural associations, the extensive domain of shared information, beliefs, and values that impinge on meaning. If we return to the word *apple* or to the iconic sign of an apple, it becomes clear that in addition to the meaning of fruit, for example, a large number of cultural assumptions and connotations pertaining to mythology, folklore, and popular beliefs can be called up for us by these sign-functions. Such ideological knowledge is picked up by constant exposure to a culture's multiple discourses and is therefore closely related to what has been termed "intertextuality," or the echoing allusions to previous texts that all texts contain. In his influential "Discourse in the Novel," written in 1934–35 and first published in the 1970s, Bakhtin (1981) calls this the "dialogic" nature of discourse. Senders orient their discourse to the conceptual horizons of the receivers, in the process reinforcing or contesting the validity of the shared knowledge. In this manner the receiver's social belief system and anticipated response, that is, the position of the receiver, is a constitutive part of the text (pp. 280–83). Consequently, what audiences need to accomplish in order to participate in the construction of meaning within discourse from a different time and a different culture from their own is a shifting back and forth between their own conceptual horizon (and age, gender, class, race, etc.) and the position of the audience with which the discourse first entered into dialogue. As we emphasized in the first part of this paper, to acquire knowledge of another culture, we must set up a similar interchange between our own perceptual, conceptual, and social moorings and the other's, in this manner constructing an intercultural discourse in which the other's position is in a dialogic relation to our own.

Knowledge of types of signifying events. Hymes (1974) suggests that one good ethnographic technique for understanding communicative events is an examination of the names given them (p. 198). In our culture these might include such speech genres as heart-to-heart talk, ad, prayer, joke, polite conversation, poem, or social situations, such as doctor's appointment, shopping, religious ceremonies, dates, and all kinds of performances and games, such as opera, baseball, bridge, and so forth. For each of these one would need to be aware of the appropriate spatial frames or settings — playing field and stadium, classroom, restaurant, for instance — temporal frames, including duration and sequencing, degree of formality, and participant roles. Finally, knowledge of the material conditions, such as technological and performance requirements, financial and institutional factors, and networks of distribution is required for an understanding of cultural events.

Ability to make appropriate stylistic choices related to topic or field. This area of cultural competence includes distinguishing technical and specialized from unmarked or general expressions, appropriate style registers, awareness of taboos associated with certain topics, and familiarity with ways of evaluating subject matter.

Understanding the effect of medium on message. This requirement takes us back to the materiality of the sign and the specific social functions of speech, writing, gesture, pictorial and musical texts and the technologically reproduced media. The ways in which the transition from print to electronic media affects social meaning is of particular importance for our times.

STRUCTURE, INTERACTION, AND SETTING

It is now time to link the seven broad contextual factors involved in the social production of meaning — (1) conversational principles, (2) participants' perspective, (3) social positioning, (4) shared cultural knowledge, (5) topic, (6) event, and (7) medium — with the structural and functional models introduced earlier. First of all, from the deictic (shifting) and dialogic nature of discourse posited in the preceding section, it has now become apparent that the participants in a communicative event cannot be tied down to fixed positions. Such a fixedness is implied, however, by Jakobson's unidirectional alignment of the addresser, message, and addressee (1960):

sender . . . . message . . . . receiver

Instead of this model, taken from communications engineers, depicting a predetermined message traveling in linear fashion from sender to receiver, our chart places social meaning-making into an interconnecting structural, interactional, and situational network (see Figure 1). In the process, we have integrated an adapted version of Jakobson's structural/functional model into a larger contextual design. Clearly, there is some overlap among the categories, and meaning is generated by interaction among all of them. It is important also to envisage the multiple intersecting and superimposed semiotic prac-

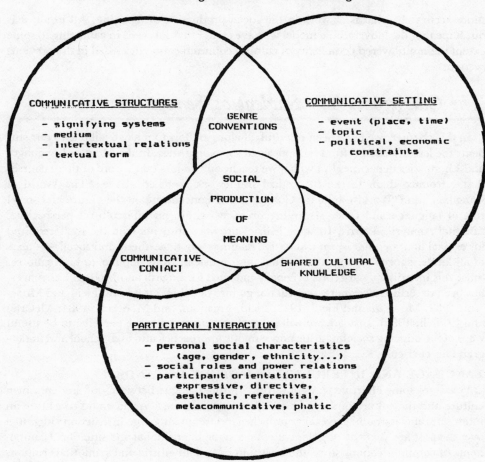

Figure 1. The social production of meaning

tices that enter into the production of meaning, so that in conversation, for instance, one must interrelate the spoken utterance with tone, timbre, volume and rhythm of voice, facial expression, look, posture, gestures, personal distance, dress, hesitation features, turn-taking signals, pauses, interactional synchronizing patterns, and so forth. In changing Jakobson's term *metalingual* to *metacommunicative* (under Participant Interaction), we had this complexity in mind. For, whereas the *metalingual* function implies language used to check on language, such as asking for the meaning of a word, the *metacommunicative* orientation extends reflexivity to all signifying practices and to their multilevel interaction. Accordingly, a painter can use color to make a statement about color, a filmmaker use film to reflect on film, and in personal interaction, a look can make a statement about the words just said, reinforcing or denying their surface meaning. Cooperation, politeness, irony, humor, and so forth are metacommunicatively signified by such superimposed commentaries. The other terminological alterations are minor: *referent* has been replaced by *topic,* and *code* by *signifying system,* since the latter term suggests more accurately what is at work in the social production of meaning. All in all, it is our hope that the labyrinthine model we have elaborated succeeds in capturing to some extent the multilayered complexity of cultural communication discussed in the previous sections.

The Classroom: The Student as Semiotician

In this chapter, we have been mindful all along of how to make available to our students the lessons learned from semiotics and sociolinguistics. In the Modern Languages and Linguistics department in which we teach, our majors take a core of three courses that introduce them to the theoretical framework sketched above. "The World of Language" and "World Language Communities" concentrate on the nature and social role of language and other signifying practices within an intercultural perspective; "Textual Analysis: Words, Images, Music" provides students with the tools required for critical literacy, that is, for evaluative readings—both aesthetic and social—of texts of all kinds, spoken and written, visual, and musical, from popular to high culture. Since this interdisciplinary core, originally intended for English and Modern Languages, has been described elsewhere, we will not go into detail about it here (Field and Moorjani, 1982; Moorjani and Field, 1983; Field, Freeman, and Moorjani, 1984; McCray and O'Neill, 1985). Instead, we will suggest in general what we perceive to be useful ways of introducing sociolinguistic and semiotic approaches into high school and undergraduate curricula.

LANGUAGE AND INTERCULTURAL STUDY IN TANDEM

What are some effective ways of setting up the dialogue between our students' own culture and the culture of the language they are acquiring? What would constitute an intercultural classroom? Several approaches to foreign language instruction suggested over the past few years do pay close attention to the interactional and situational components of communication, stress the inclusion of sociolinguistic and semiotic variation, and take into account the students' different cognitive styles. In our discussion below of language teaching on the elementary and intermediate levels, we propose that an amalgam of the "notional-functional" and "natural" approaches facilitates the intercultural and instructional dialogue we favor.

The notional-functional or communicative syllabus involves the learning of language as a culturally situated phenomenon, the very domain of sociolinguistic and semiotic inquiry. Emphasizing topic, event, and participant interaction, the situational syllabus focuses on cultural communication in specific contexts, such as the classroom, home and work, leisure and travel. (For two particularly useful thematic syllabi that integrate language and culture, see Allen, 1985, and Rosenthal and Sloane, 1987.) The natural approach, modeled on what is known about first-language acquisition, stresses that listening comprehension precedes speech production, relies on large amounts of understandable and interesting input in the target language to build proficiency, and recommends a relaxed classroom environment (Krashen and Terrell, 1982). These methodologies, then, would seem to respond most appropriately to the shift (back) to oral, nonlinear, functional modes of communication with which our students are most comfortable. They seem clearly to be a good way to begin language instruction, doing away with beginning terrors and resistances, while reserving analytical approaches for later stages of instruction.

Although notional-functional and natural methodologies, by themselves, do not guarantee intercultural dialogue, they offer a situational framework that makes it possible. By way of illustration, we might take one topic of the thematic syllabus, such as home, and suggest the ways in which sociolinguistic and semiotic approaches can lead to increased cultural literacy and understanding. At the most basic level, for example, in introducing the names for people who share a home in the target culture, the teacher might show how social roles and communication are intertwined. That is, for a middle-class family in a city, how do parents and children address each other? If children are expected to defer to their elders, what are the linguistic and cultural signs of this relation (style register, gestures, facial expression, eye contact, touch, right to initiate conversation, to interrupt)? How are affection and anger expressed both verbally and nonverbally? How do male and female family roles and expectations differ? (The family would seem the right topic under which to emphasize the cultural construction of the gendered subject and the consequent social variations in role, body language, and linguistic expression.) What are the norms of family etiquette, that is, the pragmatics of greetings, interaction rituals, table manners, use of space and objects, mutual obligations, etc.? How much time do family members spend together? What are typical family occasions? Who contributes to the family finances? How much money is spent on housing, food, clothing, entertainment? At what age are children expected, if ever, to live on their own? And how does this differ from our students' experience? How does a typical middle-class residence compare semiotically with the American equivalent (number and function of rooms, formal and informal areas, decor)? Class, ethnic, regional, traditional, and experimental variations might then be contrasted with the standard middle-class family model in order to permit the three-way dialogue beyond standard-to-standard suggested in the first section of this chapter. A few stories on the topic, either told by the teacher or assigned as reading, can help to focus on cultural information, expectations, and assumptions concerning home and family.

In beginning language classes that emphasize listening comprehension and are conducted in the target language, such an introduction to the family would serve to develop language and cultural proficiency in tandem. Both, of course, are helped along by the concurrent introduction of a variety of cultural icons — transparencies made from magazines, ads, trivia of all types, slides, segments from videos, films, television programs, videodisc, and miming, all used in the interactive mode. To encourage a cultural dialogue with these materials, it is important to direct the students' critical attention to the signifying practices at work in the texts. They might be asked to describe the models used in an ad showing a family by focusing on the parameters of cultural communication sketched in the previous paragraph, including social characteristics such as body language, dress, and props; the type of event and the social roles and relations implied by the decor; the use of cultural icons, indexes, and symbols, and the positions of the posed models. In addition to such a reading of social signs, students might be encouraged to comment on the type of audience for whom this ad is intended, i.e., one that would identify with the little drama laid out, and to pay attention to the interaction (if any) between models and audience by means of look, directive gestures and language, etc. Then too, there might be questions of how this family scenario relates to the product being sold and what this implies about social values. The questions need not be limited to picture content but should stretch the students' semiotic thinking by including inquiries about aesthetic patterns, such as use of color, sound, pictorial or filmic techniques, unconventional foregrounding, and the like. A contrast with similar American ads might follow. That students at the end of such an exercise be asked to make cultural hypotheses that may then be tested further has been suggested by Seelye (1974, pp. 124–30). Such an exercise is particularly apropos here, since, as frequently pointed out, the semiotic reading of ads gives access to a culture's mythical and ideological conception of itself.

In order to encourage a contrastive view, almost all class activities designed for a given topic may become intercultural. In accordance with the Total Physical Response method, for instance, students can be directed to carry out any set of actions as they would be performed in their home culture and then in the target culture. Some of the topics of the notional-functional syllabus, such as entertainment, suggest a large number of possibilities, such as the contrastive analysis and practice of popular games, sports, and music.

The increasingly popular interview also fits well into an intercultural approach. When people who were brought up or who have lived in the target culture come into a class to interact with students, the stage is set for the first-hand experience of the multilayered intricacies of intercultural conversation described above, such as the metacommunicative punctuation of speech that nonverbal gestures perform, differing politeness and discourse conventions, questions of social positioning, and shared and unshared cultural contexts. Since misfirings are bound to occur in this situation, the faux pas and discomfort that results can lead into a useful discussion about cultural differences, the dialogic complexity of intercultural situations, and the knowledge needed in order to avoid miscommunications.

As students become active readers of cultural signs and practices on the elementary level, they are increasingly prepared for the extended multimedia programs—videotape, film, videodisc, television via satellite—available on the intermediate and advanced levels. Since many courses on the intermediate level now make use of such media either as adjuncts or even as the major focus of the course, eclipsing the textbook, it is crucial that we take into consideration the cultural and cognitive shifts that the transition from a print to an electronic era entails. If, as has been suggested, we are internalizing the signifying structures of film and beginning to think "filmicly" instead of "bookishly," then surely such montage/collage thinking has major implications for pedagogy (Ulmer, 1985, p. 305). To go beyond the transmission or consumption of information, then, and aim for the elaboration of cultural knowledge, we must develop a postmodern pedagogy that encourages students to engage in a critical dialogue with the media, a type of contrastive montage of their own and others' views. Although obviously a rich source of cultural information, electronic programming will not lead to cultural understanding without the distanciation from automatic consumption that the dialogical orientation to cultural discourse described above provides.

INTERCULTURAL DIALOGUE AND THE MAJOR

At the advanced level, where we are very much concerned with helping students gain skill in inference and in digging out presupposition (along with improving their fluency and their mastery of language structures), the need for explicit semiotic content in cultural teaching becomes very great. It is particularly important at this level not to maintain a hypothetical "average" cultural model for the target language, but rather to present the full reality of cultural variation. A course at this level might focus on a regional or minority culture, Alsace, for example, thus permitting one form of the three-way comparative point of view recommended above (U.S. — mainstream France — region). The selection of a society with a minority language is especially useful, as it allows for unusually clear exemplification of the interaction that always exists among communicative structures, communicative setting, and participant relations. In such a context, one is led naturally to ask which settings, which social relationships, which communicative orientations require use of dialect? Which allow the use of standard German? When is French alone appropriate? What political/economic constraints are relevant? Such questions necessarily open discussion to history and sociology, as one searches for the sources of the pragmatic rules that regulate interaction. To take another example, an advanced-level course with a strong focus on the Spanish Civil War could serve to reveal some of the signs that have dominated Spanish culture for the past fifty years, along with the reasons for certain communicative practices that function today in, say, Catalonia, as opposed to Madrid. In both cases, the students' store of cultural information (their "cultural literacy") is being developed. In addition, they are refining their understanding of the nature of signifying practices, and they may also be meeting and analyzing important cultural productions (Strasbourg cathedral, Picasso's *Guernica*). Analytic thinking and work with inference and presupposition can be facilitated through a careful ordering of visual and print materials and oral and written assignments, passing from simple description to straightforward historical narrative to more complex social and cultural analysis. Thus, at the advanced level, the course can be moving actively toward all five of the goals set forth above (pp. 29–30).

Since the critical exploration of cultural productions of the target culture is one of the major thrusts of upper-level courses, training in the analysis of all types of texts and media is of crucial importance here. Such training might be provided across languages by a common course, such as our *Textual Analysis,* introducing a semiotic/dialogic approach to cultural communication. The target language major programs, then, would likewise be cross-disciplinary and multimedia. An introduction to literature and culture would, for instance, include popular and high culture, music, the pictorial arts, and social and historical context. Modern literature would be studied in relation to film and the other arts and vice versa. In order to exemplify the analytical/dialogical stance our students are encouraged to take, we give in the appendix the suggestions for a discourse analysis of a film, one of several guidelines introduced in *Textual Analysis* to help students explore intricate cultural productions. Although at first sight, the guidelines might appear daunting, they have led students who have learned to manipulate semiotic and sociolinguistic concepts to produce outstanding analyses. We suggest that certain elements of the guidelines can be adapted at all levels to stimulate the semiotic and dialogic interaction with cultural productions and processes that we have proposed as the path to cultural knowledge.

Coda: Return Home

We have suggested above that when we provide students with the tools they need to explore signifying practices in the target civilization, we are also preparing them for a fuller participation in their own culture. It is our experience that students who have worked with semiotic approaches to cultural production in the second language are much more aware of aesthetic and persuasive uses of communication in American advertising, television, and the fine arts. In addition, a firm understanding of the nature of the social production of meaning (as sketched in Figure 1, for example) can make students more critical consumers of all kinds of texts, as they come to understand how power relations are expressed and maintained through semiotic systems. Good teaching of culture can thus have an important effect on the ways students deal with political discourse and advertising, but it can also affect their ability to discuss contemporary problems of language policy and education (the U.S. English movement, censorship, bilingual education, nonstandard dialect in the classroom). Language teachers have long maintained that the exploration of a second culture can have profound effects on the way one views the world; we feel that it is precisely this potential for changing the student's outlook on life that gives the teaching of culture its depth and significance.

Appendix

GUIDELINES FOR A DISCOURSE ANALYSIS OF A FILM

1 **Discuss the film as a commodity.**
How do the economic/institutional considerations that might have contributed to the decision to make and distribute the film influence the viewer's approach to the work?
2 **Analyze the film as a dialogue between the implied author, the implied audience, and yourself as viewer.** [Note: The implied author of a film is the role into which the filmmaker shifts while producing a film addressed to a distinctive audience. Together with the scriptwriters, production artists and technicians, implied authors/filmmakers orient their view of the world toward what they consider the audience's conceptual horizon or beliefs and values to be. In the questions that follow, the word "filmmaker" is to be taken in the sense of such an implied authorial role.] **In your analysis, include:**
• *Personal deixis or shifters:*
Is the filmmaker also the film's anonymous narrator, that is, is the audience made to share primarily the authorial viewpoint? Or is point of view projected through a fictional narrator or narrators? If yes, is this narrator a distanced voice-over eye-witness or an internal narrator who is also a participant? What type of narratee corresponds to the above persona(s) of the filmmaker/narrator(s)? [Note: The narratee is the fictional or nonfictional addressee of the narrator.]
• *Spatio-temporal deixis:*
How is the audience made to anchor in the spatio-temporal point of view of the film-maker/narrator? [Note: Spatial shifts are largely effected by camera manipulation; temporal shifts depend primarily on editing and montage.] Is the point of view omniscient or limited? Does the narrator project the temporal viewpoint into the past, the future, or both? Is the passage of time communicated chronologically or achronologically? If chronologically, is the sequence linear or nonlinear, that is, disrupted by flashbacks, flashforwards, parallel actions, time compressions and extensions? If achronologically, is time circular, repetitive, involuted, associative, etc.?
• *Social deixis:*
How do the filmmaker's/narrator's and the scriptwriter's social characteristics (gender, age, class, ethnicity, geographical origin) and reputation affect their dialogue with the audience? What are the social characteristics of the spectators to whom the film is addressed? How do you position yourself as viewer in relation to the type of receiver

implied by the film? How do these social factors affect your understanding of the film? How closely does the filmmaker involve the audience in the filmic process?

• *World-sharing and evaluative deixis:*

What cultural information, assumptions, values, and texts does the filmmaker/narrator take as shared with the implied audience/narratees? (The time and place the film was made play an important role here.) What evaluative/expressive stance does the filmmaker take toward these and the film? [Note: This can be gauged largely by paying attention to (a) choice of topic (or lack thereof), (b) the overall composition, i.e., thematic selection and organization, (c) the use of cultural signs (icons, indexes, and symbols), (d) unconventional foregrounding and other means of distanciation, (e) textuality or aesthetic temporal, spatial, visual, musical, and linguistic patterns (repetitions and contrasts), (f) visual, linguistic, and musical style related to topic (this is in part communicated by sharp or soft focus, graininess of filmstock, slow motion, etc.), (g) social role and positioning of participants, (h) metacommunicative evaluative commentary, irony, humor, etc., effected partly by means of camera distance, deep versus shallow focus, high-angle versus low-angle shots, cutting, recurring images, dialogue, music, etc., (i) persuasive techniques, such as positive and negative metaphorical transfers and cultural associations of all kinds.] What is your response to the implied author's cultural constructs and evaluations?

• *Genre:*

To what genre does the film belong?

• *Communicative act:*

What type of communicative act is the film as a whole, that is, does it mostly entertain, inform, persuade, raise questions, reflect on itself, etc.?

3 **If the film is a narrative, discuss:**

• *Narrative structure:*

Does the film's title function as an abstract or is there another summary of the film? How does the film orient the audience in respect to time, place, and persons? What is the narrative sequence of events, or in the case of a story, what is the plot? Is there a complicating action and resolution? Or does the story lack a resolution? Is there a coda?

• *The participants as senders and receivers:*

What are the characters' social characteristics, roles, and status? How are the personal and social/power relationships that hold between the participants staged in the film? How do the actors' performances influence your understanding of the characters?

4 **Give your overall evaluation of the film. Discuss the areas of agreement and disagreement, aesthetic pleasure and pain, new understandings, etc.**

References

Allen, W. W. Toward cultural proficiency. In A. C. Omaggio (Ed.), *Proficiency, curriculum, articulation: The ties that bind.* Middlebury, VT: Northeast Conference, 1985.

Arizpe, V., & Aguirre, B. E. Mexican, Puerto Rican, and Cuban ethnic groups in first-year college-level Spanish textbooks. *Modern Language Journal,* 1987, *71,* 125–37.

Bakhtin, M. M. *The dialogic imagination.* Trans. C. Emerson & M. Holquist. Austin: University of Texas Press, 1981.

Barthes, R. *Mythologies.* Trans. A. Lavers. New York: Hill and Wang, 1972.

Brière, J.-F. Cultural understanding through cross-cultural analysis. *French Review,* 1987, *60,* 202–08.

Crawford-Lange, L. M., & Lange, D. L. Doing the unthinkable in the second-language classroom: A process for the integration of language and culture. In T. V. Higgs (Ed.), *Teaching for proficiency, the organizing principle*. Lincolnwood, IL: National Textbook Company, 1984.

Eco, U. *A theory of semiotics*. Bloomington: Indiana University Press, 1976.

Field, T. T., & Moorjani, A. A linguistic and semiotic approach to textual analysis. *French Review*, 1982, *55*, 593–600.

Field, T. T., Freeman, L. H., & Moorjani, A. Introducing *The World of Language:* A linguistic basis for language study. *Modern Language Journal*, 1984, *68*, 222–29.

Fillmore, C. J. *Santa Cruz lectures on deixis 1971*. Bloomington: Indiana University Linguistics Club, 1975.

Goody, J. R., & Watt, I. The consequences of literacy. *Comparative Studies in Society and History*, 1962-3, *5*, 304–45.

Greenfield, P. M. *Mind and media: The effects of television, video games, and computers*. Cambridge, MA: Harvard University Press, 1984.

Gumperz, J. J. *Discourse strategies*. New York: Cambridge University Press, 1982.

Hawkes, T. *Structuralism and semiotics*. Berkeley: University of California Press, 1977.

Henley, N. *Body politics: Power, sex, and nonverbal communication*. Englewood Cliffs, NJ: Prentice-Hall, 1977.

Hirsch, E. D. *Cultural literacy: What every American needs to know*. Boston: Houghton Mifflin, 1987.

Hymes, D. H. *On communicative competence*. Philadelphia: University of Pennsylvania Press, 1971.

Hymes, D. H. The ethnography of speaking. In B. G. Blount (Ed.), *Language, culture and society: A book of readings*. Cambridge, MA: Winthrop, 1974.

Jakobson, R. Closing statement: Linguistics and poetics. In T. A. Sebeok (Ed.), *Style in language*. Cambridge, MA: M.I.T. Press, 1960.

Jakobson, R. Language in relation to other communication systems. In *Selected writings*. Vol. II. The Hague: Mouton, 1971.

Joos, M. *The five clocks*. New York: Harcourt, Brace, and World, 1967.

Krashen, S., & Terrell, T. D. *The natural approach*. New York: Pergamon, 1982.

Leech, G. N. *Principles of pragmatics*. London and New York: Longman, 1983.

Lévi-Strauss, C. *Tristes tropiques*. Trans. J. Russell. New York: Atheneum, 1971.

Lyons, J. *Semantics*. 2 vols. Cambridge: Cambridge University Press, 1986.

McCray, S., & O'Neill, M. World language communities: Foreign language teaching and the world view. *ADFL Bulletin*, 1985, *16* (2), 53–55.

Mead, M. Discussion session on linguistics. In T. A. Sebeok, A. S. Hayes, & M. C. Bateson (Eds.), *Approaches to semiotics*. Transactions of the Indiana University Conference on Paralinguistics and Kinesics. The Hague: Mouton, 1964.

Moorjani, A., & Field, T. T. Revising and reviving textual analysis in the modern language curriculum. *ADFL Bulletin*, 1983, *15* (2), 12–18.

Ong, W. J. *Orality and literacy: The technologizing of the word*. London: Methuen, 1982.

Paoletti, M., & Steele, R. *Civilisation française contemporaine*. Paris: Hatier, 1983.

Rosenthal, A. S., & Sloane, R. A. A communicative approach to foreign language instruction: The UMBC project. *Foreign Language Annals*, 1987, *30*, 245–53.

Saussure, F. de. *Course in general linguistics*. Trans. W. Baskin. New York: Philosophical Library, 1959.

Seelye, H. N. *Teaching culture: Strategies for foreign language education*. Skokie, IL: National Textbook Company, 1974.

Tedlock, D. *The spoken word and the work of interpretation*. Philadelphia: University of Pennsylvania Press, 1983.

Ulmer, G. L. *Applied grammatology: Post(e)-pedagogy from Jacques Derrida to Joseph Beuys*. Baltimore: The Johns Hopkins University Press, 1985.

Westphal, G. F. On the teaching of culture in the FL curriculum. *Canadian Modern Language Review,* 1986, *43* (1), 87–93.

Witherspoon, G. *Language and art in the Navajo universe.* Ann Arbor: University of Michigan Press, 1977.

Wylie, L. *Village in the Vaucluse.* Cambridge, MA: Harvard University Press, 1957.

Robert C. Lafayette
Louisiana State University

Integrating the Teaching of Culture into the Foreign Language Classroom[1]

Introduction

A cursory examination of the foreign language education professional literature since 1970 as well as the programs of state, regional, and national meetings and conferences during that same period of time provides sufficient evidence of the high degree of importance accorded the teaching of culture. In fact, the present volume represents the sixth in this important collection to be devoted exclusively to culture. No other single topic has received such extensive treatment.

Given the vast amount of ink and paper spent on the subject, one would think that by now the cultural component would have been strongly implanted into the foreign language curriculum. However, such is not the case. Among the three major components of the curriculum (language, literature, and culture), the greatest amount of time and energy is still devoted to the grammar and vocabulary aspects of language, even though the area of communication has advanced considerably during the last twenty years due to activities surrounding communicative competence, the functional-notional syllabus, and proficiency. Culture, however, remains the weakest component due to its uneven treatment in textbooks and to the lack of familiarity, among teachers, with the culture itself and with the techniques needed to teach it.

History tells us that for decades grammar and literature have been the main actors on the foreign language teaching stage. It is understandable, then, that methods and materials still reflect portions of this history. Moreover, the textbooks, which perpetuate teaching strategies, still constitute (after the teacher) the most important cog in the educational process (see Chapter 4). It is thus obvious that the textbook itself represents the most powerful agent for change in language teaching. What we fail to realize, however, is that most textbook publishers are commercial enterprises, whose primary purpose is to serve the foreign language profession, not to change it. Therefore, as long as the majority of foreign language teachers demand grammar, with communication and culture as secondary interests, that is exactly what most publishers will provide. If we wish to have serious impact on increasing the cultural component in language teaching, we must try not only to influence publishers, but, more importantly, to design teacher training programs that will provide teachers with both a knowledge of culture and the ability to convey it to their students. As Allen so aptly states:

. . . Despite the talk of communication and culture, and the desire for their attain-
ment, energies are devoted instead to grammar and vocabulary. And this is understandable, for grammar offers several advantages over culture: it is the concept around
which most textbooks and materials are organized; it is finite and can be ordered
in either a linear, sequential plan of study or else in a cyclical one; mastery of it
can be easily tested and evaluated; and, finally, it is a subject matter the classroom
teacher can teach him or herself, if necessary, using an advanced grammar text,
and which, once mastered, is unlikely to change. Culture, by contrast, is diffuse;
difficult to grasp, translate into instructional goals, test, evaluate, and order;
prodigious in quantity; and ever-evolving. (1985, p. 145)

Culture: Much Dialogue but Little Action

Both Allen (1985) and Omaggio (1986) spend considerable time tracing the history
of the teaching of culture and summarizing the major ideas of Brooks (1968), Nostrand
(1967), and Seelye (1984). It would be redundant to repeat that exercise here, except
for a brief comment on the revised *ACTFL Proficiency Guidelines* (1985) from which were
deleted the guidelines for cultural understanding that appeared in the provisional 1983
version. Allen (1985) demonstrates appropriately that the culture guidelines were
unsound, from a theoretical standpoint, because they attempted to follow the same function, content, and accuracy schema used to describe the proficiency guidelines in the
four language skills. She then suggests replacing the function–content–accuracy schema
with a different conceptual tripartite framework:

1 *Information:* information about the particular culture and the organization of this
  information into a coherent whole, broken down into successive stages;
2 *Experience:* a cognitive process by means of which the learner approaches and comes
  to know the particular culture;
3 *Authenticity:* the effect upon the learner in terms of socio-economic behavior and
  attitude that results from increasing, deepening knowledge of the culture.

Allen subsequently reformulated the entire culture guidelines, but, unfortunately, in
the interim ACTFL decided to omit culture from its revised proficiency guidelines. It
might now be beneficial for the profession to reconsider the guidelines in light of Allen's
suggestions.

The works evoked above represent important attempts by members of the profession
to increase the role of culture in foreign language teaching. Unfortunately, most of the
suggestions require such a significant change from what is currently taking place in
the classroom that only the most courageous individuals will even consider attempting
any of them. What the profession needs at the moment is a simple, direct approach
to more culture in the classroom built upon content and practices which already exist.
The remainder of this paper will explore the creation and implementation of precisely
such an approach. It includes:

1 A set of suggested cultural goals from which teachers may select those that fit their
  needs;
2 A discussion of the new Indiana "Guide to Proficiency-Based Instruction" (Strasheim
  & Bartz, 1986), whose primary goal is the integration of language and culture;
3 A set of principles to help teachers and students develop a cultural mind-set;
4 A series of practical classroom suggestions for integrating culture with the teaching
  of vocabulary, grammar, listening, speaking, reading, and writing.

Suggested Goals for the Teaching of Culture

Due to the breadth and depth of culture, it is often difficult for teachers to select those aspects of it that should be included in the curriculum at various stages of instruction. The choices range from supplying students with clearly identifiable facts about a culture to bringing about subtle affective changes in their desire or ability to value people who think, dress, or act differently from themselves.

Although many experts criticize focusing on factual information, this author believes, along with Porcher (1986), that there indeed exists a basic repertoire of information necessary for the comprehension of most cultural concepts. This includes very basic geographical and historical background that provides the necessary space and time dimensions, as well as basic institutional (administrative, political, etc.) and cultural (family, professions, etc.) information which is needed to understand and process more complex cultural phenomena.

The student-oriented goals listed below may be classified in several different categories. The first four reflect what is commonly referred to as "culture with a capital C," while goals five through eight belong to the category of "everyday culture." Goals five and six distinguish between "active" everyday culture, i.e., that knowledge needed to function as a visitor in the foreign environment, and "passive" everyday culture, knowledge that would enhance the understanding of a people but might not be necessary in functioning in their environment as a temporary guest. Goal nine represents the overarching affective objective sought by most foreign language programs but attained only by focusing on several of the other stated goals. Goals ten and eleven recognize the fact that several cultures may be linked to the same language, including ethnic populations within the continental United States, and encourages teachers to venture beyond the mother country in presenting culture. Finally, goals twelve and thirteen deal with the process of studying foreign cultures.

In considering these goals, it should be noted that each is important in and of itself and that priorities in selecting them can only be determined in relation to overall course and performance goals. In addition, several of them distinguish between the ability of students to recognize a cultural pattern and the more difficult task of explaining it. It is suggested that school foreign language departments rank these goals and compare the results with present and potential cultural activities in the classroom. The student will be able to:

1 Recognize/explain major geographical monuments.
2 Recognize/explain major historical events.
3 Recognize/explain major institutions (administrative, political, religious, educational, etc.).
4 Recognize/explain major "artistic" monuments (architecture, arts, literature).
5 Recognize/explain "active" everyday cultural patterns (eating, shopping, greeting people, etc.).
6 Recognize/explain "passive" everyday cultural patterns (social stratification, marriage, work, etc.).
7 Act appropriately in common everyday situations.
8 Use appropriate common gestures.
9 Value different peoples and societies.
10 Recognize/explain culture of target language-related ethnic groups in the United States.

11 Recognize/explain culture of non-European peoples speaking target language (Canada, Africa, South America, etc.).

12 Evaluate validity of statements about culture.

13 Develop skills needed to locate and organize information about culture.

The Indiana Guide to Proficiency-Based Instruction

In 1983, a committee of Indiana high school foreign language teachers under the direction of Lorraine A. Strasheim of Indiana University and Walter H. Bartz of the Indiana Department of Education began work on a set of proficiency-based guidelines for use in their schools. One of their primary goals was to develop a model for the integration of communicative, cultural, and linguistic learning in foreign language curricula and instruction. After three years of labor, they produced, in this writer's opinion, one of the most enlightened curriculum guides in American education (Strasheim & Bartz, 1986).[2] The document includes a list of specific proficiency statements (goals) for each level of instruction, each statement being followed by "proficiency indicators," which are descriptions of student performance and are used to indicate the extent to which each goal has been met. For example, one of the five Level Two proficiency statements says: "Write short compositions on familiar topics, structured letters, outlines and synopses, and fill out some of the forms encountered in the culture." The accompanying proficiency indicators are:

1 Describe the school day.

2 Write a letter describing a day in the foreign culture.

3 Write a description of a special event in the foreign culture.

4 Identify specific places in the foreign culture(s) to be visited in order to experience a variety of opportunities.

5 Describe famous people of the foreign culture.

6 Write a letter describing meals in the foreign culture.

7 Plan and describe a day's activities for a foreign visitor.

8 Write a letter describing his or her family.

9 List appropriate clothes to wear, based on weather reports.

10 Write appropriate salutations, closings, etc., for a friendly letter.

11 Write a business letter.

Proficiency statements and indicators such as the above are extremely valuable in defining student progress and in establishing what constitutes proficiency at the end of each level of instruction. Ideally, they establish parameters for the articulation of instruction from one level to another.

The Indiana guide, however, goes much further in that it attempts to integrate culture and communication at every level of instruction. The major portion of this guide consists of more than one hundred culture-based learning goals spanning Levels One through Four. All goals are grouped under the nine following broad cultural contexts which the committee identified as reflecting the topics covered in most textbooks adopted in Indiana (the numbers that follow each context identify the levels at which it appears):

1 School and Education (1-2).

2 Leisure Time (1-2-3).

3 Family and Home (1-2-3).

4 Meeting Personal Needs (1-2-3).

5 The "World" of the Target Language (1-2-3-4).
6 Travel/Transportation (1-2-3-4).
7 World of Work (2-3).
8 History and Politics (3-4).
9 Fine Arts (3-4).

Each of these contexts is then broken down into "cultural situations" which represent a narrower topic (sports, living quarters, children's literature, etc.) or situation (ordering a meal, shopping, etc.).

None of the levels of instruction include all nine cultural concepts. Six are covered in Level One, seven in Level Two, eight in Level Three, and four in Level Four. Level One content is focused primarily on personal, everyday cultural elements such as living quarters, daily schedule of activities, city travel, and shopping, while Level Four content mainly consists of formal or capital "C" culture, such as history, literature and famous places. The only two cultural contexts to be treated at all four levels of instruction are the "World" of the Target Language and Travel/Transportation. Below are sample goals from these two contexts taken from each level of instruction. An examination of these goals will reveal a regular progression in the level of complexity of learning tasks. The goals first deal with the listing of items, then move on to identification and selection, followed by description and information gathering, and concluding with synthesis and conjecture.

THE "WORLD" OF THE TARGET LANGUAGE

Level One: Given a map of the world, the student will be able to locate and pronounce the names of ten countries (cities) in which the target language is spoken.

Level Two: The student will role-play a situation in which he/she has won a trip around the "world" to ten cities and/or countries that speak the target language, identifying the places he/she will visit in the order in which he/she plans to go.

Level Three: Given a specific country speaking the target language, the student, acting as a travel agent, will "sell" a tourist (the teacher) on visiting this country, giving the following kinds of information:
a The climate during a certain season.
b Things of interest to see.
c Major cities.
d Foods and major occupations.
e Fun things to do there.

Level Four: After listening to three conversations, each of which contains vocabulary and/or cultural allusions associated with a specific region or country, the student will identify the location of each conversation, citing the vocabulary or cultural references that influence that choice.

TRAVEL/TRANSPORTATION

Level One: Given a map of a part of a city, the student will listen to a series of directions as to how to get to a specific place, indicating the directions by drawing arrows on the map.

Level Two: Given an authentic menu and an exact amount of money to spend, the student will, with the teacher serving as waiter or waitress, order a complete meal he/she can "afford."

Level Three: Given a specific city, the student will identify three famous places to visit, describing each in a short paragraph.

Level Four: Given an opening statement such as "If I were a millionaire," the student will describe his/her fantasy trip around the world, explaining choices made.

Some Basic Principles for Integrating Language and Culture

Although we would prefer foreign language courses to be built upon a culture-based as opposed to a grammar-based syllabus, there is little doubt that most textbooks and teachers will continue to favor the grammatical syllabus for years to come. This, however, does not prevent these individuals from integrating culture into their language-based courses. The principles that follow apply to them as well as to those who favor culture-based courses.

In courses where communicative goals are paramount, it is obvious that teachers must establish an atmosphere that demonstrates the importance, indeed the very existence of communication. They must use the target language to communicate and must demand that the students do likewise; they must plan communicative activities and test for communication; they must convince the students that the language taught exists above and beyond the front and back covers of the textbook. In short, teachers must create in both themselves and each student the conviction that the language is real and that it works. The same argument applies to integrating language and culture. Teachers must create their own positive cultural mind-set, as well as that of their students. Culture will not become a reality in the foreign language classroom until teachers become convinced that they are teaching more than form, that there is indeed a content to that which is being taught, a content that is not identified in terms of grammatical descriptors. The teacher can nurture the development and assure the predominance of this mind-set by abiding by the principles outlined below.

CULTURAL OBJECTIVES AND ACTIVITIES MUST BE PLANNED AS CAREFULLY AS THEIR LANGUAGE COUNTERPARTS AND BE SPECIFICALLY INCLUDED IN LESSON PLANS

Since the average foreign language textbook is based and sequenced according to grammar, teachers view their task as "covering" a pre-established number of grammatical items. Consequently, lesson plans typically consist of a series of grammar points accompanied by a variety of appropriate activities. This tends to assure that these points are introduced and practiced during a fixed period of time.

A similar system is necessary to assure the presence of culture in the curriculum. Each class should include at least one culture objective along with suggestions for introducing and practicing it. For example, if the grammar objective consists of the verb "to be" in its function of showing location, the culture objective might be to locate various cities or other geographical elements in the target country. At first glance, this may appear simplistic, but until the answer to the often-asked question, "What am I teaching today?" includes a cultural element as well as a grammatical one, we cannot claim to be serious about the teaching of culture.

CULTURAL COMPONENTS MUST BE TESTED AS SERIOUSLY AS THEIR LANGUAGE COUNTERPARTS

Throughout most of American education, grades are based on test results, and since grades themselves carry such importance, students virtually always pay the greatest attention to that which is tested. It is therefore obvious that curricular elements not tested by the teacher carry much less value in the eyes of students, and indeed are often ignored. For example, one of the reasons that the majority of our beginning students have minimal oral communication skills is that we rarely or never formally test those skills in beginning level courses. The same is true for culture. Why should students concern themselves about culture if it is not tested and does not affect the course grade? Even good students are not usually idealistic enough to learn for the sake of learning.

Unfortunately, little has been written about testing culture and only a handful of foreign language textbooks include culture items on the tests which accompany them. In an article entitled "Evaluating cultural learnings," Lafayette and Schulz (1975) discuss and provide examples for three types of culture tests: (1) testing for knowledge, that is, the ability to recognize cultural information or patterns; (2) testing for understanding, that is, the ability to explain cultural information or patterns; (3) testing for behavior, that is, the ability to use cultural information or patterns.

TEXTBOOK PHOTOGRAPHS AND ILLUSTRATIONS MUST BE CONSIDERED AS VIABLE TEACHING CONTENT

Every modern-day textbook includes an abundance of attractive photographs taken in the target countries as well as illustrations of a variety of realia. There is often a higher incidence of culture in the photographs and realia than in the printed texts and exercises found in the book. Unfortunately, these visuals are rarely mentioned in class and are almost never supported in the text by culturally related exercises and activities.

An excellent approach for fostering the increased integration of langue and culture as well as nurturing the cultural mind-set is to make use of a basic set of questions for each illustration. The questions suggested below are grouped in three categories of ascending difficulty. The first category, description, is at the simplest level and is meant for use in learning and/or reinforcing vocabulary and basic cultural information. Depending on the content of the photograph, the focus may be on nouns, adjectives, verbs, etc. The purpose of the second category of questions, information gathering, is not limited to the acquisition of new cultural information. A second purpose of these questions is to help students learn to gather information by observation, a skill that will be of use to them in all other subject matter areas. The third level of questions, comparison, represents a higher level of cognitive processing, but it is still readily usable in the classroom. It should be noted that the ability of the students and the nature of the photographs or illustrations may not permit the use of all three levels of questioning. In addition, these questions are not meant to be all-inclusive. Individuals are encouraged to change or add to the set based on their particular classroom needs.

SAMPLE QUESTIONS

Description
1 What do you see in this picture?
2 Can you describe some of the items?
3 What are people doing?
4 How are they dressed?

Information gathering
1 Can you tell where or when this picture was taken?
2 Do some of the objects or places in this picture have historical significance?

3 Does the picture tell you anything special about life in that country?

4 Does the picture portray a certain segment of society in that country?

5 Is the picture of a general or specific nature?

6 Could a similar picture have been taken in other parts of this country?

Comparison

1 What makes this picture French, German, or Spanish, if anything?

2 Could a similar picture have been taken in the United States? Where? If not, why not?

3 Where would you go in the United States to take a picture of contrasting cultural habits?

IN ORDER TO FOCUS ON CULTURE, LANGUAGE TEACHING MUST EMPHASIZE THE TEACHING OF CONTENT AS MUCH AS IT DOES THE TEACHING OF FORM

Linguists and language teachers are virtually the only individuals alive who consider language for its own sake. The rest of the world uses language for a purpose. They are usually more concerned with the content of an utterance than its form. In order to foster a more acute cultural mind-set, language teachers must dramatically increase their attention to content. For example, it is not sufficient for a teacher to accept a student's proper use of *estar* in locating a South American city; the teacher must also verify that the city has been correctly located. Similarly, there is a significant difference between asking a student to generate any ten articles of clothing and asking the same individual to identify five that might be appropriate attire at a funeral.

Increasing the focus on content presents the problem of selecting the type of content material. Should teachers continue with textbooks or materials that present cultural facts in a synthesized and/or summarized manner or should they turn to raw, authentic materials as advocated by Beacco and Lieutaud (1985)? We are naturally attracted to the latter, not only because of their authenticity but also their attractiveness, since they are presented exactly as they appeared in their original form. They also lend themselves very well to process-oriented learning strategies. Upon closer examination, however, exclusive use of authentic materials may present serious comprehension problems. Most newspaper articles and radio and television news programs, for example, tend to assume prior knowledge of past events, along with total control of the language itself, thus making them very difficult for the average foreign language learner to comprehend.

The decision to use authentic or synthesized materials should of course depend on the background, abilities, and objectives of the students. Very often, the ideal situation is to use a combination of the two. The synthesized and edited materials provide the students with the background knowledge necessary for a better understanding of the authentic materials, while the authentic materials themselves supply real-life examples of generic cultural phenomena.

THE TEACHING OF CULTURE MUST EXTEND BEYOND FACTUAL LEARNING AND INCLUDE COMMUNITY RESOURCES, EXPERIENTIAL LEARNING AND PROCESS SKILLS

Allen (1985), Galloway (1984), Kramsch (1983), Crawford-Lange and Lange (1984), Zarate (1986), and many others all state that a "facts-only" approach to the teaching of culture is not only insufficient but may also be detrimental in that it may at times reinforce stereotypes rather than diminish them. Students need to be taught to understand culture on more than a cognitive level. In fact, they need to experience culture and learn how to process it.

Sadow (1987) states that the target culture should be approached from the outside-in. Students need to (1) engage in in-class activities and simulations that reflect the culture, (2) watch and examine people and artifacts from the target culture, (3) interact with one representative in a controlled way, (4) interact with a group of representatives, and (5) where possible, visit ethnic neighborhoods (see Chapter 9).

Not all classrooms, however, have the luxury of community resources at their disposal. Those who lack them need to make use of experiential devices such as imagery (fantasy trips), role-playing, and simulation. Hammers (1985) suggests numerous techniques for having individual students simulate the conditions in life which contribute to the development of unique personalities in every culture. They include:

- the physical conditions (the geography, climate, and objects in one's life);
- the social environment (family, friends, and all those, past and present, who make their presence felt in one's life);
- an orientation to time (including the history of one's culture and how one's life-span relates to that history);
- the unique genetic heritage with which each one is born (including the physical and mental strengths and weaknesses of that heritage).

Curtain and Pesola (1988) complement the above suggestions very well by adding experiential activities, including fantasy trips, designed for use in elementary school foreign language courses, but easily adaptable to other levels of instruction.

Crawford-Lange and Lange (1984) urge that culture be taught as a process. They describe in detail (pp. 146–50) an interactive process that relates target and native languages, cultures, and perceptions. It also integrates the teaching of culture and the teaching of language. The process incorporates the following eight basic stages, the first five of which are primarily teacher-directed and the final three student-directed:

1 Identification of a cultural theme;
2 Presentation of cultural phenomena;
3 Dialogue (target/native cultures);
4 Transition to language learning;
5 Language learning;
6 Verification of perceptions (target/native culture);
7 Cultural awareness;
8 Evaluation of language and cultural proficiency.

Galloway (1984) also suggests developing cultural understanding through process skills. She proposes organizing instruction around four basic categories:

- *Convention,* which provides students with information about the common everyday behavior of people;
- *Connotation,* which helps students develop their inferencing skills, such as recognizing that the meaning of a word is determined by each individual's frame of reference;
- *Conditioning,* which helps students develop observational and interpretive skills and understand that the actions of individuals reflect an already established cultural frame of reference;
- *Comprehension,* which helps students develop the skills of analysis and hypothesis formation, thereby recognizing that the behavior of one person does not necessarily reflect the behavior of society as a whole.

THE TARGET LANGUAGE SHOULD BE THE PRIMARY VEHICLE USED TO TEACH CULTURE

It is commonly believed that the use of English is necessary in the foreign language classroom especially when dealing with the teaching of culture and grammar. In reality, all but the most limited use of the native language in the foreign language classroom should be not only discouraged but prohibited. In fact, the native language is never necessary in foreign language teaching; ample proof of this is provided by teachers of English as a second language, a great many of whom do not know the native language or languages spoken by the students enrolled in their ESL courses. Moreover, most success stories in foreign language learning and teaching involve some form of exclusive immersion in the target language.

Exclusive use of the target language, especially in the teaching of culture, obviously entails a lowering of the intellectual level of the discussion. In the end, however, the sacrifice is beneficial, since language and culture have been viewed from the beginning as partners, and since the students will have acquired more language with which to acquire more culture. Given a simple, well-marked map of the target country, it is even possible to conduct the entire first day of class in the target language and teach a considerable amount of geography.

Language is the first and most important representation of culture, and its place in the classroom should not be relinquished. Allen says it best:

> . . . Of all the elements of the target culture, the target language is the most typical, the most unique, the most challenging, and—almost ironically—the most readily available. Its authentic use in the classroom from the beginning of instruction is therefore the primary cultural objective (p. 140).

Suggested Activities for Integrating Language and Culture

The preceding discussion makes it eminently clear that one of the most basic issues in foreign language teaching is the degree to which language and culture are integrated. It would of course be preferable if language were to be integrated into a culture-based curriculum, but, as mentioned above, the reality is that textbooks will continue to be grammar-based for some time to come. The activities suggested below can be used in either a language- or culture-based curriculum. It is left to teachers to determine how they might best accommodate their program.

In addition to the numerous activities suggested here, the reader is also referred to Omaggio (1986) who offers an abundance of suggestions organized around Seelye's seven goals of cultural instruction, and to Spinelli (1985) who proposes several ways to integrate culture with the teaching of grammar and vocabulary through the use of contextualized activities.

INTEGRATING CULTURE AND THE TEACHING OF VOCABULARY

Since vocabulary is best taught in context, it is relatively simple to make that context a cultural one. In fact, it is probably in the area of vocabulary that teachers can most easily develop the cultural mind-set discussed above. Several suggestions come to mind:

• Vocabulary should be grouped in culture-related clusters. This provides opportunities to present and discuss cultural concepts or reinforce ones already presented. For example, instead of presenting food vocabulary via traditional food groups, it would be culturally advantageous to place the items into sub-groups according to what people eat during different meals such as breakfast (cereal, eggs, toast, doughnuts, etc.), lunch (sandwich, Big Mac, hot dog, pizza, etc.), dinner (steak, potatoes, peas, stew, bread, etc.).

• Descriptive adjectives could be introduced and/or practiced by describing a famous person, monument, or work of art that is found in the target culture.

• Whenever visuals accompany the introduction of lexical items, it is important that they be culturally accurate. A photograph of a loaf of Wonder bread is not an accurate representation of the French word *pain*.

• Since students manifest varied interests, provision should be made for self-generated sets of lexical items that supplement basic sets of words dealing with a specific cultural concept. For example, basic leisure vocabulary might include such words as cinema, concert, stadium, and various sports, while individualized supplementary items might include types of films, names of positions in a particular sport, types of concerts, names of musical instruments, etc.

INTEGRATING CULTURE AND THE TEACHING OF GRAMMAR

When teaching grammar, the instructor is usually so intent on the linguistic element at hand that little thought is given to including possible cultural components in the exercises that precede or follow the grammar point. This need not be the case, however, since most grammar points easily lend themselves to a cultural context. Two examples are included below. For a complete treatment, readers should consult Allen (1985) who presents a culture-based syllabus for introductory-level French courses and includes therein the linkages between culture and grammar.

• The partitive in French is commonly used with food vocabulary. The above activity that presents the types of foods eaten at different meals could just as easily be used to practice uses of the partitive, and in doing so, would have the added advantage of reinforcing cultural information.

• You are a sixteen-year-old girl who has been given money to purchase a complete outfit. of asking students what they did yesterday or last weekend, we might ask them what William the Conqueror did in 1066, what Christopher Columbus did in 1492, what happened in France in 1789, what the Allies did on June 6, 1944, etc.

INTEGRATING CULTURE AND THE TEACHING OF LISTENING COMPREHENSION

During the past two decades, considerable research has demonstrated the importance of listening in the acquisition and learning of foreign languages. In order not to neglect the importance of this skill in developing readiness for the other skills, teachers need to include listening activities in their lesson plans. Integrating the cultural element can easily be accomplished by having students listen to cultural content. For example:

• Students can be given maps of the target country and, using Total Physical Response, they can be asked to perform different tasks related to the location of various geographical elements. These might include circling ski resorts in red and seaside ones in blue, or tracing someone's trip as it is related orally by the teacher.

• A great deal of cultural information can be transmitted orally through the use of visuals, using what Krashen and Terrell (1983) call pre-speech activities. For example, the teacher might use a transparency of a supermarket ad to ask numerous questions requiring one-word answers, thus focusing on listening rather than speaking.

• Fantasy trips mentioned above are another excellent source of cultural listening activities. Students can cross the Alps, get ready for a picnic, climb the Eiffel Tower, etc.

INTEGRATING CULTURE AND THE TEACHING OF SPEAKING

In designing communicative activities, it is important, first of all, that students have something to say. Students should be given numerous opportunities to describe and give opinions about both native- and target-language cultural concepts. In addition, they should be involved in simulations and role playing that reflect both cultures. These need not be complicated as the following two examples demonstrate.

• You are a 16-year-old girl who has been given money to purchase a complete outfit. However, the clothing must be appropriate to attend Sunday mass in a small provincial village. Go to your teacher, who is playing the role of the owner of a boutique, and make your purchases.

• You wish to purchase a book, a record, stationery, and stamps for yourself. Your mother has asked you to pick up some bread and cold ham slices on your way home. There are several store signs on your teacher's desk. When you approach the desk, pick out the appropriate sign and purchase the necessary items. Repeat this procedure until you have acquired everything mentioned above.

INTEGRATING CULTURE AND THE TEACHING OF READING

Initially it appears that the simplest skill to integrate with culture is that of reading since all that is seemingly required is to select reading texts with cultural content. Although this is partially true, the teacher must see that the texts are read first and foremost for their cultural content. Far too many cultural selections are read only for the purposes of pronunciation or sound-symbol association (reading aloud), grammar illustration, and/or translation. The primary purpose of reading a text is to learn from its content; it should be used only secondarily for the purposes mentioned above. The following suggestions will help maintain that focus:

• Every reading should be preceded by at least one culture-related pre-reading activity whose purpose is to set the scene and assure that the content of the reading will be understood and processed. One suggestion is to ask the students to reflect upon the cultural phenomena as seen in the native culture prior to reading about its implementation in the target culture.

• Similarly, post-reading activities can require students to process the information just read and compare it to the information about the native culture gathered during the pre-reading activity. The examples that follow illustrate the above suggestions. The instructions and questions are in English here for the purpose of illustration; they would normally be in the target language.

Example #1

Step 1—Before reading the following text, answer the questions below:

    1 Where do you eat most of your meals?

    2 How many meals do you eat per day?

    3 What are your favorite foods or dishes?

    4 How many times per week do you eat in a fast-food restaurant? Which ones do you like best?

    5 Can you cook? What are your specialties?

Step 2—Read the following article entitled "Food and the French/German/Spanish Student."

Step 3—Use the questions in Step 1 to interview three students in your class and prepare an oral summary of the results.

Step 4—Write a one-page composition comparing the answers you got in Step 3 with the information in the reading about students in France, Germany, or Mexico.

Example #2

Step 1—Make three lists:

1 A list of nouns to identify eating and drinking items needed at a party.

2 A list of adjectives describing the mood you prefer at a party.

3 A list of verbs describing the main activities at a party.

Step 2—Read the following article describing a party in France, Germany, or Mexico.

Step 3—Make the same three lists, this time based on the information presented in the above text.

Step 4—Compare the list in Step 1 to that in Step 3 and discuss the similarities and differences.

• Consider designing activities which ask students to identify cultural concepts as reflected in selected passages. For example, students are given five short paragraphs to read. They must then match each paragraph with one-sentence descriptions of the concept illustrated in each paragraph. A more difficult task would be to withhold the concepts and ask the students to formulate them after having read the passage.

• Consider the use of several different cultural readings on a similar topic to serve the different levels of ability in your classroom more effectively. There are numerous supplementary readers on the market, and it is not terribly difficult to assemble several readings on the same topic. The same pre-reading activity could be done with all students, followed by the simultaneous silent reading of the different passages. The content of these passages could then be discussed in small groups by the individuals who read the same passage, and finally, the content of the various passages could be compared among groups.

INTEGRATING CULTURE AND THE TEACHING OF WRITING

The writing skill offers an excellent opportunity for integrating language and culture because it can be controlled at various levels of difficulty. Two reservations are in order, however. First, teachers should be cautious about open-ended assignments such as "write a one-page composition describing eating habits in Spain" lest students get into the habit of completing such assignments by composing sophisticated essays in English that are then beyond their ability to translate. Second, integrated writing assignments should be evaluated for cultural as well as linguistic content, thereby encouraging adequate student attention to both components. The following suggested activities integrate culture and writing:

• Teach students to write personal and business letters, and have them write actual letters to individuals or companies in the foreign country. Letters to individuals could be structured by identifying the type of information sought on specific cultural topics such as class schedules, weekend leisure activities, family rules, etc. Letters soliciting information from hotels or travel agencies might first require planning a trip to a foreign country.

• Give the students one or more cultural generalizations and ask them to write sample statements illustrating the concept. For example:

Generalization: In many Latin American countries, schedules are not interpreted as literally as in the United States.

Potential student answers: (1) An individual with a 10 a.m. business appointment in Mexico City should not expect to be seen precisely at that time; (2) a person in Puerto Rico arriving at 8 p.m. for a party scheduled at that time might find the hostess taking a bath.

Generalization: The annual vacation is a sacred element in the life of the French.

Potential student answers: (1) French salaried workers are guaranteed five weeks of paid vacation per year; (2) families begin planning the next year's vacation not long after returning from their latest one; (3) highways leaving the Paris area are highly congested around July 1 and August 1.

• Prepare short, incomplete narratives describing the initial phases of a cultural episode. On the basis of the information presented and their own cultural knowledge, students complete the narrative.

Teacher segment: It is a Monday night in Paris during the summer. Mike and Sally Jones, two Americans visiting Paris, are sitting at a café planning their next day's visit to the Louvre. Having determined exactly how to get there by *métro* and which parts of the Louvre to visit, they return to their hotel near the Tour Montparnasse for a good night's sleep. The following morning . . .

Potential student answer: The following morning Mike and Sally have a leisurely breakfast in their hotel room. At ten o'clock they go to the Montparnasse Subway Station and take the *métro* to the Louvre Station, changing once along the way. When they arrive at the museum, they are disappointed to learn that, like most museums in Paris, the Louvre is closed on Tuesdays. Therefore, they sit down in the nearby Jardin des Tuileries to discuss how they will now spend this unexpected free day.

• Assign guided compositions not only on target culture topics but also on American counterpart behavior. The latter improves awareness of one's own culture and leads to a greater understanding and acceptance of the target culture.

Sample: Write a brief composition that includes the following: What, when, and where a bank secretary might eat at lunchtime in a small provincial French town, in Paris, in a small American town, and in New York City or Los Angeles.

• Make use of simulation materials such as *L'Immeuble* (Debyser, 1986) which includes some fifty mostly small group activities originally designed to write a "group novel" dealing with the daily life of thirty different apartment dwellers. This collection of oral and written activities lends itself to numerous communicative and cultural ends.

Conclusion

In the introduction it was mentioned that the teaching of culture has been one of the most discussed topics in the professional literature during the past twenty years but that its actual application in the classroom has lagged considerably. Several models for its integration in foreign language teaching have been proposed. Most, however, are still at the theoretical level or have been presented with only limited examples of implementation. Only the Indiana guide has developed a fully extended, four-level sequence—which nonetheless represents a significant beginning, considering that grammar has been the primary focus of foreign language teaching for decades, even centuries. Except for the importance granted literature, itself a cultural artifact, culture in the classroom is indeed a recent phenomenon. Perhaps we need to be somewhat more patient in our expectations. The Indiana model, the basic principles for creating a cultural mind-set, and the numerous suggestions for integrating language and culture may well lead to yet greater emphasis on culture in the classroom. Simultaneously, it is hoped that universities will produce foreign language teachers who are better trained to focus on culture, and that publishers will begin to insist on a more systematic treatment of culture in textbooks. It is most important, however, that teachers begin to view themselves not simply as teachers of language but rather as teachers of both language and culture.

Notes

1 Portions of this paper include ideas originally presented by the author in a publication no longer available entitled *Teaching culture: Strategies and techniques*. Language in Education: Theory and Practice, No. 11. Washington, D.C.: Center for Applied Linguistics, 1978.

2 Copies of *A Guide to Proficiency-Based Instruction in Modern Foreign Languages for Indiana Schools* may be obtained by writing to Dr. Walter H. Bartz, Center of School Improvement and Performance, Indiana Department of Education, Room 229, State House, Indianapolis, IN 46204. Also available, from the same source, are specific guides to proficiency-based instruction in French, German, and Spanish.

References

ACTFL Proficiency Guidelines. Hastings-on-Hudson, NY: American Council on the Teaching of Foreign Languages, 1985.

Allen, W. W. Toward cultural proficiency. In A. C. Omaggio (Ed.), *Proficiency, curriculum, articulation: The ties that bind*. Middlebury, VT: Northeast Conference, 1985.

Allison, M. A review of proposals to strengthen foreign language and international education. *Foreign Language Annals*, 1986, *19*, 533–36.

Beacco, J.-C., & Lieutaud, S. *Tours de France: Travaux pratiques de civilisation*. Paris: Hachette, 1985.

Berwald, J.-P. *Au courant: Teaching French vocabulary and culture using the mass media*. Language in Education: Theory and Practice 65. Washington, D.C.: ERIC Clearinghouse on Languages and Linguistics, 1986.

Brière, J.-F. Cultural understanding through cross-cultural analysis. *French Review*, 1987, *60*, 203–08.

Brooks, N. Teaching culture in the foreign language classroom. *Foreign Language Annals*, 1968, *1*, 204–17.

Carr, T. Contemporary culture: A model for teaching a culture's heritage. In P. B. Westphal (Ed.), *Meeting the call for excellence in the foreign language classroom*. Lincolnwood, IL: National Textbook Company, 1985.

Crawford-Lange, L., & Lange, D. L. Doing the unthinkable in the second-language classroom: A process for the integration of language and culture. In T. V. Higgs (Ed.), *Teaching for proficiency, the organizing principle*. Lincolnwood, IL: National Textbook Company, 1984.

Curtain, H. A., & Pesola, C. A. *Languages and children: Making the match*. Reading, MA: Addison-Wesley, 1988.

Debyser, F. *L'Immeuble*. Paris: Hachette, 1986.

Fantini, A. et al. *Beyond the language classroom*. Brattleboro, VT: The Experiment Press, 1985.

Galloway, V. B. Communicating in a cultural context. *ACTFL Master Lecture Series*. Monterey, CA: Defense Language Institute, 1984.

Grittner, F. *A guide to curriculum planning in foreign languages*. Madison, WI: Wisconsin Department of Public Instruction, 1985.

Halverson, R. J. Culture and vocabulary acquisition: A proposal. *Foreign Language Annals*, 1985, *18*, 327–32.

Hammers, J. Culture and language: The individual approach. *Foreign Language Annals,* 1985, *18,* 53–58.

Heusinkveld, P. R. The foreign language classroom: A forum for understanding cultural stereotypes. *Foreign Language Annals,* 1985, *18,* 321–25.

Koppe, P. G. Teaching culture and language in the beginning foreign language class: Four strategies that work. *Unterrichtspraxis,* 1985, *18,* 158–69.

Knox, E. C. Bibliography on the teaching of French civilization. *French Review,* 1985, *58,* 426–36.

Kramsch, C. J. Culture and constructs: Communicating attitudes and values in the foreign language classroom. *Foreign Language Annals,* 1983, *16,* 437–48.

Krashen, S. D., and Terrell, T. D. *The natural approach: Language acquisition in the classroom.* New York: Pergamon Press, 1983.

Lafayette, R. C. *Teaching culture: Strategies and techniques.* Language in Education: Theory and Practice, No. 11. Washington, D.C.: Center for Applied Linguistics, 1978.

Lafayette, R. C., & Buscaglia, M. Students learn language via a civilization course: A comparison of second language classroom environments. *Studies in Second Language Acquisition,* 1985, *7,* 323–42.

Lafayette, R. C., & Schulz, R. Evaluating cultural learnings. In R. C. Lafayette (Ed.), *The culture revolution in foreign language teaching.* Lincolnwood, IL: National Textbook Company, 1975.

Lafayette, R. C., & Strasheim, L. A. Foreign language curricula and materials for the twenty-first century. In D. L. Lange and C. Linder (Eds.), *Proceedings of the National Conference on Professional Priorities.* Hastings-on-Hudson, NY: ACTFL Materials Center, 1981.

Marc, E. Civilisation: l'enseignement des cultures. *Le Français dans le Monde,* 1987, *206,* 65–68.

Morain, G. *The role of culture in foreign language education.* Washington, D.C.: ERIC Clearinghouse on Languages and Linguistics, 1986.

Morain, G. Commitment to the teaching of foreign cultures. *Modern Language Journal,* 1983, *67,* 403–12.

Nostrand, H. L. (Ed.). *Background data for the teaching of French. Part A, La culture et la société françaises au XXe siècle.* Seattle: University of Washington, 1967.

Nostrand, H. L. "Horizontal" coordination, foreign languages, and social studies: An editorial. *Modern Language Journal,* 1985, *69,* 41–43.

Nuessel, F. Teaching Hispanic culture with postage stamps. *Canadian Modern Language Review,* 1984, *40,* 429–39.

Omaggio, A. *Teaching language in context: Proficiency-oriented instruction.* Boston: Heinle & Heinle, 1986.

Porcher, L. *La Civilisation.* Paris: CLE internationale, 1986.

Sadow, S. A. Experiential techniques that promote cross-cultural awareness. *Foreign Language Annals,* 1987, *20,* 25–30.

Seelye, H. N. *Teaching culture: Strategies for intercultural communication.* Lincolnwood, IL: National Textbook Company, 1984.

Spinelli, E. Increasing the functional culture content of the foreign language class. In Westphal, P. B. (Ed.), *Meeting the call for excellence in the foreign language classroom.* Lincolnwood, IL: National Textbook Company, 1985.

Strasheim, L. A. Establishing a professional agenda for integrating culture into K-12 foreign languages: An editorial. *Modern Language Journal,* 1981, *65,* 67–69.

Strasheim, L. A., & Bartz, W. H. (Eds.). *A guide to proficiency-based instruction in modern foreign languages for Indiana schools.* Indianapolis, IN: Indiana Department of Education, 1986.

Valdes, J. M. (Ed.). *Bridging the cultural gap in language teaching.* New York: Cambridge Press, 1986.

Westphal, G. F. On the teaching of culture in the FL curriculum. *Canadian Modern Language Review,* 1986, *43,* 87–93.

Zarate, G. *Enseigner une culture étrangère.* Paris: Hachette, 1986.

Claire J. Kramsch
Massachusetts Institute of Technology

The Cultural Discourse of Foreign Language Textbooks[1]

To play the violin it is necessary to possess certain habits, skills, knowledge, and talents, to be in the mood to play, and (as the old joke goes) to have a violin. But violin playing is neither the habits, skills, knowledge, and so on, nor the mood, nor (the notion believers in "material culture" apparently embrace) the violin. Clifford Geertz, *The Interpretation of Cultures* (p. 12).

Introduction

It is a truism of our profession that one cannot learn to use a language without learning something about the culture of the people who speak that language: "Language as a means of communication as opposed to an object to be analyzed is inseparable from culture" (Weatherford, 1986); "To study language without studying the culture of the native speakers of the language is a lifeless endeavor" (Crawford-Lange and Lange, 1984); "Culture is necessary to an effective understanding of language and language to an effective understanding of culture" (Hammerly, 1982). The communicative revolution and, in its trail, the proficiency movement have made clear that languages are learned in a cultural context, that is both the internal and the external context of communication. This context is the matrix in which forms get attached to meanings which are expressed, interpreted and negotiated in communication (Canale and Swain, 1980; Savignon, 1983).

Much effort has been expended in designing imaginative materials to sensitize learners to the foreign culture: culture capsules, culture clusters, cultural assimilators, cultural readings, mini-dramas. However, there is virtually no study of how first- and second-year textbooks themselves are structured so as to present an integrated study of language and culture. It is as if culture were indeed a fifth skill that needed to be added only to "stimulate interest in foreign language study" and provide a "welcome change from oral drill or grammatical exercises" (Hendon, 1980).

In the first year, whether we like it or not, the text is central to the language-learning process in the classroom. It may be used or abused, followed religiously or humorously, memorized with piety or abandoned with spite — the text remains the bedrock of syllabus design and lesson planning (Olson, 1980, p. 189). Its adoption is a major event for publishers and school boards alike, its replacement a major challenge for teachers and

students. The text creates its own folklore and its own cultural bonds among generations of alumni; it is the most frequent conversational topic among teachers ("And what
text do you use?").

In the pages that follow I will take an ethnomethodological approach to the study
of textbooks.[2] Inspired by recent theories of culture, I will first attempt to define the
parameters of the foreign language textbook as a social genre and as a cultural construct in its own right. I will next examine the textbook as a learning tool within the
larger context of its conditions of production and reception. I will then analyze in detail
some existing foreign language textbooks and explore what implications can be drawn
for authors and users of textbooks.

THE TEXTBOOK: A CULTURAL CONSTRUCT

I will use here, as a theoretical starting point, a semiotic definition of culture such
as the one given by the anthropologist Clifford Geertz (1973). According to Geertz,
culture consists of "those socially established structures of meaning" in terms of which
people do such things as perceive insults and answer them, talk and write about certain
topics and respond to them, order meals in restaurants, use the telephone and take
vacations. Understanding a culture is understanding the signs by which native speakers
of the language make sense of and give sense to the world around them. The French,
for example, "wave their arms when they talk" (Bateson, 1972) not because their culture
requires them to do so, but because they wish to convey a meaning that can only be
understood in relation to all the other signs in the environment (such as the attention
shown by French interlocutors, the importance given to gestures, French ways of expressing feelings, etc.). Culture is not a collection of isolated facts and behaviors dictated
by some strange higher principle. "As interworked systems of construable signs [. . .]
culture is not a power, something to which social events, behaviors, institutions or
processes can be causally attributed; it is a context, something within which they can
be intelligibly [. . .] described" (Geertz, 1973, p. 14).

How can I, as an American, know whether the wink of a stranger in the Paris *métro*
is a sign of complicity, a flirtatious move, an involuntary twitch or the parody of a twitch
[. . .] or even the rehearsal of a parody? By putting this wink in relation with other
cues in the situation and with everything I have learned about French culture and society.
What most prevents people from one culture "who grew up winking other winks" from
grasping what people are up to is not ignorance of the forms of their language or of
their ways and customs, but "a lack of familiarity with the imaginative universe within
which their acts are signs" (Geertz, 1973, p. 13). Learning to understand a people's
culture entails, therefore, understanding the set of assumptions, expectations and perceptions normal for and common to a social group engaged in a given activity. It entails
learning to perceive, so to speak, "[the people's] normalness without reducing their particularity" (p. 14).

This view of culture encompasses both the "small c" everyday life events and the "capital
C" artistic, intellectual and political phenomena. For art forms too are embedded in
what Geertz (1983) calls the "social history of the imagination," "the common world
in which men look, name, listen and make" (p. 119). Even given a mastery of the country's language we often do not understand the people because we do not share common
bearings. A textbook whose aim is to teach language and culture, as do our first- and
second-year texts, has therefore to present a foreign world of signs through which students
can find their bearings in another imaginative universe.

That a textbook does not present language and culture as they are in real life is obvious, even though beginning learners tend to believe it does. Like any work of art, it is a construct, one that represents the way author and publisher conceive of language, culture and learning, and the way they construe an integrated world of foreign reality for instructional purposes. Despite the increased sense of immediacy of genuine photographs, authentic texts, audio and video tapes, a text is not the authentic experience, but a culturally coded educational construct.

The foreign language textbook, as a cultural phenomenon itself, is a complex nexus of various forces, requiring the collaboration of a variety of people: linguists and educators, authors, reviewers, publishers, school boards, teachers and students. It is the product of at least five different cultures:

- the target culture to be learned (hereafter referred to as C2), composed of the normal behaviors, events, and thoughts expected by and of native speakers in the target culture;
- the source culture (hereafter referred to as C1), made up of the implicit and explicit phenomena that are part of the universe of the learners;
- the educational culture of the country where the book was published, formed of all the signs of institutional learning (type and structure of knowledge presented, format, usage, etc.) expected from and imposed upon the users of American textbooks;
- the classroom culture in which the book is used, consisting of the expected rules of student/student and student/teacher interaction during the lesson;
- the interculture, or stages of acquisition of C2 in the learner, made up of a developing universe in which C1 meanings are slowly being relativized in light of C2, but C2 is still viewed with C1 structures of meaning.

Thus the text is a cultural system in itself, as valid as the conviction of its validity held by those who use it. By giving learners access to a body of "local knowledge," i.e., knowledge embedded in a certain foreign cultural context (Geertz, 1983), it suggests to them that its educational culture will help them pass from their C1 mental universe to a C2 representation of the world.

Indeed, that is what textbooks' prefaces and introductions mean when they claim that their text will "lead to an understanding and appreciation of differences between individuals and cultures in a pluralistic, interdependent world" (Corl, Jurasek and Jurasek, 1985), or that it will "introduce students to contemporary life and culture in German-speaking countries and make them aware of their own language and culture" (Moeller and Liedloff, 1986).

CHARACTERISTICS OF THE GENRE

Unlike reference grammars, activities handbooks, cultural or literary readers, audio or video ancillary materials and computer software, foreign language textbooks are characterized by four major features that they have in common with texts in other subjects. They are:

1 *Principle-oriented*. They provide the learner with basic principles of knowledge. Webster defines a textbook as a "book containing a presentation of the principles of a subject, a source providing an introduction or a basis." Larousse points to the "notions essentielles" given by a textbook. In fact, texts differ in what they consider essential knowledge and what principles they identify as forming the basis of cultural understanding through a foreign language.

2 *Methodical.* The organization and progression of textbooks is methodical. They embody the notion that knowledge is itemizable and classifiable and that learning is sequential and cumulative.

3 *Authoritative.* Textbooks are sources of authority (Olson, 1980, p. 192). They are by essence normative (Königs, 1983, p. 400), above criticism. They present the language as it should be spoken and written by the learners, cultural information as it should be viewed and interpreted by the reader. The idea that a text could contain misprints or even errors is inconceivable for most learners. By contrast with noneducational material, a foreign language text imparts knowledge that is viewed by its users as ultimately imperative, not declarative, knowledge. The message it gives is: "Master the material between the covers and you will do well on the test and in real-life situations." The knowledge it imparts is meant to be displayed, first in class to show that one has learned the material, then in real-life situations. Thus, knowledge that will not be tested, such as the less quantifiable "intercultural understanding," is usually viewed as the decorative, cosmetic enhancement of the "real stuff," namely, grammar rules and vocabulary.

4 *Literal.* Unlike a work of fiction, a textbook is usually intended to be taken literally, at face value. Everything is the way it is depicted and no other way: "Texts say what they mean and mean precisely neither more nor less than what they say" (Olson, 1980, p. 190). For example, conjugations are not a metaphor for something else, as in concrete poetry. Their truth value lies in their referential relationship to a firmly established outside world of literal forms and meanings. Learners are not supposed to read any subtext into their textbook.

THE CULTURAL DILEMMA OF FOREIGN LANGUAGE TEXTS

Unlike other teaching materials, a text whose purpose is to teach a foreign language and culture is caught in an interesting dilemma that arises from the discrepancy between its monocultural educational parameters and its multicultural educational goals. This dilemma can be captured by the following questions relating to the principles of knowledge, the selection of topics and the authority of the genre.

What rules should be taught? Besides the essential logic of grammatical and lexical rules, a text that integrates language and culture should teach also the logic of the particular way in which native speakers say what they say and behave the way they do. It should help the students make C2-relevant inferences and build C2-relevant connections between various lexical items (Müller, 1980). However, how can it do so if it is immersed in the educational culture of C1? Shouldn't the discourse and the perspective be that of C2 also?

What cultural topics should be covered? A language and culture text should help the learner understand what is important for a person of that culture and what is not. If, for example, students in Germany are first and foremost concerned with the threat of nuclear war and with environmental issues, then these should be the topics covered in German textbooks; only then can our students learn to communicate competently with their counterparts in Germany. But how can the interest of American learners be aroused by events that do not concern them personally? One could argue, for example, that an American student of French *should* learn how to appreciate the central value of vacation in France and decide accordingly to give that topic a central position in the book. However, if an American student is not as concerned as the French about what to do and where to go during "les vacances," but is far more interested in finding and holding a job, what should be given priority — C1 concerns or C2 values? The difficulty of using foreign texts (e.g., *Deutsch Aktiv, Archipel*, etc.) lies often in their different educational emphasis.

If, however, the educational culture is itself considered an important aspect of C2 — for example, the intellectual style instilled in French students (Bourdieu, 1967; Clyne, 1984; Galtung, 1981) — should we not, at some point, consciously expose the student to that different style? But at what point?

Which culture(s) should we teach? That of the middle-class, the educated elite or the less-educated working class? The native French culture or that of France's immigrants? How can cultural relativism be taught via a normative learning tool? Here again, the foreign language text is caught in a dilemma.

We have seen up to now that the objectivity of textbooks is usually as taken for granted as the native culture they implicitly assume the student knows. In fact, they are no more objective than any other cultural event. They are rather a complex construct of subjective views by authors, publishers, teachers and learners of what is worth learning and how it is worth learning. We have also seen that our initial concept of learning culture as the negotiation of subjective meanings or signs is insufficient to serve as a guide for the composition and utilization of textbooks. Individuals do not communicate meanings in a social vacuum; each student is embedded in the cultural discourse of his or her family and social background, ethnic origin and education. The meanings that are expressed, interpreted and negotiated in communication are social constructions, culturally (i.e., affectively and cognitively) loaded and acquired through the primary socialization of the learners. As the sociologist Peter Berger expresses it: "Culture is at base an all-embracing socially constructed world of subjectively and INTER-subjectively experienced meanings" (Wuthnow, 1986, p. 25). The textbook genre itself has its laws that determine much of the exchange of meanings that should take place.

If textbooks are not only to describe linguistic and cultural facts, but to actually help learners become communicatively competent in their interaction with target culture speakers, then the textbook should initiate a process of secondary socialization in the second language and culture. To what degree, however, do foreign language textbooks reproduce and reinforce the primary socialization, and to what extent can they foster the social awareness necessary to begin the learner's socialization in a foreign culture?

To attempt to answer that question, we have to examine the social determinants of the textbook culture. These will be found in its conditions of production (i.e., in the educational culture) and in its conditions of reception (i.e., in the classroom culture).

Conditions of Production: The Educational Culture

The foreign language textbook is at the intersection of conflicting discourse worlds at all levels of the educational enterprise.

A POSITIVISTIC VIEW OF EDUCATION

In its lockstep, rational structure, the American textbook is a product of a whole educational culture that is, as many have pointed out, fundamentally positivistic (Hofstadter, 1963; Giroux, 1981; Singer, 1986). Education in this country has traditionally emphasized the managerial aspect of schooling, or "social engineering," provided by experts or professionals in the possession of a certain knowledge that they are uniquely qualified to transmit. The notion of a competency-based curriculum reflects the view that the acquisition of knowledge is the mastery of skills, that it is a task-oriented activity concerned with the solving of practical problems of a technical variety. Giroux traces this form of rationality to the American scientific management movement of the 1920's and to the demands of mass education, but it is typical, of course, of many other Western industrialized societies.

In its carefully orchestrated sequence of activities, the textbook thus exhibits a technocratic bias that is both pervasive and controversial. If positivism is indeed the dominant ideology of American education, it has been challenged repeatedly by such counter-ideologies as Freire's conscientization pedagogy (Crawford-Lange, 1981), the open schools of the sixties and movements to do away with textbooks altogether, such as the Community Language Learning, The Silent Way or Suggestopaedia.

In a country which has no central federal board of education and where the sixteen hundred school boards represent not the educational establishment but the local elites, textbooks insure the controlled acquisition of a selected body of knowledge that both preserves and reinforces the cultural and social status quo (Postman and Weingartner, 1969). They serve the needs of a variety of interest groups in the national economy: corporate and technocratic representatives on school boards, professional educators and administrators, intellectuals in search of cultural information, fundamentalists, etc.

PUBLISHERS

The publishers themselves play a critical role with respect to the conditions of production of textbooks. An informal survey of five of the major foreign language publishers in the United States yields a rather startling picture of the implicit censorship that publishers routinely impose upon themselves in order not to offend the myriad private and public interests that have a stake in foreign language education.[3] Trend-followers and trend-setters, they have to issue textbooks that both respond to the needs of the market and create those needs, both teach the students and train the teachers. They are commercial enterprises, trying to satisfy both the conservative and the progressive forces in American society, and many of them are painfully aware of the fine line they have to tread between the two.

The American educational tradition of inculcating moral values in all aspects of the curriculum (Shaver and Strong, 1982), including the teaching of a foreign culture, and the fear of losing substantial sales if they lose lawsuits brought by parents or public interest groups, lead many publishers to censor an astounding assortment of potentially "dangerous" topics or illustrations, especially in high school texts.

Here are, for instance, some of the items on the unwritten black list of publishing houses, especially for high school texts. Holiday customs (e.g., Christmas, Easter, Rosh Hashana) should be downplayed for fear of provoking the charge of religious bias; horoscopes are to be avoided for fear that they might encourage superstition or sorcery; birthday cake traditions (such as, in Germany, a *Geburtstagstorte*) are best dropped, for no textbook should condone the consumption of junk food—unless it is counterbalanced by a picture of "healthy" foods such as orange juice or milk. Of course, no mention or depiction of weapons is tolerated, nor cigarette ads in France and beer ads in Germany. Mention of the pre-marital sexual relationships of French teenagers can be made only at great risk. A current college text teaches the parts of the body with a drawing representing the emasculated contours of a naked male body. One publisher had to airbrush the unshaven legs and armpits of Mediterranean women in bikinis going down to the sea to bathe, for fear of offending or shocking high school learners. Others go so far as to ask the authors of short stories to change a wording or a part of the story that might be offensive to American students, such as the word "Neger" in a German story or the ending of Luise Rinser's story, *Die rote Katze,* in which one of the protagonists kills the cat. Since the topic of death is to be avoided, at least at the high school level, a number of Latin American readings that deal with death have to be chosen with great care. The censorship not only imposes American values on foreign cultures, it also "protects" students from developing too great a sympathy for cultures of which this country does not approve. Thus, too many positive remarks about East Germany's cultural ways have provoked complaints, forcing a political stance on a publisher whose sole intent may have been to offer a balanced representation of German-speaking countries. Complaints about American ethnocentric biases in the depiction of the target culture are rarely voiced (see, however, Arizpe and Aguirre, 1987).

The very enforcement of American laws can sometimes interfere in the development of intercultural educational goals. For example, affirmative action demands proportional representation of minority groups in the United States. In Germany, the dominant minorities are not Blacks or Hispanics, but Turks, while in France they are North Africans. Will the states' adoption committees accept, for example, a proportional representation of Turks in German textbooks, or will they still require that Blacks, Hispanics and handicapped persons be represented? A recent regulation within one publishing company cautions all editors and authors against using the names of real people, companies or other organizations without formal permission from those individuals for fear of law suits or embarrassment to the company. (But what if the laws are different in the target country?) It is equally unacceptable to insert a dialogue line or caption under photographs of any individuals without securing their explicit authorization to do so. Since many photographs are taken anonymously and at different times in the target country, either by a photoagency or by the publishing house itself, it becomes very difficult to use these photographs in any other way than in a touristic or *National Geographic* display fashion.

It is important for students and teachers to be aware that our overlitigious and ideological society has built up its own defenses against intercultural understanding. Publishers have to first satisfy native culture interest groups, feminists, fundamentalists, intellectuals, businessmen, and the potential consumers before they can even start representing the foreign culture as it really is. Their major concern is bidding for and getting admitted to the major states' adoption committees' lists for the usual six years. For this they have to abide by the states' official guidelines for the manufacturing of textbooks. But the language of the required content designations is itself difficult to interpret. To quote but one example, the Texas State Board of Education's advertising for bids on textbooks requires the following cultural content in German texts for grades 9–12: "Concepts that result in knowledge and awareness of the history and culture of another people within a range of situations. Textbooks shall contain material relating to (a) culturally-conditioned behavior, (b) cultural connotations of common words and phrases, (c) cultural generalizations." It is no wonder that the cultural aspect of language textbooks has been dealt with in a rather cautious, if not conservative, manner by most publishers. What they look for primarily is authenticity, accuracy, updatedness and typicalness of cultural facts, attractiveness, relevancy to students' lives, survival value, fair representation of target countries speaking the language, and sensitivity to sexist and ethnic stereotypes. Hardly taken into account, if at all, are whether the discourse, i.e., the logic of presentation, reflects C1 or C2 patterns of thought, whether the cultural facts are presented and explained from a C1 or a C2 perspective, nor what cognitive/affective abilities should be developed to elicit from the students a critical analysis of their own culture through the presentation of the target culture. Among those publishing houses that publish both foreign language and English texts, none has, for example, any consistent policy in the development of skills necessary to analyze critically the American culture in the English texts and the foreign culture in the foreign language texts. Sociology texts do provide such an analysis (see, for example, Wallace and Wallace, 1985) but there is no guarantee that the foreign language student will be offered, or take, an appropriate course in sociology to compensate for the lack of cultural analysis in the foreign language textbook.

Another aspect of the educational culture pertains to the authors themselves. Most foreign language textbooks, high school and college texts alike, are written by teams of authors. Some are high school teachers or supervisors, but most of the teams are comprised predominantly of college or university professors. The majority have a literary or linguistic background; they are not sociologists, anthropologists or political scientists. Most college professors do not get academic recognition for writing textbooks, and they do so, in many cases, only once they have been given tenure. They generally write texts as a lucrative task, rarely to put into practice their own theoretical research in linguistics or sociology. They are often bilingual individuals with an American view of education and a good deal of experience in both cultures, but no knowledge of theories of culture. Although they do not shy away from using the appropriate specialized terminology of grammar and syntax, and more recently even functional-notional nomenclature, they generally present cultural facts and events in the anecdotal language of people who have experienced the culture, but not reflected upon it or consciously made sense of it. Many feel that "interpreting" aspects of the foreign culture is too intellectual or elitist an activity for high school or even for college texts (Müller, 1981).

STATE DEPARTMENTS OF EDUCATION

The adoption of textbooks generally occurs at the state level in "state adoption" states such as Texas, California or Indiana, or by local school boards in "open territory" states like Massachusetts. The criteria vary with the moral, religious, political, and educational interests represented in the state. In California, for example, the official goals of foreign language education in public schools are stated as follows: "A consensus exists among foreign language professionals, in the body politic, among students and parents and among educators in general that the main goal of foreign language learning should be the ability to demonstrate practical meaningful use of the language [. . .] Communication in the foreign language should be the major objective and the dominant activity in foreign language classrooms" (California State Department of Education, 1985, p. 32). Critical analytic skills or understanding of the native and the target cultural contexts is, apparently, secondary. In Michigan, where foreign languages are good for the automobile industry, this fact is reflected in the state's guidelines. Textbooks should impart "skills to participate in the international business market, for foreign language study is a vital factor in Michigan's economy. Foreign languages mean employability, effective participation in a democratic society" (Michigan State Board of Education, 1983). In Texas, "students should develop a deeper comprehension of their own culture by exploring another." Foreign language study should bring about "awareness of self and reassessment of personal values" (Texas Educational Agency, 1978).

Currently, most of the states are revising their guidelines in the spirit of the ACTFL proficiency guidelines, which, as we know, have not yet integrated culture nor the development of intercultural understanding at their various levels of language proficiency.

TEACHERS

Finally we have to look at the teachers. In the American free-market educational economy, where local needs and values prompt students to study foreign languages or to ignore them, foreign language teachers have to compete for students. Thus, motivating their students is a top priority on their agenda. This concern reinforces the image that the American teacher has been given by society of a professional whose major skill should be the rigorous and carefully planned management of lessons. However, overburdened by paperwork, community service, and committee work, most foreign language teachers have neither the time nor the desire to design their own materials. They expect the textbook to give them the syllabus they need. This, by the way, is true of foreign language teachers in other countries too, as indicated in a recent report by Krumm (1985). Most of their concerns being managerial, teachers who do have a say in the selection of the text attend first to its methodological aspects and only secondarily to its cultural elements.

The teachers' view of the target culture is heavily influenced by their own experience as American tourists or students, or as native speakers. This experience they tend to consider the true, authentic one, and they are critical of any text that does not reflect "their" France or "their" Latin American country. Frequently, they share the cultural background of the country they teach, but they or their ancestors chose to or were forced to leave it and emigrate to the United States. The foreign culture they want to teach and that many of their students of similar ancestry want to learn is often historically, socially, and politically different from that of the people currently speaking the language.

The reviews of first- and second-year textbooks in *The French Review, Hispania, Unterrichtspraxis* and in *The Modern Language Journal* respond to the above-mentioned priorities of the teacher. The main focus of these reviews over the last five years has been the methodological features of the books: lay-out, sequencing of material, clarity of grammatical explanations, authenticity of the language of the texts, choice and introduction of vocabulary, respective value given the four skills, usability in real life, amount of meaningful communicative activities, recycling of vocabulary, and affirmative action in the representation of women, minorities, and traditionally underrepresented countries. Review of the cultural content is usually limited to the presence or absence of important cultural information, the degree of "information" contained in the culture capsules, and the factual accuracy of the information given (see also Schulz, 1987). There is absolutely no critique of potential American or white Anglo-Saxon biases in the presentation of the target culture, nor of the possible absence of a target culture perspective. No reviewer even notices the lack of a cultural theoretical standpoint, nor does anyone question the social or political slant of any of the textbooks reviewed. Foreign language texts get reviewed exclusively in foreign language journals by foreign language educators, not by anthropologists or sociologists.

In sum, the educational culture of textbooks imposes a variety of power structures—

financial, political, professional—on all those involved in building and validating the construct "textbook." If there is to be meaningful change in the cultural content of the latter, it can only come through the joint efforts of textbook producers and consumers (the classroom teachers). To understand the full dimensions of textbook learning, let us turn now from its conditions of production to its conditions of reception, both in the culture of the classroom and in the minds of the learners.

Conditions of Reception: The Classroom Culture

Studies of the way texts are used in foreign language classrooms (Krumm, 1985; Krampikowski, forthcoming) suggest that although there are many exceptions, teachers in general, in this country and elsewhere, deviate little from the text once they have built their syllabus around it. We have seen some of the constraints that can account for that fact. This is why the professional journals abound in practical suggestions on how to adapt or supplement the textbook (e.g., Guntermann and Phillips, 1982), but very rarely do we find suggestions for the total abolition or a fundamental restructuring of texts (see, however, Stevick, 1980; Valdman and Warriner-Burke, 1980; Crawford, 1981; Lafayette and Strasheim, 1984).

In the same manner that interest in discourse phenomena has focused public attention on the cultural aspects of language learning and has brought to light the cultural dilemma of textbooks, so does it lead us to examine what role the textbook plays in the social context of the classroom. In a recent article, Breen (1985, p. 142) describes the classroom as "coral gardens" that have to be viewed and respected with "anthropological humility." He distinguishes eight essential features of discourse in the foreign language classroom:

1 *It is interactive.* It is motivated by the assumption that people can learn together in a group. However, that group usually consists of members from very different social, ethnic, family, and religious backgrounds who all speak different "languages." This creates a sometimes implicit, sometimes explicit struggle between individual perceptions of the foreign culture and the official culture portrayed in the textbook. "This means that a high premium is placed upon consensus whilst misunderstandings, alternative interpretations, and negotiable meaning will paradoxically be the norm, and from which participants will seek to make their own sense and upon which participants will impose their own purposes" (p. 143).

2 *It is differentiated.* There is no one social reality in the language classroom; it is a different social context for each participant. The foreign culture is learned against a background of multiple native cultures. In her study of pre-school children in the Piedmont Carolinas, Heath (1984) shows how children at an early age are socialized into different kinds of literacy, i.e., they differ in the way they have learned how to extract knowledge from books. She shows that, depending on their social and ethnic background, learners will either identify with the type of schooled literacy conveyed by the text or not; they will either integrate their textbook knowledge into the larger context of their life experiences or not.

3 *It is collective.* "An individual learner in a classroom is engaged in both an individual learning process and a group teaching-learning process. Therefore individual psychological change will continually relate to group psychological forces [. . .] To infer individual learning process from classroom process or vice-versa will lead to a partial

understanding of classroom language learning" (p. 145). Thus the impact of the textbook on the individual learner includes the impact of the group learning achieved in the classroom.

4 *It is highly normative.* The language classroom categorizes the persons who participate within it as "good" learners and "bad" learners, "good" teachers and "bad" teachers, "beginners" and "advanced," "high" participators and "low" participators, etc. (p. 145). This normative nature of the foreign language environment, combined with the authoritative character of the text, is what makes the teaching of cultural relativism in classrooms a particularly difficult endeavor.

5 *It is asymmetrical.* Asymmetrical relationships do not only exist between teacher and student. The class is also made up of subgroups which develop for themselves mainly covert, though sometimes overtly expressed, roles and identities which are potentially asymmetrical with both the dominant culture and with other subgroupings in the class. Although the textbooks are part of the dominant culture, the fact that students scribble on them, poke fun at them, deface the photographs, lose them or sell them — or, on the contrary, carefully wrap them, keep them for future reference, and carry them at all times — makes them part of the cultural asymmetry of the classroom.

6 *It is inherently conservative.* Given the anxiety created by the foreign language, the group will tend to seek security and relative harmony in the belief that learning a language is like learning any other subject and that the textbook holds the key to successful learning.

7 *It is jointly constructed.* Lessons are successfully carried out and textbooks used through the collaborative decisions of students and teacher to define what part of the text is worth attending to, how to learn it, and how to define progress.

8 *It is immediately significant.* Ultimately, the meaning of texts must be viewed in their role as catalysts in the general "interplay between the individual, the individual as group member and the group which represents and generates the social and psychological nexus" which Breen defines as the "culture of the language classroom" (p. 149).

Any study of the impact or effectiveness of foreign language textbooks on the intercultural development of the learner will have to take into account the culture of the classroom in which it is used.

Conditions of Learning: The Learner's Interculture

Before we analyze existing texts in greater detail, we have to examine the key factor in the reception of textbooks, that is, the learners and their modes of acquisition of cross-cultural competence.

ACQUISITION OF CULTURAL MEANINGS

Just as the culture of the classroom is formed of a variety of individual and group assumptions and perceptions, constantly in flux and in reassessment, both a petri dish of foreign cultural meanings and the real world of native cultural values and signs, so the individual learner attempts to acquire simultaneously the forms of the new language and endow them with meaning. The notion that language learning proceeds from focus on form to focus on meaning (Littlewood, 1980) and that the world expressed by the foreign language is the same world as that of the native language, only with different labels attached (to paraphrase Sapir) is, however, tenacious. It can be as much an obstacle for learners trying to make sense of and behave appropriately in a foreign culture as would be their linguistic inadequacies.

In a series of recent studies on the concept development of language learners, Müller (1981, p. 116) examined the adjustments learners have to make in order to understand their environment when in a foreign country. For example, a foreigner has the opportunity to discover that Spanish *familia* means "family" plus a number of additional relatives, that French *vin* usually means "wine" but that it also represents something to eat along with the wine, or that the American expression "Why don't you stop by sometime?" is usually not a request or an invitation, but rather a polite conversational formula. Thus learners acquire foreign meanings by experiencing the foreign words in their total context, according to the heuristic formula: foreign language meaning = native language meaning plus foreign culture particularity. So, it must be learned through experience, for example, that with a *car* (in the USA) one may go on weekend trips of over 800 km, but that this is entirely unthinkable with a German *Auto,* or that while *breakfast* (in America) may not be an early morning family get-together, this is precisely the connotation of the German *Frühstück* (the source of many crises in intercultural marriages!) and that entering a *casa* requires a different pattern of behavior from entering a *house.*

Classroom learners who have a textbook knowledge of the language, i.e., who lack the socialization base that naturally goes along with language acquisition, will try to interpret the signs according to their native language meaning system. Müller gives an anecdotal example, which is only one of the many incidents that any foreigner experiences abroad. "A German student is invited in Spain by a Spanish family. In the room he takes to be the *Wohnzimmer* or living room and in which he carried on an animated discussion with a number of family members (in the sense of Spanish *familia*), he notices a *nevera* or refrigerator. The hostess, and sometimes also the host and the children, take cold beverages and ice out of it. The presence of this 'refrigerator in the living room,' and especially the fact that his hosts offer no word of apology or explanation about it, give him the feeling that this must be a family of very unconventional people. The conversation, which proceeds with hardly any polite formulaic elements—as would be usual in Germany—confirms this impression. The guest sees these proofs of an 'unconventional definition of roles' as something positive and 'liberating' for him—and helps himself to two ice cubes out of the *nevera.* There follows an awkward silence in the room" (p. 116). The guest has evidently misbehaved.

This Spanish learner has given the Spanish word *nevera* the same meaning as the word for refrigerator in his native language. Faced with a situation that was unusual to him, namely a refrigerator in a living room and an unexpectedly informal atmosphere, he misread the signs of what he took for an invitation to be "unconventional" and just imitated the behavior of his hosts. One might argue that he was rude not to ask for permission, but in fact all he did was to act in accordance with what he saw and grasped in the here-and-now of a culturally new situation: a well-known kitchen appliance with a specific function and people helping themselves freely from it. To complicate matters, "rudeness" is a culturally relative term; a direct request for permission might have been perceived as equally rude, if what was expected from the guest was modesty and unobtrusiveness. The right behavior in this context depended on a number of factors to which the guest needed to be sensitive, such as the social class of his hosts, their age, the degree of his acquaintanceship with them, whether men and women or only women were helping themselves from the refrigerator. The faux pas consisted in taking an object in the foreign culture and either reducing it to its pragmatic function or giving it the social symbolic meaning of one's native cultural environment. The student did not take into account the complex social meaning that object might have in another cultural environment.

One of the major difficulties for learners of a foreign culture is what Giroux calls "the reification or objectifiedness of native culture relations," the unquestioned assumptions of the native culture and the fundamental lack of social, historical and political knowledge of foreign language teachers and learners (1981, p. 20). If we want learners to be able to behave appropriately in the target culture, they have to learn not only the dictionary definitions of words, but their social meanings as well, for, as Bourdieu remarks, "le mot à toutes fins du dictionnaire n'a aucune existence sociale" ["the all-purpose dictionary word has no social existence"] (1982, p. 16). The acquisition of these social meanings is predicated on a change in perspective that does not occur by itself, nor through the mere fact of learning new lexical items in the classroom, nor even by living the culture in the target country. It has to be developed consciously through such cross-cultural skills as putting things in relation with one another and exposing socially significant meaning systems. Rather than a linear sequence of intercultural development along a scale from total native culture perspective to total foreign culture perspective — analogous to the model of interlanguage development from first to second language through various stages of interlanguage, as suggested by Selinker (1972) and others — sociologists and anthropologists envisage such a concept formation as a slow and progressive discovery of the "logic" of foreign cultural phenomena, an overcoming of the cognitive isomorphism of language structures (*nevera = refrigerator*) and, ultimately, the achieving of a cultural perspective which is neither totally native nor totally foreign, but a synthesis of the two.

MODELS OF SEMANTIC INTERLANGUAGE

Learners acquire foreign meanings through the various forms of the language: vocabulary, grammar, syntax, pronunciation, gestures, etc. Focusing on the acquisition of vocabulary, Müller (1981) describes five models of the acquisition of foreign meanings through various learning strategies:

1 *Bicoding.* The learner acquires vocabulary without recourse to context. Ex. An American student of French finds the word *chien* in the dictionary as a translation of dog. This acquisition type reflects a purely formal bicoding learning strategy on the part of the learner (How do you say "dog" in French?).

2 *Integration.* The learner tries to integrate the C2 phenomenon as an isolated item into an otherwise totally C1 perspective as in the above-mentioned example with *nevera.* The integration-type acquisition can be recognized by the fact that the learner behaves like a bicoder and keeps C1 and C2 strictly separate. Thus, an American learner might say things like: "We were in France in a café but a jukebox was playing," or "The hostess was quite friendly, even though she never showed us around the house."

3 *Relativization.* The learner tries to relate all new meaning units only to the situational and cultural context in which they are encountered. Ex. A young Turkish woman categorizes *kissing in public* as a human behavior pattern which she relates to *social tolerance, young Americans, expression of tenderness, summer,* etc.; that is, a phe-

nomenon distinct from her home pattern. Learners using a relativizing approach are aware of the relativity of their perceptions, which they organize in a nonhierarchical fashion, based on isolated observations. They do not put these observations into relation with their native culture because they want to avoid the conflict that often occurs when native norms and values (in the example, those for *öpüsmek*) are carried over onto the new situation (*kissing*). Relativization can lead to parallelization, if the learner keeps the two domains of cultural behavior totally separate; for example, if the woman adopts in America an "American" behavior and in Turkey a "Turkish" behavior with respect to *kissing in public*.

4 *Separation.* The learner is exposed to concepts which have yet no social meaning for him/her in the native culture. The foreign concept thus becomes the "continuation" of the socialization process started in the first language. Ex. A young French woman marries an American and emigrates to the United States. The words "my husband" acquire a meaning that is particular to the American environment in which she acquired it and have for her quite different connotations from their French equivalents "mon mari." She will probably not be aware of the cognitive separation of her two conceptual systems until she returns to France and people ask her: "Comment va votre mari?" It is then that she realizes that her identity as a married woman is linked to a network of social meanings acquired in an English-speaking environment and that her French identity does not contain the concept *mari*. The change in social meaning from *husband* to *mari* might require quite a bit of restructuring, for, depending on the social group in which these two concepts are used, "mon mari" might carry connotations of authority, superiority, and family responsibility that "my husband" does not have. This acquisition type is characterized by the fact that learners can talk about certain foreign cultural phenomena only in the foreign language.

5 *Confrontation.* Müller defines this acquisition type as follows: "The learner consciously leaves new concepts as parts of the whole situational context and determines internal meaning relationships of the key concepts. He/she also constructs hypotheses about the historical development of the concept, seeks a functional equivalent in the native culture, and then places this equivalent concept into its culture-specific context and sees it as a product of historical development" (p. 134). For example, a young French college student notes that American students seem obsessed with *work* (French: *le travail*); they don't ever seem to take a vacation, but are all looking for a summer job. After an initial reaction of rejection ("Ils sont fous, ces Américains!" ["Americans are nuts!"]) she begins to establish relationships and categorizes *work* into a relational system along with *making money, paying tuition, holding a job,* etc., and thinks about how *work* may have acquired its meaning in the course of the historical development of the United States. She reconstructs the situation in her home environment as follows: there, *le travail* is not linked to *money* since she doesn't have to pay for her studies, but is closely related to *faire des études* ("*Ce soir il faut que je travaille*" ["Tonight I have to study"]). It is embedded in the concept *formation intellectuelle* and is linked to *lecture* [reading], *voyages, culture.* For this situation, too, she asks herself now why these functions have developed in this way. She discovers that both *work* and *le travail,* from a student's perspective, have a common—but not identical—function. This she expresses as *education,* a concept that has traditionally been given different definitions in both societies. The "confrontational"

learner can be recognized by his understanding of socio-historical relationships, a mature nonjudgmental attitude toward foreign culture situations and a willingness to reexamine his/her own cultural meaning system in the light of the foreign culture.

EXISTING APPROACHES TO TEACHING CULTURAL MEANINGS

We have seen possible models of how learners attempt to acquire cross-cultural competence through a foreign language. Returning to the classroom, the question is now: Which of these models is promoted by the way teachers and textbooks present foreign meanings? In a survey of 12 anglophone authors of German textbooks, Müller (1981, p. 136) tried to find out whether these authors were aware of the problems created by socio-cultural semantic differentials such as those discussed above. Almost all the authors equated complexity of cultural meaning with linguistic complexity, stating that complex semantic explanations belonged only in advanced courses. Most of their texts used linguistic parameters to clarify cultural meanings: cognates, word context, lexical stems and translation; teaching the development of the new concepts was not deemed necessary nor possible. In general, these authors were either unable or unwilling to give everyday cultural occurrences in the Federal Republic any social meaning. For example, to explain the concept *Vater* (father), most authors favored the first of the following strings of associations:

- *Mutter* (mother), *Kind* (child), *Großvater* (grandfather), *Onkel* (uncle), *Bruder* (brother);
- *Vaterland* (fatherland), *Vaterschaft* (paternity), *Doktorvater* (thesis advisor), *Väterlich* (paternal);
- *Autorität* (authority), *Familienvorstand* (head of family), *Geldverdiener* (wage earner);
- *Aktiv in politik* (politically active), *Spielkamerad* (playmate), *Technisch begabt* (technically gifted).

The first string defines *Vater* in strictly biological terms, while the other three attempt to capture the German affective, political, social meanings of the word. Textbook authors seemed to ignore the latter three.

The results of this survey were confirmed by a study of the strategies used to teach the meaning of words in the course of lessons. Müller and his team observed ten German teachers in adult classes in Germany. Four were teachers of German as a foreign language, two were teachers of English, two taught Italian and two Spanish. The most frequently used cognitive technique to clarify the meaning of a word or an expression was reference to a denotated object, i.e., an object isolated from its situational and cultural properties such as "a *vegetable* is, for example, carrots, beans, cauliflower" (thirty-seven percent). Twenty-seven percent of the techniques did not refer to any content. For example: "The *weekend* is the end of the week," or "*Auto* means *car*." In thirteen percent of the cases, the teacher compared objects in C2 with objects in C1 such as "*Krankenversicherung* is the insurance that pays the bill when one is sick, like health insurance in the USA." In six percent of the cases teachers used explanations that made reference to configurational-quantitative features, like "This is a *dog;* you can find dogs everywhere in the world." These four techniques, that amounted to eighty-two percent of the cases, seem to encourage bicoding and integration and to convey the message that between the foreign and native cultural concepts there are really no cultural differences worth mentioning.

The textbook authors and teachers in the Müller study represent the prevalent view that students should learn mainly the forms and the culturally universal meanings of foreign words. We will examine in the next section how this view translates into the actual structure of language textbooks.

What's in a Text?

A textbook can be viewed as a carefully constructed "ideational scaffolding" for the organization and interpretation of a new linguistic and cultural experience (Brown and Yule, 1983, p. 247). It is constituted of a variety of voices and constructs that are expressed through the different chapter segments. Let us first examine how the textbook achieves its purpose through the interaction of various voices.

COEXISTING DISCOURSE WORLDS

It has been noted that the foreign language classroom is at the intersection of several "coexisting discourse worlds" (Edmondson, 1985), i.e., the talk that teachers and learners engage in as they do lessons together has a variety of meanings and functions according to how the participants perceive each other's purposes and goals. Consider, for example, the following fabricated exchange:

T. Who can tell me what this is? There are many of them in Germany.
S. This is a dog.
T. Right, do you have a dog?
S. Yes, two!
T. Oh, really? That must be fun. And this is the dog's tail. Repeat: This is the dog's tail.
S. This is the dog's tail.
T. Yes, and the dog is wagging its tail. What do you think it means, to "wag a tail"? Heidi?
S. He is happy.

This exchange can be seen as a polyphonic dialog of at least four different voices. The teacher acts here as the narrator, who uses the foreign language to teach the students something about the language and the culture. He or she also acts as the master, whose purpose is to carry out the successful management of the lesson and elicit responses from the students. The master is, in addition, the communication partner or native speaker representative who conveys information through the language, not only about the language. Learners attend to what he or she says, not only to how it is said. And then there is the voice of the learners, mediated at first by the master, then becoming more and more autonomous as they use the language for their own purposes, sometimes even to challenge one of the teacher's voices.

Like a classroom, a language textbook has many voices. We can identify in first- and second-year textbooks the same four voices we discovered in the classroom.

1 *The narrator's voice.* This voice not only orchestrates all the others via the lay-out of each chapter, but it is the authorial voice of the omniscient representative of the target culture who provides the basic information about the language (rules of grammar, lexical meanings, cultural information and interpretation) and who illustrates it through photographs, realia, and other visuals. The language of the narrator is made mostly of declarative statements of unquestioned truth. By saying, for example, that "the German school system provides little room for individual development" (Halverson, 1985, p. 331), the narrator makes the learner believe that this statement is true by the sheer virtue of the authorial nature of the text-

book genre. If such a statement had been read in the press, the reader might have questioned its objectivity.

2 *The master's voice.* This voice models for the learner how the language is used (through grammatical examples, pattern drills, etc.), how the learners are to proceed (instructions, guidelines for activities), and how they are to interpret the linguistic and cultural facts presented by the narrator. This voice also occasionally teaches learners how to learn and how to reflect upon the way the textbook helps them learn. The master's voice uses mostly imperative and interrogative statements of the type: "Put the following sentences in the past tense," or "What were the two friends doing in the park?"

3 *The native speaker's voice.* This voice gives evidence of how the language and the culture exist in the target world outside the textbook. Whether it be the transcription of naturally recorded dialogs, a selection of readings not fabricated for foreign learners or a series of follow-up activities involving native speakers, a foreign language textbook often incorporates, either between its two covers or through its extensions in the real world, the target culture's own voice.

4 *The learner's voice.* Asked to read aloud, repeat, transform, substitute, respond, manipulate, and create, the learner's voice is present throughout the chapters. It is, at first, a composite of the other voices that the learner imitates, but it progressively becomes autonomous and acquires a unique personality, as the learner becomes able to make linguistic and cultural choices according to his or her needs and desires.

It is through the orchestration of these different voices that textbooks build both the linguistic and the cultural competence of learners across chapters and chapter segments. The following section will examine in detail how such an orchestration takes place.

ANATOMY OF SOME EXISTING TEXTBOOKS: A CASE STUDY

A study conducted by this writer (forthcoming) focuses on eight current first-year college textbooks of German in the United States and analyzes the one chapter that all these texts have in common, namely the chapter on sports. By choosing college-level texts it was hoped that the study would yield a clearer picture of what textbooks can do when they are less subject to the type of censorship that is imposed on them at the high school level. Concentrating on a common topic obviously facilitated the comparison of the textbooks.

Macroanalysis. The first observation is that "each textbook builds its view on sports with remarkable consistency across the different chapter segments. Culture is taught not only through cultural footnotes and readings but is carefully woven into every aspect of the instructional process." All texts explicitly claim in some way to foster cultural understanding through an understanding of cultural differences. Comparisons between native culture and foreign culture are frequent; they are even encouraged by the grammar point chosen in some of the textbooks that emphasize the competitive aspect of sports: comparatives and superlatives. However, the constructs are built at low levels of abstraction and often lack an explicit analogical component, as the following example taken from *Deutsch für Alle* (Haas and Mathieu, 1987) will show.

In this textbook the competitive aspect of sports is built into the chapter first through a dialog between an American student, Craig, and a German student, Uwe, in an American college dorm. They voice their opinions about tennis and jogging. We hear that Craig prefers the fun of a competitive game of tennis rather than the organized, boring push-up gymnastics of the German fitness trails. Uwe says he prefers jogging, but only because tennis is too expensive in Germany. Each stays with his opinion in the end. "Ich bleibe bei meinem Tennis," says Craig, "Und ich bei meinem Laufen," answers Uwe.

The grammar explanations focus accordingly on *da-* and *wo-* compounds, of the type "to be for or against something," that are particularly useful in argumentative discourse, as well as on reflexive verbs such as *sich trimmen* (to stay fit), *sich ändern* (to change), and *sich interessieren* (to be interested in). The latter is particularly appropriate to point out differences in interests, tastes and values.

The reading reinforces the focus on competitiveness that was already apparent in the dialog; this time, however, represented by the GDR, a superpower in sports. The reading heavily stresses the state-controlled and state-supported nature of GDR sports versus the self-supported nature of "true" amateur sports and traces the origins of the *Staatsamateur* to national socialism. It explains the successes of GDR athletes in international competition by "the mixture of leninist marxism, strong nationalism and German thoroughness" (p. 227).

No attempt is made to go beyond these simple low-level dichotomies to try to understand each cultural system within its own frame of reference in order to find bridges between them. What is being taught here is American culture in German words, not German culture.

Whose voice? A microanalysis at the level of discourse attempts to find out at what junctures in the texts concept formation was initiated and fostered. In all textbooks, the target culture is represented by the full range of subjective and objective voices mentioned above: the native speaker's voice of protagonists in the dialog; the narrator's voice in the reading and the cultural notes; the master's voice in the instructions, drills, and exercises; the learner's voice, uttering pre-programmed sentences, using prescribed grammatical structures, answering comprehension questions, and also expressing personal opinions and native culture experiences. By contrast, American cultural facts are presented almost exclusively through two subjective voices: American protagonists in dialogs and the learners themselves as they answer personalized questions of the type: "And you, what sports do you like to engage in?" Textbooks rarely offer any native counterparts to the foreign facts presented (comparative percentages, statistics, sociological facts), nor do they offer, as in the example we have just seen, any interpretation of American reality together with any higher level construction of the target cultural reality. Yet, as we know, one of the major handicaps of students learning to conceptualize a foreign culture is the fact that they have not learned to conceptualize their own. Thus the development of an intercultural voice in the learners is impeded by the fact that they are not given the tools to develop that voice.

Target versus native culture. The dialogs act as a cultural introduction to the chapter, by coaxing the learners into trying on new cultural ways of doing things. They make it look as if only minor adjustments are needed to participate in the foreign culture and one doesn't need to change one's views. In fact, five out of the eight texts are based on the assumption that German culture is basically the same as the American and if, for the moment, it is still slightly inferior, it is becoming more and more like the American. One text states explicitly that both German and American cultures are based on common activities (such as shopping and engaging in sports) that correspond to different sets of habits in the two cultures. Only two texts present German culture in its historical development, from the old traditions to the new face of present-day Germany, but even they fail to construct both German reality *and* American reality within their respective frames of reference.

Microanalysis: dialogs and readings. In *Deutsch für Alle,* the competitive aspect of sports is built into the ninth chapter roughly through the following constructs:

Dialog:	Craig (American)		Uwe (West German)
	1. tennis	vs.	fitness trails
	2. game	vs.	push-ups
	3. fun	vs.	boring
	4. inexpensive	vs.	inexpensive
Reading:	United States		G.D.R.
	5. fewer medals	vs.	many medals
	6. true amateurs	vs.	state amateurs
	7. self-supported	vs.	state-supported
	8. (origins ?)	vs.	origins: national socialism
	9. (sports = ?)	vs.	sports = politics
	10. (financed by?)	vs.	financed by nationalized industry

We observe that the constructs used in the dialog are all low-level constructs that include such judgmental attributes as "fun" vs. "boring" or statements of fact such as "inexpensive." The reading introduces higher-level constructs of a more interpretive nature, but by not exploring fully either the GDR construct of "State Amateur" (i.e., by not mentioning other related cultural aspects of the GDR) nor the American construct of "True Amateur," the textbook leads the learner to build a series of stereotypical constructs which do not help "understand" either culture, but only reinforce current American clichés. It suggests that there are differences in views and opinions between Americans and Germans concerning sports, that these views are unbridgeable, and that of course students have to be tolerant of other viewpoints, but that the American view is "better," "more democratic," and "more fun." The illustrations confirm the fact that an Americanized Germany is the only "fun" one. Such an approach does not help learners make sense of the foreign culture, nor does it show them how to make sense of their own in the light of the foreign culture.

Classification of constructs. Analysis of the readings in the eight textbooks showed three different constructs at work:

• Explicit low-level reference to C1, without evaluation: pointing to a similarity between C2 and C1 ("The rowdys among the German soccer fans can be as aggressive as many Americans"), or stressing the differences ("The so-called Golf, that is called the Rabbit in America"), or focusing on a deficit in C2 as compared to C1 ("Driver education courses are not offered in the public schools, so one must go to a *Fahrschule,* which is expensive");

• Implicit low-level reference to C1, with or without evaluation: emphasizing the commonality of C2 and C1 ("The German Sports Federation, which is partially subsidized, but in no way controlled, by the federal government"); stressing the differences ("School sports are intramural rather than intermural"); or showing what C2 is lacking as compared with C1 ("In the GDR sports are financed by publicly owned industry, i.e., the nationalized industry"), meaning that the GDR does not have private industry

• Higher-level interpretations of facts within a C2 framework, either with no explicit reference to C1 ("Family memberships have become popular because the clubs now offer many social and athletic activities . . ."), or implying similarities with C1 ("That success in sports is linked to national pride is nothing new"), or implying a negative match with C1 ("When the average German buys himself a car, he takes loving care of it because it is something special and because he wants to show it with pride to his friends"), implying a status-conscious tendency in Europeans. Seventy-eight percent of all constructs belong to the third category, i.e., they explain cultural facts within C2 with no explicit reference to C1. Of these, thirty-eight percent imply a negative match with C1. More recent texts offer much less interpretive activity than older texts; they tend to offer mostly intracultural explanations of C2 without any reference to C1.

Thus, in a sense, we notice a progress in the attempt of recent texts to construct the target culture through historical and sociological information. However, events are still not related to one another across chapters, nor is there any conscious effort to help the students construct concepts based on the facts given. Native cultural facts are still rarely provided or used to construct concepts.

Grammar exercises. The study showed that with the exception of one text that tries to keep language exercises as culture-free as possible, most texts use grammatical drills and pattern sentences to further reinforce the cultural information given in other parts of the chapter. This is done through the master's voice by (1) requesting of the learners that they make comparisons (e.g., between an American football game and a European soccer game) and then state whether they prefer one or the other; (2) directly modelling the learner's utterances ("Say that you are for the same thing: I am for democracy—What are you for? Frau Strauss is against state amateurs. Against whom is she?"); (3) indirectly modelling learners' utterances, particularly through comprehension checks; e.g., Narrator: "Few people doubt that East German sports show a successful mixture of leninist marxism, strong nationalism and German thoroughness"/Master: "What do East German sports show?" The learners can only answer with the construct suggested by the master's voice, which transforms the narrator's modulated statement into a statement of truth.

The above study revealed three important points. First, existing foreign language textbooks, however much they purport to teach the principles of both language and culture, still teach only language in any "principled" way. Culture is conveyed in an anecdotal non-reflective manner. Second, textbooks foster bicoding or integrative culture-learning strategies. It is assumed that the foreign culture is basically the same as the native culture with a few variations. Vocabulary only needs to be "glossed" with foreign language equivalences; C2 facts are integrated as exceptions into an otherwise C1 view of the world. Third, learners' voices are often used not only to inculcate the forms of the language, but also to indoctrinate the students with a view of the foreign culture that reinforces mainstream American ethnocentrism.

Implications for Textbook Writers and Users

In this paper we went from a view of culture that was based on the interpersonal negotiation of signs to a realization that those signs are determined by larger social and political power structures. In the case of textbooks, the constraints of the genre, of the American educational culture, of state and school boards, of the training and professional situation of teachers, and of classroom conditions all come to bear on how culture is defined and presented in American texts. If we want foreign language textbooks really to teach language and culture, if we want students to become not only linguistically, but also socioculturally proficient in the foreign language, then we must reexamine a few traditional concepts in foreign language education.

FOUR CONCEPTS REVISITED

Culture. It is clear that culture is not only a collection of facts but a system of meanings. If, as Kelly (1963) reminds us, no bridges of understanding emerge from the mere gathering of facts, but only from assigning meaning to those facts, our interpretation must be informed by the full range of related facts both in the target and in the native culture to avoid reinforcing cultural prejudices rather than promoting cross-cultural understanding. Thus the depiction of culture in language textbooks needs to be rethought around four main points:

• *Factual information.* Texts should provide explicit information about the target culture seen both from a C1 and a C2 perspective. They should provide equally explicit information about the native culture of the learner, likewise seen both from a C1 and a C2 perspective.

• *Relations between facts.* Texts should also bring to light the socio-political links between the cultural facts presented throughout the book.

• *Construction of concepts from facts.* Relations between facts should be sought at a sufficiently high level of abstraction to allow generalizations and meaningful contrast and analogy between the target and the native culture. Meanings should be constructed along the full range of human experience: social, political, moral, symbolic, and esthetic, not just along the axis of tourist survival.

The question naturally arises as to which language should be used to present and discuss this cultural information: the native or the target language? Current communicative methodologies advocate immersing the students totally in the target language, which should be used exclusively in the classroom both for the content and for the management of lessons. While it is certainly not recommended to switch back and forth from the native to the foreign language in the course of the lesson, it is also a fact that first-year students cannot be expected to understand lengthy explanations in the foreign language, be they grammatical or cultural. As in the case of grammar or syntax, most of the cultural information has to be presented in the native language, at least in first-year textbooks. This cultural information should be tied as much as possible to the forms of the language introduced in the chapter. For example, when presenting the French *tu/vous* distinction, some contrastive cultural information concerning historical relationships of private and public spheres, and regarding power and solidarity in American and French society, is in order (Brown and Gilman, 1960, pp. 253–76). If the students are assigned to read this cultural information at home, it can then be discussed briefly in class either in English or in French, making sure to introduce gradually the necessary cultural concepts into the students' French vocabulary and contrasting them with the American. Cultural information should be tested in the native language as long as the students do not have the tools to do so in the target language.

• *Cognitive and affective abilities.* Learners should be given exercises that foster relational thinking, abstraction, and metaphor and that promote critical analysis of facts and of their presentation. Textbooks should also, and this cannot be stressed enough, stimulate the learners' fantasy, their ability to dream other cultures' dreams, to enter other peoples' imaginative universes and open themselves to novel connotations and feelings.

Culture will then cease to be either "big C" or "little c," the three F's of food, fairs, and folklore, survival skills or the culture of the "educated native speaker," but rather that system of social and symbolic meanings in the target culture that has its analogy in but is different from that of the native culture.

Authentic materials. Given our new definition of culture, authentic materials are materials that not only use language in real life, i.e., for nonpedagogical purposes, but also express and convey meanings and intentions that cannot be isolated from their social context. Thus, for example, a German menu is indeed an authentic text, but if it is used only to retrieve lexical or grammatical information (to practice reading numbers or decoding words on a page through skimming and scanning techniques), it is still used to teach linguistic forms, not cultural meanings. The cultural authenticity of menus derives from their being embedded in a host of social and symbolic relations in the C2 — price of food, taxes and tips, restaurant-going habits of customers, food and drug regulations, waiter's wages, trade unions, standard of living, the rituals and metaphors of eating and dining out — that all have their counterparts in the native culture.

Helping students understand authentic materials means bringing those relations explicitly to light throughout the book. "The most authentic language-learning tasks (in a classroom) are those which require the learner to undertake communication and metacommunication" (Breen, 1985, p. 68). Students could be required, for example, to pull together several cultural facts learned in different chapters (price of a meal in one, unemployment and wages in another, German trade unions in the other) and be encouraged to speculate how all these facts combined "make sense" within the society they are studying.

Contextualized learning. If we want to integrate language and culture, it is not enough to provide an authentic sounding, contextual frame for exercises and activities and then have the students "behave appropriately" in that context. The classroom environment has its unique cultural authenticity and is misused if it attempts to make participants forget as much as possible that it is a classroom. Simulating and role playing authentic contexts are excellent activities, but only if they serve the purpose of raising the consciousness of the learners about their native cultural patterns of thought and those of the foreign culture.

Learning the language in its cultural context means explicitly and systematically attending not only to English linguistic equivalents of foreign words, as do traditional vocabulary lists, but to the cultural concepts associated with those words (as in the case of *nevera* above). Hog, Müller, and Wessling (1984) propose "meaning collages" to slowly help learners acquire not only foreign words but the networks of foreign meanings in which they are embedded.

Personalized learning. If we mean by "personalized learning" making the learning of a foreign language and culture relevant to our students' lives and experience, it is not enough to ask questions such as "And you, what do you do during vacation?" This may make the students talk but doesn't insure that they realize how culturally determined their answer is, nor how a speaker of the target culture would "understand" what they say.

Personalized learning should mean reflection on one's own personal experience and how it is related to a host of native cultural relations. It means comparing those relations with that of the other students in the class. It means also having many more "free spaces" for the learners' voices in the textbook, not only to repeat and manipulate others' meanings, but to express and interpret their own as their new intercultural identity emerges (Börsch, 1987, p. 197). This entails taking into account the different social "cultures" of the learners and the different styles of learning that have resulted from their particular socialization (Heath, 1984).

THE C1 CONNECTION

Ultimately students cannot attempt to understand a foreign culture if they don't understand their own. Most American high school and college students live their culture but are insufficiently prepared to explain it, to interpret it historically, socially, and politically to speakers of other cultures. They are given facts about the foreign culture in their textbooks, but, as mentioned above, do not know which facts in their own culture have an analogous or contrasting social and political meaning. Textbooks should provide them with relevant facts about their own society, so that they can start constructing C1 and C2 realities in a truly intercultural perspective.

The C1 connection should be based on contrast and analogy, not on opposition and similarity. For example, it might be more appropriate to compare the European unemployment problem with the American poverty problem than with the American high employment rate (Dahrendorf, 1987). The equivalent of American students' summer work is arguably not the French students' summer leisure but the French state support for education. Textbook authors must draw on studies in sociology, political science, and anthropology to deepen their understanding of societal phenomena in both the native and the target culture.

Publishers are beginning to draw on the resources offered by scholars outside the field of linguistics or literary studies in the elaboration of textbooks. Greater numbers of social and political scientists should join the teams of foreign language text authors and should participate in the reviewing of textbooks, along with foreign language educators (Arizpe and Aguirre, 1987).

THE TEXTBOOK: A CATALYST FOR LEARNING

The role of the foreign language textbook is unique among its peers in the textbook culture. It must be grounded in the native culture of the users and at the same time show them a way out of their native culture and into a foreign mode of thought and behavior that will eventually change their native ways. Education always implies change, but foreign language education implies social change.

As we have seen, American educational culture puts a high premium on the management of learning, on methodology, and on procedure. But cultural understanding, unlike discrete points of linguistic knowledge, does not develop from well-designed maps and fool-proof instructions that lead the student through the forest of foreign meanings. It thrives on speculation, on successful and unsuccessful attempts to bring isolated facts and events into relation with one another, on multiple perspectives and interpretations, on a sensitivity to ambiguity, and on the search for meaning itself. Rather than trying to improve the textbook as a medium and goal of instruction, we should enhance its role as a conveyor of information and as a critical analyst of that information. We should also develop its unique ability to foster the imaginative and creative powers that alone can bridge the gap between two cultures. We must, of course, remind ourselves that we are all — teachers, learners, textbook authors, and publishers — caught in cultural networks that it is not in the power of any one person to change. But we can plant and nurture the seeds of intercultural understanding in the conviction that the final product will be far more than the sum of its parts.

Notes

1 Parts of this article are to appear in Lothar Bredella (Ed.). *Mutual Perceptions and Misperceptions between the US and Germany: Approaches to Intercultural Understanding.* Giessen: Giessener Beiträge zur Fremdsprachen-didaktik (forthcoming).

2 Ethnomethodology is that domain of sociolinguistics that is concerned with speech in personal interaction (Garfinkel, 1967), here the interaction of learners and teachers with texts.

3 I wish to thank the publishing teams from Harcourt Brace Jovanovich, Heinle and Heinle, Holt Rinehart, Houghton Mifflin, and Random House for generously providing me with valuable information on the conditions of textbook production.

References

Arizpe, V., & Aguirre, B. E. Mexican, Puerto Rican and Cuban ethnic groups in first-year college-level Spanish textbooks. *Modern Language Journal,* 1987, *71,* 125–37.

Bateson, G. *Steps to an ecology of mind.* New York: Ballantine Books, 1972.

Börsch, S. (Ed.). *Die Rolle der Psychologie in der Sprachlehrforschung.* Tübingen: Gunter Narr, 1986.

Bourdieu, P. Systems of education and systems of thought. *International Society of Science Journal,* UNESCO, Vol. XIX, No. 3, 338–58.

Bourdieu, P. *Ce que parler veut dire. L'économie des échanges linguistiques.* Paris: Fayard, 1982.

Brière, J.-F. Cultural understanding through cross-cultural analysis. *French Review,* 1980, *60,* 203–08.

Breen, M. P. The social context for language learning—a neglected situation? *Studies in Second Language Acquisition,* 1985, *7,* 135–158.

Breen, M. P. Authenticity in the language classroom. *Applied Linguistics,* 1985, *61,* 60–70.

Brown, G., & Yule, G. *Discourse Analysis.* Cambridge: Cambridge University Press. 1983.

Brown, R., & Gilman, A. "The pronouns of power and solidarity," in T. A. Sebeok (Ed.), *Style in Language.* Cambridge, MA: M.I.T. Press, 1960, 253–76.

Canale, M., & Swain, M. Theoretical bases of communicative approaches to second language teaching and testing. *Applied Linguistics,* 1980, *1,* 1–47.

Clyne, M. The cultural bias in discourse structure: Academic texts by English and German speaking scholars. Paper presented at the 7th World Congress of Applied Linguistics, Brussels, 1984.

Corl, K., Jurasek, B., & Jurasek, R. *Sprechen wir Deutsch.* New York: Holt Rinehart, 1985.

Crawford, L. M. Redirecting second language curricula: Paulo Freire's contribution. *Foreign Language Annals,* 1981, *14,* 257–73.

Crawford-Lange, L. M., & Lange, D. L. Doing the unthinkable in the second language classroom: A process for the integration of language and culture. In T. V. Higgs (Ed.), *Proficiency, the Organizing Principle.* Lincolnwood, IL: National Textbook Co., 1984.

Dahrendorf, R. Poverty in industrialized countries. Paper presented at the Kennedy School of Government, May 1, 1987.

Dorwick, T. Global demands on language: The experience of one Spanish textbook author-editor. Unpublished ms.

Edmondson, W. J. Discourse worlds in the classroom and in foreign language learning. *Studies in Second Language Acquisition,* 1985, *7,* 159–68.

Galtung, J. Structure, culture and intellectual style: An essay comparing saxonic, teutonic, gallic and nipponic approaches. *Social Science Information,* 1981, *20,* 817–56.

Garfinkel, H. *Studies in ethnomethodology.* Englewood Cliffs, NJ: Prentice-Hall, 1967.

Geertz, C. *The interpretation of cultures.* New York: Basic Books, 1973.

Geertz, C. *Local knowledge.* New York: Basic Books, 1983.

Giroux, H. *Ideology, culture and the process of schooling.* London: The Falmer Press, 1981.

Gumperz, J. J. *Discourse strategies.* Cambridge: Cambridge University Press, 1982.

Guntermann, G., & Phillips, J. K. *Functional-notional concepts: Adapting the foreign language textbook.* Language in education: Theory and practice 44. Washington, D.C.: Center for Applied Linguistics, 1982.

Haas, W., & Mathieu, G. B. *Deutsch für alle.* Third edition. New York: John Wiley, 1987.

Halverson, R. Culture and vocabulary acquisition: A proposal. *Foreign Language Annals,* 1985, *18,* 327–32.

Hammerly, H. *Synthesis in second language teaching: An introduction to linguistics.* Blaine, WA: Second Language Publications, 1982.

Heath, S. B. *Ways with words. Language, life and work in communities and classrooms.* Cambridge: Cambridge University Press, 1984.

Hendon, U. S. Introducing culture in the high school foreign language class. *Foreign Language Annals,* 1980, *13,* 191–99.

Hofstadter, R. *Anti-intellectualism in American life.* New York: Vintage Books, 1963.

Hog, M., Müller, B. D., & Wessling, G. *Sichtwechsel. Elf Kapitel zur Sprachsensibilisierung.* Stuttgart: Klett, 1984. (See review by Kramsch, C. J., in *Unterrichtspraxis,* 1986, *2,* pp. 268–70.)

Kelly, G. A. *A theory of personality—the psychology of personal constructs.* New York: W. W. Norton, 1963.

Königs, F. G. *Normenaspekte im Fremdsprachenunterricht.* Tübingen: Gunter Narr, 1983.

Krampikowski, F. *Das Deutschlandbild im Deutschunterricht am amerikanischen College* (Schwerpunkt: Analyse der Lehrwerke). Baltmannsweiler (forthcoming).

Kramsch, C. J. Culture and constructs: Communicating attitudes and values in the foreign language classroom. *Foreign Language Annals,* 1983, *16,* 437–48.

Kramsch, C. J. Textbooks' construction of foreign reality. *Canadian Modern Language Review* (forthcoming).

Krumm, H. J. Zur Situation der Lehrwerkkritik und Lehrwerkforschung Deutsch als Fremdsprache. *Stockholmer Kriterienkatalog zur Beurteilung von Lehrwerken des Faches Deutsch als Fremdsprache in den nordischen Ländern.* Stockholm: Goethe Institut, 1985.

Lafayette, R. D., & Strasheim, L. A. The standard sequence and the non-traditional methodologies. *Foreign Language Annals,* 1984, *17,* 567–74.

Littlewood, W. Form and meaning in language teaching methodology. *Modern Language Journal,* 1980, *64,* 441–45.

Moeller, H., & Liedloff, J. *Deutsch Heute.* Third edition. Boston: Houghton Mifflin, 1986.

Müller, B. D. Bedeutungserwerb—ein Lernprozeß in Etappen. In B. D. Müller (Ed.), *Konfrontative Semantik.* Tübingen: Gunter Narr, 1981, pp. 113–54. In translation: Culture learning strategies and concept formation. Paper presented at SIETAR conference, Washington, D.C., 1984.

Olson, D. R. On the language and authority of textbooks. *Journal of Communication,* 1980, *30,* 186–96.

Postman, N., & Weingartner, C. *Teaching as a subversive activity.* New York: Dell, 1969.

Sapir, E. *Culture, language and personality: Selected essays.* D. G. Mandelbaum (Ed.). Berkeley, CA: University of California Press, 1970.

Savignon, S. *Communicative competence: Theory and classroom practice.* Reading, MA: Addison-Wesley, 1983.

Schulz, R. A. The FRG and the U.S. as portrayed in foreign language textbooks: A comparative study. *Unterrichtspraxis,* 1987, *20,* 95–101.

Selinker, L. Interlanguage. *IRAL,* 1972, *10,* 209–30.

Shaver, J. P., & Strong, W. *Facing value decisions: Rationale-building for teachers.* 2d edition. New York: Teachers College Press, 1982.

Singer, J. *The American school 1642–1985.* New York: Longman, 1986.

Stevick, E. *Teaching languages: A way and ways.* Rowley, MA: Newbury House, 1980.

Valdman, A., & Warriner-Burke, H. P. Major surgery due: Redesigning the syllabus and texts. *Foreign Language Annals,* 1980, *13,* 261–70.

Van Dijk, T. A. Discourse studies and education. *Applied Linguistics,* 1981, *2,* 11–25.

Wallace, R. C., & Wallace, W. D. *Sociology.* Boston: Allyn and Bacon, 1985.

Weatherford, H. J. Culture in the FL classroom. What, why, when, how? *The Beacon,* 1986, *20,* 1.

Wuthnow, R., Hunter, J. D., Bergesen, A., & Kurzweil, E. *Cultural analysis. The work of Peter L. Berger, Mary Douglas, Michel Foucault and Jürgen Habermas.* London: Routledge & Kegan Paul, 1986.

Jean-Pierre Berwald
University of Massachusetts at Amherst

Mass Media and Authentic Documents: Language in Cultural Context

Introduction

The audio-lingual era of the late 1950's and the ensuing decade introduced a much more serious concern with culture than had previously been the case. Although there had always been reference made to cities, monuments, personalities, and artistic triumphs, only passing reference had ever been made to the daily lives of those whose language was being studied. Nelson Brooks, one of the more outspoken participants of this methodological revolution, focused his attention on what he referred to as "large C" culture, pertaining to the history/fine arts aspects, and "small c" culture for the every-day sociological elements. In general terms, he considers culture to be everything people do, think, and believe. The inclusion of culture into the curriculum, because of its inextricable relationship with language and literature, marked a major advance in foreign language teaching. The focus on spoken language and contemporary dialogs gave impetus to a youth-oriented vocabulary which was culture-laden. Even if dialogs were contrived, they were used to emphasize the patterns of daily living and value systems of a people (Morain, 1983).

While dialogs introduced a more modern vocabulary as well as reference to the daily lives of its speakers, more specific information on contemporary culture was presented through culture capsules, reading passages, pictures, and reproductions of realia and documents (such as tickets, train schedules, menus, etc.). In recent years, the role of culture in the foreign language classroom has taken on an even greater significance as language teachers have taken some ideas from anthropologists and introduced such techniques as cultural assimilators and mini-dramas, to enable students to experience a mild form of culture shock in their own country. In addition to these specific techniques, they also began to use a wide variety of printed and taped materials never intended for the classroom. As more and more teachers went abroad to study and travel, not only did they appreciate cultural distinctions observed while traveling, but they learned to deal with various "institutions" intended for the inhabitants of these countries: filling out forms, telephoning, traveling by train, renting cars, watching television, going to the movies, listening to the radio, eating—in short, enjoying a full life in another culture. A complete range of activities was open to those who were more than casual travelers to a country. Teachers discovered that these experiences were so vital to their own ability to cope in a foreign culture that they were able to use them as instructional tools. They were to find that the "souvenirs" they picked up while traveling—telephone books, tickets, catalogs, bills and menus—served as excellent motivational devices for both themselves and their students. They were not just a series of artifacts that described the customs and traditions of another culture but also a set of teaching aids which facilitated the simulation of experience in the target culture.

Why Use Mass Media to Teach Foreign Languages When Textbooks Have "Sufficed" for Such a Long Time!

The major advantage of authentic documents and mass media is that they contain current language on all topics imaginable and are constant reinforcement of grammatical forms learned in the classroom. In addition to containing traditional vocabulary learned in the first two years of language instruction, they also contain neologisms as well as extensive vocabulary for sports, politics, cooking, music, etc. Perhaps most importantly, mass media allow students to read or hear items of great personal interest including, of course, many youth-oriented topics of current interest. Furthermore, there is nothing artificial or contrived about foreign media; they have been created for inhabitants and consumers in authentic settings, not for foreign language teachers or students.

One of the most compelling reasons for using mass media is the instructor's participation in the selection and development of the material. The interest and enthusiasm generated for such projects can easily be shared with students; the teacher is presenting a class with his or her very own text. In addition, the material preparation is an excellent way for teachers themselves to develop their vocabulary and to gain further insight into the culture under study.

All forms of contemporary culture can be observed in mass media—the clothes people wear, the food they eat, their interests, preferences, personalities and residences, to name but a few. Different media reveal different facets of a given culture and will be illustrated in the sections to follow. The list of exploitable media is endless. It consists of a complete range of public communication in written and spoken form, including the obvious newspapers, magazines, radio, telecasts, films, and mail-order catalogs, while extending to other less-heralded realia such as wine bottle labels, postage stamps, menus, and product directions.

One key advantage of using mass media is to dispel stereotypes. Mollica (1979) suggests that if textbooks and teachers often reinforce nationalistic stereotypes, contemporary media representations help correct these notions. Students working with media have a chance to see for themselves that some of the more commonly held beliefs of other groups can be erroneous. Santoni (1983), for instance, uses feature films to break stereotypes by having students analyze footage from two different angles—the French and the American. Students are asked to categorize films by cultural content (which often reveals more about the student than the featured culture). In another exercise involving cultural stereotypes, Santoni uses a set of photographic portraits of French people in various walks of life. Students are asked to determine visually their age and profession and to match them up with a series of other photographs that include wine preference, living quarters, stores, cafés, and television programs. They are shown one set of slides of individuals and another of various living quarters such as a château, a single family house, a housing project, etc. The two sets are projected simultaneously with students expected to match each portrait with the respective residences. His technique involves getting students to use media in order to discover for themselves cultural notions refuting stereotypes.

The Pedagogical Exploitation of Authentic Materials

The first question to be asked is whether authentic materials should be "exploited" in the first place. One point of view is that they were not intended for a student population and should be given to students "unadulterated," without commentary, for their interest and appreciation. Kienbaum (1986) describes the implementation of courses based on mass media at Purdue University. Materials were thematically organized and prepared by instructors for two-year programs of French, German, and Spanish. The materials were *not* simplified or otherwise pre-digested for students since it was felt that the lack of help would be better for their self-confidence in understanding the language and coping with the culture. On the other hand, there is good justification for professional intervention at all levels — especially since a teacher can select materials, explain difficulties of grammar and vocabulary, and point out cultural distinctions. The well-traveled, informed teacher is in the best position to explain hundreds of points of culture as they relate to content and vocabulary. Who else could explain to the students the curious artifact referred to as a "bidet" in a mail-order catalog? When in doubt, of course, the best idea is to experiment with both prepared and unprepared materials; there are advantages to using both.

The preparation of written pedagogical materials generally consists of vocabulary study and a series of content questions and exercises designed to help students understand and describe the cultural distinctions the instructor wishes to emphasize. The initial step in preparing materials is to isolate and gloss a dozen or so useful vocabulary items for oral and written practice and personalization. This exercise immediately creates a focus on cultural distinctions. In addition, one can prepare content and multiple-choice questions on the corpus, at various levels of difficulty, to develop language skills, review grammar and provide additional cultural insights.

The instructor can also prepare quite easily his or her own audio-visual teaching aids. In the case of sound recordings, for instance, one can simply copy one audiocassette onto another cassette, building in one to two second pauses at the end of each breath group. This allows students to concentrate on material being heard and gives them time to focus on small units of speech. When exploiting videocassette recordings, the instructor can copy the sound portion onto an audiocassette and prepare from this another audiocassette with pauses, as suggested above. In addition, 35mm slides can be taken directly off the video screen by placing a single-lens reflex camera on a tripod or table, in a dark room, and setting it at the light value given by the camera (generally 1/30 to 1/60 of a second). The slides can then be used to introduce characters, action and dialog prior to viewing the video; they can also be used, of course, to review the same material.

The Projection of Slides

Slides have been a favorite standby of foreign language teachers for introducing culture. The simplest form of use is to project them one after another while offering live commentary during the presentation. If a teacher doesn't have slides to illustrate a certain point of culture, he can always copy a magazine, postcard, or calendar picture with a 35mm single-lens reflex camera and close-up lens. Most audio-visual departments have the facilities to prepare slides from pictures. A somewhat more advanced presentation involves the simultaneous running of a slide projector and tape recorder. The instructor has to listen to the tape to know when to change each slide. Music can be incorporated into a sound track by playing it softly during the narration and by bringing the microphone close to the music source for several seconds between paragraphs. A slide/tape presentation can be automated by setting the projector to change a slide every X seconds; this is easily done with a switch on the projector itself. The projection has to be coordinated, of course, with the tape.

A more sophisticated presentation makes use of a stereo cassette player, two slide projectors and a dissolve unit. Pictures are placed on alternate carousels and are advanced by a noiseless electronic signal placed on both sound tracks of the stereo after the tape has been recorded. The mechanism of the dissolve unit is such that each slide can be presented for as long as is desired. Furthermore, this machine creates an artistic effect by fading in and out each slide shown: as the light on one projector goes on, the light on the other goes off, and vice-versa. Ryan and Schunk (1984) describe a slide/tape presentation where two hundred and thirty slides are shown using two projectors, a sound synchronizer, a dissolve unit, and an audible tone on the tape to signal slide changes. They recommend showing multiple slides of any item of interest—the same picture as viewed from several angles—and also suggest taking horizontal shots in case the presentation is to be transferred later onto a videocassette format. In addition to the usual tourist shots of buildings, monuments, and streets, the authors recommend scenes such as unwrapped bread protruding from a shopping net, a typical meal, washing clothes, ads, billboards, and other pictures which reveal the culture. Scanlan (1980) points out that even in a single shot of an outdoor café a great deal of comparisons and contrasts can be made. One can comment on such matters as the age of the clients, their drinks, the drinking laws of the country, and the role of the café in a particular culture. Scanlan shows students pictures and asks them to speculate on what they see and to create possible stories of the individuals shown using the local culture as a framework for their invention.

Another useful approach consists of preparing subtitles to accompany a slide presentation. Titles are helpful in introducing and reinforcing spoken dialog and showing students how words are spelled. Again, two projectors are used for simultaneous presentation: while one shows a picture, the other shows subtitles, generally a shortened version of the taped narration. In a previous study, this writer (1979) describes several procedures for preparing titles. The first involves taking pictures of typewritten titles with black and white Kodalith film. The negatives, showing white titles on a black background, are then mounted and projected. Another technique makes use of color film to shoot Dymo labels consisting of white letters on a black tape. One can also take color slides of white transfer letters on a black cardboard background; such lettering kits are available in most art and photo stores. Titles are flexible; they can be shown with just an audiotape to focus on the message or they can accompany a visual presentation and be discarded when they are no longer needed. After students have studied a particular slide/tape presentation, they should be able to understand the tape without any visual or written support. This written support can also be prepared on a transparency for overhead projection; it is certainly easy enough to prepare, but lacks the sophistication of the slide-projected titles. Using the overhead projector may also necessitate the help of an additional person.

Techniques of Working with Film

Some of the techniques of creating pedagogical materials for video are applicable in the case of film as well. One can use a single-lens reflex camera to take still shots in the form of slides directly from a screen, and the film sound track can easily be copied onto an audiocassette by means of a patch cord. Again, once the audio portion is on a cassette, it can be copied, along with pauses, onto another cassette.

Feature films often have accompanying scripts, either in separate volumes or in magazines. The French publication *Avant-Scène Cinéma,* for example, has published the scripts of many well-known international films since the 1960's. These scripts along with the films are an additional source of linguistic and cultural enrichment that can be exploited in the classroom. Morain (1972) lists a series of cultural characteristics to look for when viewing films or televised materials. Although Morain first considered these characteristics for a series of commercials, they are certainly applicable to any film or videocassette presentation. They include the following:

1 *Art:* Examine the materials for artistic use of language as well as for artistic use of form and design.
2 *Artifacts:* What physical objects of the culture are visible (household appliances, automobiles, fashion accessories, etc.)? Are they used differently? Do their characteristics in any way reflect the culture of the country?
3 *Attitudes:* How are cultural attitudes shown in the material (i.e., the French concern with the liver; the American concern with getting fat)?
4 *Background setting:* Does the setting depict locations of geographic or historical interest?
5 *Clothing:* What conclusions can the viewer draw as to social level, occupation, and geographic region from the clothing worn in the film?
6 *Gestures:* Note examples of gestures, posture, and facial meaning which convey cultural meaning. Are there equivalents in American culture?
7 *Humor:* What type of humor is shown in the film? Is it slapstick or sophisticated? Is it possible to make generalizations about a "national humor"?
8 *Interpersonal relationships:* Note significant relationships between parent and child, between teenagers, between men and women, between members of one occupation interacting with members of another.
9 *Onomatopoeia:* Does the foreign culture use the same or different sounds to portray a yawn, a sneeze, a sob? How does the culture express pleasure in taste, fragrance, and sight?
10 *Proverbs and sayings:* Examine the script for examples of proverbs or proverbial similes and metaphors.
11 *Social customs:* Do the films present examples of table manners? of greetings? of techniques for such social amenities as lighting cigarettes, entering rooms, holding chairs, opening doors, and proposing toasts? What traditional customs are revealed (birthday and anniversary celebrations, holiday observations, etc.)?
12 *Stereotypes:* Do the materials illustrate stereotypes held by the foreign culture? How

are doctors, athletes, clergymen, and in-laws characterized? Be alert for foreign equivalents of "the dumb blonde," "the old maid librarian," "the hayseed," "the used car salesman," and other stereotypes.

Capretz (1979) describes a film viewing situation in a language laboratory where students view images on two screens and regulate volume in individual booths. He advocates showing a film in fifteen-minute segments in the following manner:

1 Show the film without subtitles.

2 Listen to the sound track or to a recording of the dialog without sound effects or music. The left screen shows a printed version of the text and the right, a series of still shots.

The presentation makes use of pauses for explaining difficult words which have been underlined. The viewing of the presentation is followed by a series of written exercises.

As Capretz demonstrates, culture can be explained visually by projecting original documents alongside a film. He shows a film about the French poet Apollinaire, for instance, accompanied by a simultaneous projection of various aspects of his life, poem quotations, etc.

The Use of Advertisements

There are many reasons why advertisements are enjoyable to work with. Print ads often have the advantage of a visual element that makes them easy to comprehend. The pictures can reveal the nature of a product, and headlines offer other clues to comprehension. In addition, the text itself is very often short and designed to catch the reader's attention and encourage immediate understanding. Since they are often written in an emphatic, breezy style, using contemporary language, they are an excellent resource for practical vocabulary enrichment. We recall, for instance, an ad for a Hewlett-Packard touch screen computer that includes a complete series of technical terms not yet incorporated in major dictionaries.

Mollica (1979) finds advertisements particularly rich in culture and establishes a number of categories for exploitation, such as linguistic "curiosities," comparing how two cultures with a common language translate the same vocabulary items. For example:

- The North American influence on the translation of "soft drink": the Québecois *liqueur douce* and the French *boisson gazeuse*.
- The pun: *L'Eclat c'est Moi* for a dishwashing soap ad (reference to Louis XIV's *L'Etat c'est moi*).
- Different interpretations of international ads: e.g., "Put a tiger in your tank" in the U.S. advertisements as opposed to "Put a tiger in your motor" in other cultures.
- Translation of film titles (of particular interest since direct translations from one language to another don't always have the same impact from one culture to another). A good example of this is the film *Jaws* which was translated into French as *Teeth of the Sea;* the literal translation of "jaws" would have been meaningless.

Lawrence (1987) finds television commercials particularly rich as a source of culture. As annoying as commercials may be, they do have their pedagogical value. While showing specific differences between products, they also reflect differences in social values — such as allowing nudity in television commercials or showing knitting as a form of recreation for women of various social classes and ages (as opposed to its American perception as a grandmother's occupation). She gives several examples of symbols, abbreviations, and acronyms that can be used for giving information about products, institutions, and services, such as a squirrel used by a savings bank or yellow and brown stripes of *métro* tickets to advertise the Paris subway system. Lawrence found cheese advertisements to be a particularly rich source of culture since they discuss a variety of goat, sheep, and cow cheeses and the geographical regions they represent. She also makes reference to French attitudes toward other cultures as evidenced by their stereotypical representations of the American Wild West or ghetto gangsters.

Exploiting Radio

The ubiquitous radio is one of the best devices for students to perfect their listening comprehension. Radio/cassette players can easily be taken abroad to record a variety of programs directly off the air. The instructor can then play back a tape as often as is necessary to understand fully a particular segment. For class use, it is a good idea to copy a short segment, inserting brief pauses as suggested above. I usually play a text three times: once through for general comprehension, a second time with pauses, and a third time again straight through. If satisfactory comprehension has still not been achieved, the instructor can explain key words, expressions, and cultural factors and, eventually, provide a complete written version of the text.

Savignon (1972) made use of radio by exploiting "France-Inter," a daily news, information, and music program in France. The language laboratory technicians at the University of Illinois were able to receive it on short wave and record it daily. Students had twenty-four-hour telephone access to the seven-minute playback devoted to a variety of topics. Class follow-up included summaries, map study, cultural capsules, and general discussion. Savignon distributed in addition a written text of the preceding day's segment, which was used as a check for comprehension.

Mail-Order Catalogs

The mail-order catalog is an excellent source of information for a variety of topics taught in elementary and intermediate foreign language classes. The most extensive vocabulary in general catalogs is reserved for clothing. These items are usually displayed in color photos, described in a few sentences, and priced. Students can go through a catalog "selecting" items they want by name and price. They can determine the price in American dollars by checking the latest exchange rates (in most large city daily newspapers) and their size in the metric system by referring to guide book conversion tables or measuring instructions given in catalogs.

When there are not enough catalogs for use by an entire class, individual pages can be photocopied and distributed or made into transparencies for class viewing. The instructor can also remove selected pages and distribute one to everyone in class along with a set of general and personalized questions based on color, size, and style. In addition to the rubric on clothing, general catalogs also contain many objects covered in the first two years of a language. One can easily furnish a home with the sections devoted to various rooms in a house. Once students have learned about the parts of a house, they can use the catalog to place appropriate furnishings in all of the rooms. They can design a home and furnish it individually or, with selected xeroxed pages, participate collectively as a teacher stands by a board or overhead projector and draws in the items as they are mentioned. The items used can be priced in foreign currency and in dollars; these can be compared with prices from an American catalog, making for some interesting revelations. For those wishing to make comparisons involving the metric system, it might be interesting to compare foreign and American refrigerators for price and size. The traditional small size of foreign refrigerators can itself be used as a reflection of cultural differences: the eating and shopping habits in other countries.

Catalogs lend themselves to the preparation of color slides. I would suggest making two slides for each item: one with accompanying description and price and the other without. I project the undescribed picture to probe the students' understanding and emphasize cultural features. The second slide is then shown to reinforce the aspects of the picture that have just been discussed. After students have made their selections, they can then "place an order," using the instructions found in the back of the catalog, either by telephone or by mail. This gives them an opportunity to work with measurements, dimensions, weights, sizes, and colors. It also offers good practice in referring to postal codes for their own fictional addresses and phone numbers of the regional catalog office. This exercise would certainly be useful also for reviewing numbers and for learning how to telephone from one place in the country to another (Scanlan, 1978).

The Telephone Directory and The Yellow Pages

The telephone directory is another storehouse of information that can be used in early levels of language instruction. Of particular interest are the explanatory sections on telephone use and rates in the front part of the directory. Information gleaned from the directory serves a valuable function, since students learn and retain material by actually dialing numbers and using French charts and price structures to calculate rates for telephone calls placed throughout the world. In addition to telephone information, introductory pages often contain maps, population statistics, tourist information and details about government services.

The Yellow Pages are an institution well known throughout the world. They are still another source of authentic material that can be used to review a variety of topics. These include product categories, names, addresses, phone numbers, and a great deal of supplementary information. In addition to learning about the various types of professional listings in such a directory, there is information for the prospective traveler; there are useful references, for instance, to hotels, restaurants, and auto rental agencies. In the section devoted to hotels, one finds not only names and addresses, but occasional accompanying ads which offer additional information regarding location, services, and the all important rating. In France, for instance, hotels are rated according to quality and price, with no stars representing the most modest accommodations and four stars the finest and most expensive. As with other media, the yellow pages can be photocopied, enlarged, made into transparencies, and highlighted with a yellow marking pen to focus on desired features. Scanlan (1986) uses the ads for business terms, logos, symbols, and postal codes. On the basis of scant information, he is able to generate a great deal of discussion on cultural institutions and differences. He allows certain topics to lead naturally to others. A student wishing to drive in France first needs to "take lessons" from an "Auto-Ecole," "buy" an automobile from the many dealers listed in the directory, and then "purchase" insurance. Many details, including essential vocabulary concerning these products and services, are already listed in the pertinent directory ads (one can find approximate prices in corresponding newspaper ads). Scanlan finds that the ads refer to "a vast network of cultural traits and linguistic or historical facts with which the native French can be expected to be familiar" (p. 382).

Newspapers

From the point of view of variety and timeliness, the newspapers are probably the best of all mass media for cultural and linguistic exploitation. They contain sections on all fields of endeavor, use the latest vocabulary, and provide the reader with useful information. Mariet (1985) points out that one should not be restricted to the important national newspapers of a country but should also try to get regional and local papers for practical information, local events, schedules, and local color in general. From a cultural point of view, Mariet finds local newspapers more down-to-earth and less haughty and snobbish than the major papers.

There is no single way of exploiting a newspaper for language or culture. Certainly every section has unique aspects that suggest a variety of techniques. Since the general topic of cultural exploitation is too vast to be covered in detail in this article, we will limit the discussion to some of the most obvious features that lend themselves to classroom use.

HEADLINES

Headlines have excellent value in reviewing grammar. They can be used to change tenses or to go from singular to plural and vice versa. Adjectival and verbal endings as well as prepositions can be whited out and filled in on an overhead transparency. Headlines often contain a good deal of culture as well. One such example is the title "NEW IDENTITY CARDS WILL BE ISSUED," which certainly deals with a concept not known in the United States, where the driver's license is our identity card. One often has to be familiar with a culture in order to understand the headlines. Examples abound in the American press itself. Some years ago, one of the *New York Daily News* headlines read as follows: "FEMS SHAPE UP ON DOCKS BUT FACE PIER PRESSURE." The title refers to the selection of female stevedores and the reluctance of male dock workers to accept them in their ranks. In order to appreciate fully this headline, it is necessary to know that "shape-up" is the term used for the daily early morning selection of those who will work on a given day. Other *Daily News* headlines which exhibit a combination of puns and cultural information include the following:
- "DORSETT DOESN'T FUMBLE FOR WORDS" (referring to Tony Dorsett, the football player, and playing on the word "fumble");
- "WHAT'S UP IN PARIS?" (an article on women's skirts, playing on the expression "What's up?");
- "ONE MOOD IN IRAN. JUST STRING 'EM UP" (a Wild West metaphor used to refer to Iranian feelings toward American hostages in 1980).

A fanciful headline relating to a clean sidewalk campaign read as follows:
- "MAYOR: POLICE WILL PUT FOOT DOWN ON DOG-DOO DON'TS" (playing on the two expressions "do's and don't's" and "putting your foot down").

The article, incidentally, was finished on another page titled "POOP FINES TO BE ORDURE OF THE DAY" (!).

Calbris (1982) has made a detailed study of titles found in newspapers, magazines, books, and advertisements. Like the *Daily News* headlines, many use metaphor, puns, and deviations from well-known proverbs and expressions, and often refer to matters of a cultural nature. Here are some French examples:

- "UNE NOUVELLE FORCE DE FRAPPE" (an ad for a typewriter—the term *force de frappe* usually refers to French military power; *la frappe* means "typing");
- "NE VOUS SERREZ PAS LA CEINTURE" (an ad for the French railroads that has a double meaning: (1) You don't have to buckle up in a train and (2) you don't have to worry about money).

In addition, there is an advertisement for *Le Point* magazine that contains the expression *faire le point*, a pun which not only means to buy that particular magazine but also to evaluate a situation. It reminds one of the slogan used by the *Village Voice:* "KEEP AHEAD OF THE TIMES," an obvious reference to its illustrious New York competitor.

MOVIE REVIEWS

Since it often contains ads and reviews for American films they have already seen, students often enjoy the movie section of a foreign language newspaper. They usually recognize the names of the actors and are already familiar with the story line. One simple listening comprehension exercise is for the instructor to take the movie section of a foreign language newspaper and to read aloud various descriptive blurbs of films that have been shown in this country. Students then call out the American title. An assignment given by this writer in a grammar review course was to have the students themselves find film reviews in any French language newspaper or magazine (generally available at our university library). Although each student has a separate review, they all answer a series of general questions that have been asked in French. They are simple content questions, whose answers are readily found in the text. Students must make use of the vocabulary in the questions as well as the vocabulary they discover in their texts. Typical questions include the following:

1 What is the name of the film?
2 Who are the actors?
3 Where does the action take place?
4 Where was the film shot?
5 In three or four sentences, explain what the film was about.
6 What did the critic like and dislike about the film?

In addition to answering questions, students are asked to take ten unknown vocabulary words out of context, find their definitions in a *monolingual* dictionary, and write them down. They also provide two original sentences which show they understand the meaning of the words. They then submit the answers and vocabulary work to the instructor who returns them to students, with comments and corrections, for use in preparing for a quiz. The day of the quiz, students are asked to bring to class two ten-word lists. The first contains ten key words students have chosen to guide them in preparing a summary of the article. The other list consists of the ten vocabulary words mentioned above without definitions or sentences. The instructor circulates around the class during the quiz and chooses two words from each vocabulary list for which definitions and original sentences are to be given. This is a convenient and effective way to test students on work of their own choosing. Similar assignments are given to students in other areas such as music and crime.

Schulz (1974) has described an interesting cross-cultural assignment for the elementary level that asks students to answer the following questions from a newspaper movie section:

1 How many theaters are there?

2 What are the show times?

3 What does it cost to go to the movies?

4 What types of films are shown? (What do the titles imply about the content?)

5 What U.S. films seem popular?

6 Are the films rated as to who can see them?

7 Are there special children's or youth films?

It is best if the questions are prepared in the target language since students are able to use essential vocabulary found in the questions for their replies.

TELEVISION

In addition to working with the actual medium, one should not overlook the television pages of foreign newspapers or television guides. They contain program listings as well as synopses of special programs and feature films. Schulz, again, has suggested some pertinent questions as a means of developing reading and vocabulary and of focusing on various cultural differences (p. 12):

1 How many channels are there?

2 What are these stations called?

3 How many programs are available in the morning, afternoon, and evening?

4 What hours can you watch television?

5 Do any programs seem to be of U.S. or other "foreign" origin? (Check titles, actors, country of origin.)

CLASSIFIED AND DISPLAY ADS: HOUSING AND REAL ESTATE

The topics of housing and real estate are useful at the beginning and intermediate levels of foreign language study; large and small ads for apartments and houses contain information on the various topics ordinarily mentioned in first- and second-year texts. They include floor plans, room nomenclature, location and prices, and vocabulary related to rental and purchase. This information can be articulated with the section on mail-order catalogs for "ordering" furniture and appliances. It also goes well with a unit on verbs to show where common domestic activities are performed: "I wash in the bathroom, I cook in the kitchen," etc.

Most information on housing in newspapers and magazines comes in the form of ads, both large and classified. The large ads, often for luxury apartments, will occasionally include a properly labeled floor plan complete with dimensions. This type of ad can be used to ask a series of questions relating to the functions of the rooms. Additional information can be sought with regard to the name, address, and phone number of the building in question. Large ads without a floor plan will contain detailed information on location, prices, facilities, and special advantages. A certain amount of problem solving can also be done, again, in converting prices to dollars and metric dimensions to the American system.

The topic of housing allows for exploitation of want ads also. All the important information regarding an apartment is condensed into a four- to six-line ad consisting of a series of abbreviations—some easy to understand, some not. Another interesting matter concerns the price per house or apartment. In France, housing is often sold by the square meter. This information, in itself, is useful for some problem-solving activities where students multiply the area in square meters by the price per square meter in order to find the total cost in francs (which can then be converted to dollars). The instructor may wish to prepare a set of general questions in the target language applicable to all classified ads for housing, whether it be for an apartment or a house.

1 How many rooms does it have? What is the purpose of each?

2 Where is it located?

3 How many bathrooms does it have?

4 What is the surface area?

5 What are the good and bad features?

6 Whom does one contact (address and telephone number)?

It is interesting to compare ads in various countries using the same foreign language to see how the culture affects housing concerns and, consequently, the vocabulary involved. For instance, there is a great difference between ads in Quebec and in France. In French-Canadian newspapers, one immediately recognizes the strong influence of the North American culture: Blurbs will include "low taxes," "near schools," "finished basement," "9% mortgage," etc. The French leave financial considerations to banks. On the other hand, the French almost always mention square meter dimensions, generally ignored in Canadian ads except for new houses or condos.

COMIC STRIPS

Comic strips are a staple of newspapers in many parts of the world. In addition to strips found within a particular country, there are also a certain number of international favorites. American products such as "Peanuts" and "Hagar the Horrible" have been translated into many languages; perusal of the dialog and situations of these strips reveals some very distinct facets of American culture. In France and Belgium, among other countries, comic strips have become a serious art form, better known and appreciated as separate albums, such as *Astérix* and *Tintin,* than as newspaper strips. Although these albums have been translated into English and sold in North America, comics in album form have never attained the popularity here that they have abroad.

Brown (1977) believes an entire course on French culture could be taught through the medium of comics. They indirectly convey information reflecting cultural specificity, regarding, for example, such matters as hero worship and ethical values. He finds that culture is communicated by eating habits, clothes, gestures, and architecture found in the comics. The *Astérix* series is most likely the best known example of a culture-bound cartoon strip for its mixture of puns, social satire, and history. Pinet's perceptive study (1977) explores the world of *Astérix,* highlighting its cultural themes and stereotypes throughout.

SPORTS

From a cultural perspective, there are two types of sports: (1) those that are international, such as tennis and soccer, and thus known to everyone throughout the world, and (2) those that are local or regional in nature, such as bullfighting or pelota, which are familiar only to certain population groups. Although all sports may be fascinating, the latter seem more culturally "interesting," since they reveal more about a given people than would international sports. Of particular interest, for example, is how bullfighting can be so popular in Spain or other Hispanic cultures and so poorly understood, or downright vilified, by North Americans.

Another sport that is particularly rich in culture is the Tour de France bicycle race (Berwald, 1987). Not only do newspaper accounts deal with the rules of the sport, the special uniforms, and the various ways points are earned, they also focus on the participants, their home countries, and their sponsoring business firms. In addition, the entire geography of France and its neighboring countries comes into play. Newspaper accounts describe the terrain of each area covered, distances between stages, the height of the mountains climbed, the cities forming the itinerary, and even the local gastronomy!

There are, of course, other newspaper sections exploitable for cultural content, such as editorials, classified employment ads, the financial pages, etc. And we have not even mentioned the area of current events. Topics such as crime, wars, natural disasters, politics, and international events are certainly a rich source of specialized vocabulary. They also give us good insight as to how other countries and governments react to national and international incidents of a controversial nature. On a more sophisticated level, several newspapers in any given country can be compared with each other and analyzed on the basis of their political orientation. It is particularly interesting, in this respect, to compare the treatment of a single news event in several different newspapers within this culture. This certainly allows for a more in-depth analysis of the target culture.

Conclusion

In recent years, more and more interest and attention have been devoted to the inclusion of mass media, authentic documents, and realia in the foreign language classroom. Geltrich-Ludgate and Tovar (1987), for instance, have prepared an extensive listing of over fifty media, with suggestions for linguistic and cultural exploitation, at various levels of instruction. Such culture-rich materials, because of their inherent interest, authenticity, and instructional features, lend themselves to the foreign language classroom. They are the products of current, dynamic societies, and their study allows for a more realistic contact with foreign cultures.

Again, the teacher's role in selecting materials and preparing them for class use cannot be overstated. It is the teacher's interest in and experience with the culture that are expressed thereby, and it is his or her time and enthusiasm in developing and using these materials that create a successful and interesting learning experience.

References

Berwald, J.-P. *Au courant: Teaching French vocabulary and culture using the mass media.* Washington, D.C.: Center for Applied Linguistics, 1986.

Berwald, J.-P. Teaching foreign languages by means of subtitled visuals. *Foreign Language Annals,* 1979, *12,* 375–78.

Berwald, J.-P. Teaching French language, culture and geography with the Tour de France bicycle race. Hastings-on-Hudson, ACTFL Materials Center, 1987.

Berwald, J.-P. Teaching French via driver education. *Foreign Language Annals,* 1980, *13,* 205–08.

Berwald, J.-P. Teaching French language skills with commercial television. *French Review,* 1976, *L,* 222–26.

Brown, J. W. Comics in the foreign language classroom: Pedagogical perspectives. *Foreign Language Annals,* 1977, *10,* 18–25.

Calbris, G. Structure des titres et enseignes. *Le français dans le monde,* 1982, *166,* 26–54.

Capretz, P. Une expérience d'utilisation du film en tant que document sonore dans l'enseignement du français. *Le français dans le monde,* 1979, *141,* 90–93.

Geltrich-Ludgate, B., & Tovar, D. Authentic text types and corresponding strategies: A list for the foreign language instructor. *Unterrichtspraxis,* 1987, *1,* 80–93.

Kienbaum, B. E. Communicative competency in foreign language learning with authentic materials: Final project report. 1966. (ERIC Document Reproduction Service No. ED 275 200).

Lawrence, K. D. The French TV commercial as a pedagogical tool in the classroom. *French Review*, 1977, *60*, 835–44.

Loew, H. Foreign language magazines plus planning equal up-to-date culture units. *Accent on ACTFL*, 1973, *3(4)*, 6–8.

Mollica, A. Cartoons in the language classroom. *Canadian Modern Language Review*, 1976, *32*, 424–44.

Mollica, A. Print and non-print materials: Adapting for classroom use. In J. K. Phillips (Ed.), *Building on Experience—Building for Success*. Skokie, IL: National Textbook Company, 1979.

Mollica, A. A tiger in your tank: Advertisements in the language classroom. *Canadian Modern Language Review*, 1979, *35*, 691–743.

Morain, G. Commitment to the teaching of foreign cultures. *Modern Language Journal*, 1983, *67*, 403–12.

Morain, G. Language in the marketplace: A cultural analysis, n.d. Publication prepared for the American/Swiss Foundation and presented at the ACTFL meeting in Atlanta, 1972.

Morain, G. The role of culture in foreign language education. *Q & A*, ERIC Clearinghouse on Languages and Linguistics, 1986.

Pinet, C. Myths and stereotypes in Astérix le Gaulois. *Contemporary French Civilization*, 1977, *1*, 317–336.

Ryan, H. L., & Schunk, S. J. Creating cultural units through locally produced slide/sound presentations. *Hispania*, 1984, *67*, 633–40.

Santoni, G. Stéréotypes, contextes visuels et dimensions sociales. *Le français dans le monde*, 1983, *181*, 84–94.

Savignon, S. A l'écoute de France-Inter: The use of radio in a student-centered oral French class. *French Review*, 1972, *46*, 342–49.

Scanlan, T. Another foreign language skill: Analyzing photographs. *Foreign Language Annals*, 1980, *13*, 209–13.

Scanlan, T. French mail-order catalogues as teaching tools: Vocabulary, culture and conversation. *French Review*, 1978, *LII*, 217–41.

Scanlan, T. Looking up French language and culture in the Paris Pages Jaunes. *French Review*, 1986, *LIX*, 355–88.

Schulz, R. A. Comparative culture study: An approach through the printed news media. *The American Foreign Language Teacher*, 1974, *4*, (4), 11–13.

Simon, R. H. Images publicitaires, images culturelles. *French Review*, 1980, *54*, 1–27.

Trescases, P. L'utilisation de la page publicitaire: l'instantané (ou le flash) culturel. *Le français dans le monde*, 1982, *166*, 18–25.

Seiichi Makino
University of Illinois at Urbana-Champaign

Integrating Language and Culture Through Video: A Case Study from the Teaching of Japanese

Introduction: Toward a Contextualization of Language and Culture

During the past decade many and varied efforts have been made to integrate culture into language instruction; most of them seem to have failed to achieve the intended goal. This failure, in my opinion, is related primarily to pedagogical assumptions. In particular, if the philosophy of language instruction is not oriented towards contextualization, the possibility of integration of culture into language is largely eliminated or, at best, taken into consideration only sporadically. In fact, the majority of language instructors still put into practice the philosophy of the grammar-translation method and/or the audio-lingual approach. If your basic philosophy of language instruction accommodates the "contextualizing" method (which is, of course, used in conjunction with other teaching methodologies), you can vastly increase the authenticity of your students' command of the language.

Let's take a simple example from Japanese. The English "Thank you" is *Arigatoogozaimasu,* as some readers may know. What the reader may not know is how to use it in a proper way. Suppose a person younger than you (say, a child) has given you chocolate. If you think you can use *Arigatoogozaimasu,* you are wrong, because you are supposed to use the shorter, familiar version *Arigatoo* with a child. You may argue that this is less a cultural fact than a simple matter of linguistic usage. But what about the following case? Suppose someone who is much older than you compliments you on what you wear. An ordinary native speaker of English would feel no qualms about using *Arigatoogozaimasu.* You would be wrong again: what an ordinary Japanese says in such a context is *Iee, doo itashimashite* (Oh, no! It's nothing). This is a case where language and culture meet in a very intriguing way. A Japanese, being human, must also be very happy when he is complimented by his superior (i.e., a person older than he and perhaps higher in social rank), but he is not supposed to express appreciation in any explicit way. If he does so, he is violating an underlying cultural principle which says "when you are complimented by your superior, you are supposed to deny any merit." Suppose, on the other hand, that your *wife* is complimented by your superior on her cooking. If you think that you can use *Arigatoogozaimasu,* that is a reasonable assumption according to the above cultural principle: the person being complimented is not yourself, it is your wife. Unfortunately, you would be dead wrong for the third time, because a person with whom you are closely associated is regarded as a part of your "extended ego." This in itself constitutes an important phenomenon in Japanese culture. The original cultural principle should therefore read: "When you or any person with whom you are closely associated is complimented by a superior, you are supposed to refuse the compliment." This principle, however, is actually a derivative of the more general principles of "indirectness" and "ego extension." These two major cultural principles intersect crucially with the use of the Japanese language and should be taught simultaneously with usage. In my judgment, it is possible to teach culture by integrating it into language instruction if the instructor both possesses adequate knowledge of the culture in question and adopts a "contextualizing" approach which highlights the underlying cultural principles of communication (see, for instance, Omaggio, 1986). It is not, however, "contextualizing" enough simply to teach language in the context of discourse; the ultimate goal should be the teaching of culture-in-language (or, for that matter, language-in-culture) as indissociable components of a unique phenomenon.

The Preparation of Video Teaching Materials

Among the possible means of contextualizing language and culture, video (ideally, interactive video) is particularly effective by the very fact of its visual impact. The major challenge, of course, is the preparation of video teaching materials. In the following presentation, I will discuss the materials I have actually used, since 1980, in teaching elementary and advanced Japanese courses at the University of Illinois at Urbana-Champaign and at the Japanese School of Middlebury College in Vermont.

In the teaching of Japanese, the video age came into full swing in the eighties. The most frequently used video materials are based on television melodramas (of approximately one hour length) prepared as a series by the Japanese Language Section of the Japan Foundation. Each set of video materials consists of a U-matic video, a vocabulary list, notes on usage (which are basically grammatical explanations), notes on socio-cultural background, and the script of the entire drama. The usage and socio-cultural notes are carefully prepared for each segment (or each chapter) of the drama. The notes range from simple explanations of phenomena (such as Japanese chess, called *shoogi*, or an apartment complex, called *danchi*) to explanations of some cultural principle (such as the Japanese inordinate concern for what other people (*seken*) think, or the Japanese practice of taking a gift of candy or fruit when visiting someone's home). The best choice in the Japan Foundation series of video materials is, in my view, "My Dear Friend," which features a three-generation middle-class family and its internal communication gap. Since it happens that this particular television drama is done in an artistic manner, the students' enjoyment is intensified as the language and culture are learned. While this series does not have any prepared drills, other video materials, prepared by Sakuma and Fujimura (1981) have effective previewing and post-viewing activities. After learning a set of key vocabulary items appearing in a video segment viewed only twice, the student is asked to answer a set of true/false questions about the context. He or she is then required to listen to the sound track tape in the lab and to fill in blanks in the transcribed scripts. Afterwards, the student watches the video again at his own pace and checks his initial answers to the context questions. The material is taken from a popular television drama series of the Japan Broadcasting Company (NHK) dealing with a typical white-collar home with two small children. The students can learn much about the current concerns of a typical nuclear family through pertinent video images supplemented by socio-cultural notes.

These video materials are ideal for the advanced student (fourth-year Japanese), because they are completely authentic; they have been produced for consumption by a native audience. But what about students at lower levels? Can't we teach them through quasi-authentic video materials? Some of the film materials prepared in the sixties and seventies by the Department of Culture (Bunkachoo) and the National Language Institute (Kokuritsu Kokugo Kenkyuujo) were transformed into videotapes. But these materials are totally grammar-centered and acultural, each lesson being embedded in a most unnatural, contrived drama.

In 1979, I decided to prepare more "contextualized" and "natural" teaching materials for elementary Japanese for the students at the University of Illinois and at the Japanese School of Middlebury College. Instead of starting with elementary Japanese grammar items, I began with a basic set of communicative functions and contexts such as self-introduction at a party, answering basic yes-no biographical questions, inviting people to go to a football game, giving information about one's school life, telephoning to make plans, comparing the strength of the football teams, ordering foods at a restaurant, inquiring after a patient at the hospital and hesitating or politely declining when offered something. The separate units, twenty in all, were connected by a common story line and became the textbook for the course. I then created my own videotapes articulated with each lesson and based on the *same vocabulary* (thus avoiding one of the problems posed by ready-made videotapes on the market).

In the first half of the story (Lessons 1 through 11), two American college students (one male, one female) and two Japanese college students (one male, one female) meet each other at an American university. Both of the American students are studying Japanese, and they become good friends with the Japanese students. There is the suggestion of a rivalry between the two boys over the affections of the Japanese girl student, a factor which seems to help keep students interested in the story until the end of the course. In addition to the four protagonists, there is a Japanese language instructor who plays the typical role of the native Japanese professor. After a series of American episodes in this half of the story (like the hospitalization of the American boy, who suffers an injury from a car accident), the American girl goes to Japan to study art history while teaching English at a company in Tokyo. She lives with a host family, where she learns all sorts of cultural facts about Japan. Towards the end of the story, all four of the students get together in Kyoto on New Year's Eve.

Integrating Culture into Language

NONVERBAL CULTURAL ELEMENTS

Beginning with non-verbal cultural elements that are most effectively taught with videotapes, I would like to demonstrate how I integrated culture into language. Among the elements highlighted by video, the "textbook" (which became known as the Middlebury Elementary Japanese Textbook) contains physical gestures, eye contact, proxemics (the distance between two interactants, seating arrangement, and other spatial arrange-ments), environmental factors (especially the interior of the room), artifacts (clothing), and various realia. Lesson numbers are hereafter designated L.1, L.2, etc.

Gestures. Bowing, the most fundamental movement of the body (L.1, L.3, L.18), tensing the body in front of one's superior (L.2), eating with both hands on the table (L.4, L.5), sitting correctly in front of one's superiors (L.6), holding a teacup properly, (L.13), and chewing gum in class (L.17).

It should be noted that bowing is such a basic greeting that it has to be integrated as early as possible; the Japanese even bow while talking on the telephone. Tensing one's body in front of one's superior is an automatic kinesic movement in Japan; to show relaxed body movement in front of one's superior may be interpreted as being impolite or disobedient. For the same reason, chewing gum in a formal classroom situa-tion is also unacceptable in Japan. The Japanese, just as Europeans, eat with both hands on the table. Holding a teacup (without a handle) with one hand is unacceptable if the holder is female.

Eye contact. Avoidance of direct eye contact with one's superior (L.2, L.6, L.11). In Japan, even among equals, eye contact is avoided as much as possible. It is unaccept-able for you to engage in prolonged eye contact with your superior; if you do so, you will be viewed as arrogant. This is one of the crucial differences between the Japanese and American cultures.

Proxemics and environmental factors. Conversational distance of two (or more) interacting speakers (L.1, L.20), seating arrangement (L.14, L.17), flower arrange-ment (L.13), and spatial arrangement of the interior and exterior of a Japanese house (L.13, L.16, L.20). The normal conversational distance is approximately twenty to twenty-five inches, although this will change according to the particular relationship of the interactants. The Japanese culture is very sensitive to seating arrangement. At the breakfast and dinner table, the grandfather of our three-generation family, following tradition, always sits at the shorter side of the rectangular table. The floral arrangement (*ikebana*) which is placed in the alcove (*tokonoma*) of the Japanese style room, in the video, is an artistic expression of the Japanese sense of space. In three lessons we manage to recreate the interior and exterior of a typical Japanese house. No matter how small it is, a Japanese house is always surrounded by a wall or a hedge with a gate. The interior spatial arrangement is cocoon-like: each space is surrounded by another layer of space and so on. We could not show this specifically on the videotape, but the images lend themselves to discussion of this fact by the instructor.

Artifacts. A housewife wearing an apron (L.13) and the grandparents of the host family in their kimonos (L.14, L.17). A Japanese housewife usually wears an apron when she cooks, as well as when she does household chores. The kimono is seldom worn by the younger generation, except on special occasions such as New Year's Day or marriage ceremonies. Older people, however, still wear somber-colored kimonos.

Realia. Representative Japanese dictionaries (L.9), a Japanese calendar (L.10), a Japanese doll (L.10), a floral arrangement (L.13), a Japanese teacup (L.13), a Japanese tea pot (L.13), traditional Japanese dishes (L.14), slides of a railway station in Tokyo and downtown Tokyo (L.15), a slide of Mt. Fuji (L.19), a slide of Ryooanji Temple's garden, a famous rock garden in Kyoto (L.19), a Japanese foot warmer with a quilt over it (L.20), a recording of temple bells on New Year's Eve (L.20), and a slide of the Yasaka shrine (L.20).

In my experience with hundreds of students who have used these materials, the above visual representations of culture awaken keen interest in Japanese culture as an integral part of language instruction. One can elaborate more on the cultural points of interest, as I have indicated, by using slides or, of course, other films and videotapes dealing with Japan.

CUSTOMS AND SOCIAL STRUCTURES

Customs. The text includes, among others, the following customs: driving on the left side of the street (L.12), taking off one's shoes at the foyer before entering the house (L.13), bringing a gift to a house you visit (L.13), going to bed without taking a shower or bath when you have caught cold (L.17), eating *soba* noodles, listening to temple bells, and going to a shrine on New Year's Day (L.18, L.20). Most of the examples above are straightforward customs with practically no important cultural implications. "Taking off one's shoes at the foyer before entering the house" and "bringing a gift to a house you visit," however, are culturally significant in the sense that they are a manifestation of a more general cultural principle. Both of them are based on the well-known principle of the inside (*uchi*)/outside (*soto*) dichotomy (see below). This is part of such a long tradition that the ordinary Japanese is no longer aware that each time he takes off his footgear at the entrance, he is reinforcing an underlying cultural opposition. Gift exchange is a universal phenomenon, but it is part of a very intricate system in Japan: it has an important role in consolidating human relations within *uchi*.

Social structure. Depending on how you integrate social structures into the language textbook, you can increase or decrease the number of ingredients. The Middlebury Textbook incorporates only two. One is the three-generation family (L.14, etc.) and the other is the Japanese educational system, especially the role of the entrance examinations (L.14). The learner is normally surprised that in our story the grandparents are living with their son, daughter-in-law, and grandchildren under the same roof. There are still a sizable number of three-generation families in Japan, despite the fact that the current trend is in the direction of the nuclear family. Whenever the learner is disturbed or surprised by the behavior of the people of the target language, the instructor should, of course, seize the opportunity to explain the cultural rationale behind the particular behavior. The typical American learner of Japanese language is well-informed on the so-called "entrance examination hell," but he may not know about the Japanese educational system. I usually take some time to explain some of the basic facts in this area, using, if necessary, an independent video program on Japan, such as Reishauer (1976).

IMAGE-RESISTANT CULTURAL INGREDIENTS: PSYCHO-BEHAVIORAL PATTERNS

Now, let me move on to discuss some image-resistant ingredients of culture which I have incorporated into the main text. By "image-resistant" I mean those cultural elements that are not easily translated into video images, primarily because of their psychological nature. One might argue that even the most image-resistant ingredients can be transformed into images if only the actors and actresses are sufficiently competent. I would agree, but there is no doubt that compared to the nonverbal elements discussed above, the psycho-behavioral patterns are both more difficult to analyze and harder to translate into images—especially when neither the videographers nor the actors are professionals. I believe, however, that the story line throughout the text induces the learner to focus on the behavioral patterns of the characters and, further, prompts him or her to ask relevant cultural questions; as the lesson proceeds, the learner begins to ask which part of each character's behavior is idiosyncratic and culture-bound and which is universal. Let me discuss now some of the richest behavioral patterns included in the text and their underlying cultural principles.

Uchi (inside) and soto (outside). The dichotomy of *uchi* and *soto* has already been mentioned in reference to taking off one's footgear at home and to gift-exchange behavior. In the contextualized example, an American student in our text has her foot stepped on in the crowded train and is bothered by the fact that the person who steps on her foot does not apologize to her. She becomes aware that there is a sharp contrast between typical American behavior and typical Japanese behavior in public. Her host father's explanation, on the videotape, is that the Japanese behavior can be radically different depending on where he is; that is to say, depending on whether he is in *uchi* or *soto*. A perfect gentleman in *uchi* space can change into a Rambo in *soto* space in extreme cases. In another example (L.15), an American student goes to the Japanese girl's dorm to pick her up to take her to a football game. There he sees a Japanese boy whom he has not met before. He becomes upset by two things: the girl was not alone, and she did not attempt to introduce the boy to him. What he did not understand is that in Japan it is normal for you not to introduce person A to person B when (1) you know A but B doesn't know A, and (2) you have been with A for some time before B comes along. You might eventually want to introduce A to B, but you have to take more time before deciding to make both A and B insiders. The operative principle here is definitely the *uchi/soto* opposition. The principle can be rephrased in the following way: the Japanese tend to distinguish two types of people; one is *uchi,* people whom you can see practically every day, can touch if you want, can have fun with regularly (i.e., can identify with), and the other is *soto,* people whom you can hardly see, cannot touch even if you want to. The true Japanese self tends to emerge not in the *soto* space but in the *uchi* space. Since the learner usually poses questions whenever he or she encounters "strange" behavior in the story, the two above-mentioned episodes provoke pertinent cultural questions.

The humility principle. In the introductory section, I explained in some detail the proper use of "Thank you." The text includes behavior directly related to this. Our female American student goes to see a Japanese student in her dorm room (L.10). The Japanese student compliments her on her Japanese proficiency: "Have you ever been to Japan?" "No." "But your Japanese is so good!" "Thank . . . oops! No, not at all. I have a long way to go." In this situation, I intentionally had our American student say the first two syllables of *Arigatoo* and then remember the right way to react to the compliment. The learner always asks me why the student cannot say "Thank you," and I naturally take this opportunity to explain the psycho-behavioral pattern behind this seemingly insignificant use of *Arigatoo.* Other equally baffling contexts are presented elsewhere. Just before the American student is complimented by the Japanese student for her linguistic performance, for example, the Japanese student remarks, referring to her room: "My room is untidy, because I seldom put things in order." The observant student cannot understand this because her room looks very tidy. The normal American reaction would be: "Gee, why is she lying about her room?" The explanation process constitutes, of course, an integral part of teaching culture in language instruction. In this case, the instructor must explain that Japanese culture forces you to say something humble about yourself, your family members, or your possessions, regardless of your true feelings. In a sense it is a lie, but is not regarded as such in Japan. In another illustration, our American student gives a T-shirt with her college shield to the host family (L.14). Assuming that she had acquired the Japanese culture principle prior to coming to Japan, I had her say: "This is uninteresting stuff, but please take it," while handing the T-shirt to the Japanese. This, of course, does not make sense at all to the learner. Why does she dare to give uninteresting, trivial stuff to the family? What nerve!! But exactly the same cultural logic as in the previous example is operating here. The donor is supposed to make one or two humble comments about a gift before he or she gives it to someone. This behavior sharply contrasts with typical American behavior in the same circumstances: "Here. I think you'll like this." Towards the end of Elementary Japanese, the learner usually assimilates the grammar for humble and polite expressions. Unless he or she understands the underlying psycho-behavioral principle, however, the expression itself is meaningless. Spontaneous rejection of someone's compliment and humble remarks about oneself and one's belongings have a common thread, the practice of "indirectness." The Japanese cultural bond seems to force Japanese to approach a given goal in a more indirect way than is done in America. Yes, Japanese do want to say "Thank you" when complimented. Yes, Japanese do want to be proud of their performance, possessions, wife, children, parents, etc. But they are supposed to restrain the direct expression of human emotion. How do Japanese know the underlying sentiment? In two ways: by scrutinizing facial and other non-verbal cues and by paying attention to the degree of humility or negativity in the expressions. Normally, the humbler or the more negative the expression, the stronger the emotion of thankfulness and pride is judged to be. The principle of indirectness explains another form of behavior. On the day of our American student's arrival in Japan (L.13), the daughter of the host family offers her something to eat, provoking the following exchange: "No, thank you." "Please, don't hesitate." "No, thank you, really. I ate a lot on the plane." The typical American version would probably go simply like this: "Do you want to eat something?" "No, thank you." And that would be that. In Japan, however, as it is traditional to decline offers, sometimes at great length, the host family, assuming the American student is just following custom, reiterates the offer.

Psychological dependency. Japanese culture is said to exhibit a relatively high degree of psychological dependency as regards, in particular, the relationship between "inferior" and "superior," whether it be a child-parent or an employer-employee context. It has been demonstrated that Japanese infants stay with their mother longer, are breast-fed longer and are fed solid food much later than white American infants. Japanese children continue to sleep and bathe with their parents much longer than white American children, which tends to increase psychological dependency. To illustrate this cultural difference, our American student Jane is surprised (L.17) when the host family daughter, a junior in high school, tells her father that he will have to pay if she decides to study abroad in America. Another baffling thing that happens to Jane on the same day is that her host mother tells her that it is her (the mother's) responsibility to keep her (Jane) healthy. She could not understand the logic of psychological dependency behind the words of the daughter and the host mother; a logic according to which children should depend upon the parents, who like to be depended upon.

Visual orientation. It is now well known in America that Japanese tend to display foods very artistically on plates. They take extra care to make prepared food visually attractive. This is first brought to our students' attention when one of the Japanese students says, while eating at a restaurant in America (L.5), that you eat Japanese food first with your eyes and then with your mouth. The visual orientation of Japanese culture, one of its most salient features, is demonstrated again (L.16), in a more abstract way, when the American student and the host mother discuss the reason why Japanese have such difficulty learning to speak English in spite of the many years spent on English in school. The mother explains that since the time of modernization (around 1868), Japanese have only learned how to *read* foreign languages. One of the underlying cultural reasons is the visual orientation in question.

"**Looking back.**" The last lesson (L.20) deals with another important cultural principle referred to as *miren* (a lingering attachment to something or someone who has become part of the past — or is on the verge of doing so). Briefly put, Japanese culture is a culture that tends to "look back," whereas in Western culture "looking back" is generally perceived negatively. In this lesson, students learn about New Year's Eve from the Japanese viewpoint. They watch our characters eat "passing year noodles," listen to the bells of the temples and enjoy a song with a lot of *miren* thematics. The *miren* principle can explain many aspects of Japanese behavior that are otherwise hard to understand. Consider, for example, the Japanese love of taking pictures, the composition of *haiku* (a 5-7-5 syllable poem), or diary keeping. Through these activities, Japanese can preserve a person or thing which has disappeared. The same psychology can also explain the way Japanese take leave of people, a much more time-consuming process than for Americans. A host and hostess tend to go with the guest to the nearby train station or bus stop and, in extreme cases, may go out onto the platform and wait there with him or her until the train leaves the station.

Conclusion

The notion of *miren* is, of course, not unrelated to the general visual orientation of the Japanese culture emphasized above. If my characterization of Japanese culture is correct in this respect, the use of video for the instruction of Japanese language and culture is all the more appropriate. Visual images through the medium of video can capture the Japanese culture (or any other culture belonging to the visual type) much more easily and much more comprehensively than other, "nonvisual" cultures (such as, in my judgment, American culture). Unfortunately, due in part to unclear or incorrect understanding of Japanese culture, Japanese language instructors in the United States and elsewhere (including Japan) have failed to make the best use of video for the purpose of integrating language and culture.

Supposing that my assumption of a "conspiratory" relationship between language and culture is valid, how can we maximize the utilization of video in the language-cum-culture courses? If I limit the question to Elementary Japanese, the first thing we might do is combine the approach demonstrated in the Middlebury Elementary Japanese Textbook with the functional approach of the so-called "proficiency" philosophy. Under the functional approach, we start with supposedly pan-human functions such as personal identification, greeting, asking for information, giving orders, expressing emotions, voicing desires and preferences, and so on. For each of these basic functions we could then integrate relevant cultural elements and, as I have demonstrated in the preceding discussion, create video dramatizations to illustrate each point. While it is true that, as a profession, we should be moving in the direction of interactional materials, I believe that we can still make a great deal of practical contributions to the integration of language and culture in our classroom through the use of conventional video.

References

Caudill, W., & Plath, D. Who sleeps by whom? Parent-child involvement in urban families. *Psychiatry,* 1966, *29,* 344–66.

Caudill, W., & Weinstein, H. Maternal care and infant behavior in Japan and America. *Psychiatry,* 1969, *32,* 12–43.

Gallaway, V. B. *A design for the improvement of culture in foreign language classrooms.* Hastings-on-Hudson, NY: American Council on the Teaching of Foreign Languages, 1985.

Gillespie, J. B. (Ed.). Video and second language learning. Special issue of *Studies in Language Learning,* 1985, *5* (1).

Makino, S. *Kotoba to kuukan.* Tokyo: Tokai University Press, 1978.

Makino, S. How sensitive is the Japanese language to directly perceptible phenomena? In Inoue, K. (Ed.), *Issues in syntax and semantics.* Festschrift for Masatake Muraki. Tokyo: Sanshusha, 1983.

Omaggio, A. *Teaching language in context: proficiency-oriented instruction.* Boston: Heinle & Heinle, 1986.

Reischauer, E. (Ed.). *Japan: The changing tradition.* Columbia Heights, Minnesota: University of Mid-America Press, 1976.

Sakuma, K., & Motofuji, F. *Advanced spoken Japanese: Tonari no shibafu.* 2 vols. Berkeley: University of California Press, 1980.

Seelye, H. N. *Teaching culture: Strategies for intercultural communication.* Lincolnwood, IL: National Textbook Co., 1984.

Aleidine J. Moeller
Omaha Public Schools

Linguistic and Cultural Immersion: Study Abroad for the Younger Student

"Travel is fatal to prejudice, bigotry, and narrowmindedness, and many of our people need it sorely on these accounts. Broad, wholesome, charitable views of men and things cannot be acquired by vegetating in one little corner of the earth all one's lifetime."

Mark Twain, *The Innocents Abroad*

Introduction

One of the greatest reasons and motivators for students continuing language study beyond the first two years has been the opportunity for direct contact with the language and culture of the people whose language they have studied. A study abroad trip can thus contribute vitally to the success of a foreign language program, increasing both high school and college foreign language enrollments while improving the programs themselves. This has been clearly demonstrated, for instance, by the Indiana University Honors Program in Foreign Languages for High School Students as described by Armstrong (1982). Their cross-cultural immersion experience for advanced students of French, German, and Spanish was created in 1962 in order to foster in students a knowledge and appreciation of the host country, while simultaneously improving their second-language skills. This program combined the immersion experience, in which students live with local families, with the academic component of four hours of daily instruction in the target language. This allowed for both natural acquisition and formal learning in the development of second-language proficiency. The classroom learning reinforced skills acquired outside the classroom, sparking linguistic curiosity and enthusiasm that facilitated formal learning.

Armstrong's study was carried out with the intent of finding out exactly what effects the Honors Program experience had on the student participants both during and after their home stay. Using a pretest/posttest design, he first tested the Spanish high school students in the Honors Program in San Luis Potosi, Mexico, during the summers of 1979 and 1980. The MLA Cooperative Spanish Language Proficiency Test Form MA, Advanced, was used to assess listening, reading, and writing. These tests were administered on the first day of classes and again, six weeks later, on the last day of classes. Oral proficiency was tested using a system of teacher ratings (p. 367). Ratings were assigned at the end of the first two weeks and at the end of the sixth week. The results indicated clearly that these students gained more in listening, reading and writing skills than students enrolled in one full year of traditional high school Spanish. Statistics are reported below in Table 1.

Table 1. Statistics for the MLA Cooperative Spanish Tests in Listening, Reading, and Writing.

	Listening	Reading	Writing
Pretest Mean	21.05	21.13	68.43
Posttest Mean	31.23	30.33	83.43
Skills Gains	10.18	9.2	15

Source: "Language Study Abroad for High School Students: Indiana's Program for Proficiency and Recruitment" by G. K. Armstrong, in *Foreign Language Annals*, 1983, *16*, p. 367. Used by permission.

Armstrong did a follow-up study to determine long-range effects of the Honors Program on participants. One hundred and twenty participants from 1976–79 were asked to complete a sixteen-item questionnaire regarding their placement in college Spanish courses, perseverance in language study, career and educational objectives, and additional participation in overseas study and travel. Of the seventy-one completed and returned questionnaires, sixty-two reported having begun college Spanish at advanced levels (third year or above). Thirty-two had taken the CEEB College Placement Test in Spanish, achieving a group mean score of 710. This score compared with a group mean of 566 for students who had had four years of traditional high school Spanish and had never lived or studied in a foreign country. Eighty-two percent of the respondents planned to continue the study of Spanish beyond the semester in which they were surveyed. Thirty-four students (thirty-eight percent) were Spanish majors and nine had declared a Spanish minor (p. 368).

Another important finding of this study was that the students felt they had acquired a greater degree of self-confidence and better understanding of themselves as a result of their study abroad. The majority felt they had become more open-minded and objective in their thinking. It would follow then that such an improved self-concept would increase the students' desire to seek additional language study and cross-cultural experiences. Thirty-five respondents confirmed this expectation by indicating that they had travelled or studied abroad since their summer in the Honors Program. All students planned additional travel or study in foreign countries (p. 369).

It is not surprising to find in Armstrong's follow-up study that one-third of the high school students (ten students) who participated in the Honors Program in Mexico later attended Indiana University-Bloomington, the sponsoring institution. All enrolled in Spanish courses. Assuming similar results for German and French students, thirty students a year would be enrolling in upper-level language classes at Indiana after having participated in the Honors Program.

A group of high school French students was similarly pretested and posttested utilizing the MLA Cooperative Achievement Tests after a short-term intensive summer travel/study program in France (Hoeh, Spuck, 1975, p. 225). Significant gains were seen, especially in the areas of listening and reading. Hoeh and Spuck reported, in addition, meaningful attitudinal changes toward French people and culture and recorded an improved self-concept much like that found in the more recent study of Spanish referred to above.

One of the most convincing studies regarding the actual educational benefits of student exchange programs was carried out by the American Field Service (AFS) International/ Intercultural Program (Hansel, Grove, 1980). In 1978, the AFS conducted a research project "to determine if exchange students actually learn and develop more rapidly than similar students who do not have an intercultural experience and to identify specific ways in which students developed over the course of their experience travelling abroad" (p. 84). The results revealed that students who went abroad showed significant pretest to posttest increases in all seventeen personal characteristics (i.e., critical thinking, international awareness) tested. Appendix A contains a listing and description of these personal characteristics as well as the chart comparing the pretest and posttest increases for AFS participants and students with no study abroad experience.

The AFS students showed the most dramatic increases in the areas of "Awareness and appreciation of the host country and culture," "Understanding other cultures," and "International awareness." The students also showed significant increases in "Foreign language appreciation and ability," although, as might be expected, those who went to English-speaking countries showed much less of an increase: "The research findings suggest, but do not confirm, that without the experience of going abroad, an adolescent's foreign language appreciation and ability may continue to decrease over time" (p. 88).

The report further concludes that students who have studied abroad exhibit more impressive personal characteristics, a greater awareness and appreciation of their own culture, and an increased regard for spiritual values rather than material things. Hansel and Grove encourage educators to support study abroad and, in particular, intercultural homestay programs in the high schools. It has thus become clear that a major key to motivating students to continue foreign language study beyond the rudimentary levels lies in making full use of those immersion programs that are available, or developing additional exchange programs for our students. As Williamson suggests (1978), "a study abroad program may be the essential element in the promotion of foreign language study" (p. 87).

Study and exchange programs have recently experienced significant support and growth, due in large part to the efforts of politicians (such as Paul Simon) and foreign language organizations (JNCL, ACTFL), as well as numerous articles and books (Simon, 1980; Naisbitt, 1982) that have pointed out the drastic need not only for second-language acquisition and proficiency, but for educating globally responsible citizens. It is generally accepted that the earlier a student's experience abroad occurs, the better and more lasting the effect (Dodge, 1972, p. 28). President Reagan articulated this philosophy in the following statement (President's International Youth Exchange Initiative, 1982):

> . . . there is a flickering spark in us all which, if struck at just the right age, I think, can light the rest of our lives, elevating our ideals, deepening our tolerance, and sharpening our appetite for knowledge about the rest of the world. Education and cultural exchanges, especially among our young, provide a perfect opportunity for this precious spark to grow, making us more sensitive and wiser international citizens throughout our careers.

Standards for Study Abroad Programs

With the federal Youth Exchange Initiative of 1982, the sense of need was heightened; more schools and communities were encouraged to become involved in youth exchange programs. A study was commissioned by the Council of Chief State School Officers whose purpose was to assess the need for exchange standards and to develop a recommendation as to how such standards could best be formulated and implemented. As a result, the Council on Standards for International Educational Travel (CSIET) was established in 1984. This private non-profit organization is committed to developing standards, providing a system of evaluating programs in terms of these standards and publishing periodically a listing of programs that meet the criteria. Its *Advisory List* (1987–88) provides educators and the public with a listing and brief description of programs that have met the standards and suggests nine standards by which educators and the public might consider programs that are not listed at the time: (1) organizational profile and educational perspective, (2) promotion, (3) participant selections, (4) participant placement, (5) insurance, (6) operations, (7) financial, (8) adherence to government placement, and (9) agreement to annual review by council. In Appendix B is a listing of all programs reviewed by the Council in 1987–88 and relevant information pertaining to these programs. The CSIET operates through a broad-based network of national educational associations, educational travel organizations, and community volunteer groups. The *Advisory List* provides an invaluable resource from which prospective exchange students and/or their parents and school leaders can confidently gain an understanding of the scope, background, and operating character of programs that have been reviewed.

Raymond E. Wicks (1986), Assistant Principal for Academics at Rosary High School in St. Louis, developed a set of guidelines designed for teachers, school administrators, parents, and students to aid in their selection of foreign exchange programs (p. 35). These guidelines can assist in determining individual requirements and selecting the program that best serves individual needs. In order to make optimum use of the guidelines, one is asked to review the potential program thoroughly through literature, discussions with sponsors and, if possible, meetings with previous participants and group leaders. After the investigation has been completed, the user reacts to each statement in the guidelines, circling the number that most accurately reflects one's knowledge about the program feature described: (1) the feature is present in the program to a very satisfactory extent; (2) the feature is present, but is only satisfactory or marginally acceptable; (3) the feature is present but unsatisfactory, or it is not a regular program feature (p. 35). An effective program that provides a safe and educational experience will merit a "1" for the majority of the statements. The Wicks guidelines serve as a good supplement to the *Advisory List* and can be found in Appendix C.

Federally Supported Exchange Programs

Numerous exchange programs have been established and others have grown because of joint efforts on the part of the governments of several countries who have realized the importance and need for youth exchanges. This attitude is reflected in the following entry in the *Congressional Record:*

> Looking to the reality of the future of our societies, *it is obviously important to foster sensible dialogue among young people at an early stage of their intellectual development.* Attitudes in both our societies are often formed before youngsters reach the university level [. . .] in view of that, it would be especially useful to provide larger opportunities for teenagers—say those between 16–19—to spend some time in the partner country [. . .] A young person who has spent a school year or so in the partner country will have a real opportunity to learn to understand its society (July 13, 1983, S 9907; emphasis added).

One outstanding and successful example of such a joint effort is the Congress-Bundestag Exchange. This unique intercultural educational program for American and German youth is supported, as well as funded, by the United States Congress and West German Bundestag. The number of scholarships allocated to each state is based on state representation in Congress. Four hundred and thirty-six American students a year attend a Gymnasium and 420 German students attend high schools in the United States. All expenses are paid except passport and visa fees. Students must be fifteen years of age, United States citizens, and in the tenth or eleventh grade to qualify. This special program is conducted under the auspices of three recognized leaders in the field of youth exchange: Youth for Understanding (YFU), American Field Service International/Intercultural Programs (AFS), and the Experiment in International Living (EIL). The program is designed to strengthen ties between the successor generations of each country. The friendships developed will deepen each participant's understanding of the similarities and differences in German and American social, economic, and political institutions. Students are expected to complete a project on United States–West German relations to be presented during their visit to Washington, D.C. upon their return.

Similar programs exist that are partially funded by federal money and/or administered by federal agencies. One such very recent program is the Fulbright-Cologne German American Cultural Exchange. This program offers an Easter Exchange program in which German students live with American host families and attend school from March 18 to April 8; the American students' return visit takes place from late June to the middle of July. It also administers a three-month school exchange program extending from September to December and a return trip from January to April. The unique feature offered by this short-term program is that these arrangements are also made for single students, not merely groups, allowing for rural areas to participate in such exchanges. Host families are also partially reimbursed for their participation.

The Pädagogischer Austauschdienst (PAD)—Pedagogical Exchange Service under the direction of the German Ministry of Education—provides an invaluable opportunity to American students of German. It offers an all-expense-paid four-week program to secondary school students who have achieved top scores on a German language exam administered by the American Association of Teachers of German (AATG). The three- to four-week language program permits this select group of students to attend a German school to enhance their language skills. The students are housed with families to make this a true immersion program. In addition, the PAD financially supports a trip to Berlin to allow the participants to become acquainted with that important city. The primary role of the PAD is, of course, to facilitate and coordinate exchange programs with other countries. In 1982 alone, the number of German and American students who participated in its exchanges reached eleven thousand.

Another federally funded German program that deserves mention is the Bavarian

Youth Council under the auspices of the Bavarian Ministry of Education (Bayerischer Jugendring). They are currently seeking long-term partners to participate in an annual four-week exchange. Their program consists of two distinct parts: culture and language. The culture is divided by topics and discussed in English, while the foreign language is used to converse on specific themes, such as daily life, the host family, free time, and school. The cost of this program is considerably less than most other educational exchange programs. The Arkansas International Center of the University of Arkansas, Little Rock, administers such a program in their area for students ages sixteen to eighteen. One of the primary advantages is that the dates for the American students' stay in Germany (July 26–August 20) do not interfere with the academic school year.

As must seem apparent, a particularly large number of youth exchanges exists between West Germany and the United States; Janes and Scher (1987) report that they account, in fact, for forty percent of all youth exchanges sponsored by the President's Council for International Youth Exchange. In addition to these programs, there are numerous German–American public and private organizations—including religious groups and athletic teams—that regularly sponsor visits and exchanges.

Work Exchange Programs

Work exchange programs offer a unique cultural and linguistic immersion option as well as a very economical approach to a foreign experience. They can promote maximal language skill development and cultural understanding and build global awareness among the participants and the communities in which they live and work. The University of Louisville has had a work exchange program with one of Louisville's five sister cities, Montpellier, France, since 1979. The program has proven to be so successful that the city is looking into expanding the program to its other four sister cities. Their program attracts a broad range of participants. High school and college students, foreign language teachers and community members make for a rich mixture and provide a "good view of the citizenry of a typical American community such as Louisville" (Hershberg and Van Fleet, 1987, p. 175). Every participant is matched with a host family, and employment is found in corporations, government, and other organizations within the community. All have one thing in common: they must speak the target language well enough to "survive" the everyday job situation. Hershberg and Van Fleet offer a wealth of information for those seeking to establish such work exchange programs. Included are legal considerations, how to rally community support, and a thorough list of pointers designed to help in developing the program (pp. 178–79).

Hershberg and Van Fleet reported rapid gains in cultural sensitivity and self-confidence, in addition to the expected sharp increase in linguistic competence. New job skills were learned and new ways of doing things were discovered. The participants came back "with another important realization—that different is not necessarily worse [. . .] they were more tolerant, more open-minded and more receptive to diverse ideas and procedures than when they left the often secure insularity of their previous existence" (p. 177).

One very recent, innovative, and highly successful program, the Student Conservation International Exchange Program, allows ten American students to live and work with ten German students in a national park in Bavaria. The American students live in the homes of their German counterparts and attend classes with them. The whole group is then housed in the Tummelplatz, a large backcountry crew cabin, while they work together on trail conservation projects in a Bavarian national park. After five weeks, both the American and German students (twenty in all) fly to Washington D.C., where they are divided into two groups (Yellowstone and North Cascades national parks). Each group then undertakes trail construction projects in their respective park. The Student Conservation Association (SCA) is a public, non-profit educational organization that provides high school and college students with opportunities to volunteer their services for the better management and conservation of our nation's parks, public lands, and natural resources. The International Exchange Program, in cooperation with the Bayerischer Wald National Park, offers the additional opportunity to engage in a cross-cultural exchange with youth from another country. This special program not only promotes cultural and linguistic immersion, but centers on the theme of conservation, answering the need for international cooperation in this area. It has been suggested that experiencing another political, cultural, social, and economic milieu can be a powerful factor in initiating social change (Barnett, 1953, p. 30). Such global themes as conservation, pollution, and nuclear energy can all serve as excellent catalysts for cross-cultural cooperative projects.

Exchanges in the Elementary and Middle Schools

With the appearance of numerous bilingual academies and schools throughout the United States, many exchange programs have developed in the middle schools. The Fairview German Bilingual School (Cincinnati Public Schools) has an annual exchange with Donaueschingen in the province of Baden-Württemberg in Germany (Jacoby and Veidt, 1984). Approximately fifteen students, ranging in age from twelve to fourteen, participate in a four-week exchange. The organization of the curriculum is a cooperative effort on the part of the German school and its American counterpart. The classes are taught jointly by instructors from both schools for three hours each morning, or five class periods. The strength of this exchange lies in the continuity that is provided by the ongoing nature of the program. The same communities, schools, and teachers plan, coordinate, and lead the yearly exchange. Another strength is the extensive orientation that takes place prior to departure. The students are prepared on a daily basis in the classroom, in addition to participating in five intensive one-hour orientation sessions. One of the goals of the program is to reduce stereotyping and, as noted above, to help the students understand that different is not synonymous with inferior. The program also aims at developing confidence in use of the target language.

For several years Homewood School District (K-8) in Illinois has been participating with France in an exchange program for fifth and sixth graders (Miller, 1983). The program is predicated on the premise that younger children (ages ten and eleven) are more open-minded and flexible in their beliefs and attitudes (p. 36). It is affiliated with Back-to-Back, an exchange program sponsored by Campus International of Westmont, Illinois. Approximately twenty school districts in the United States participate in this program, whose total cost is underwritten by the French government. Irving Miller, Superintendent of Schools in Homewood, cites positive effects of the exchange on the school and community, similar to those reported by other short-term exchanges, adding that "the program proves that a small school system in the Midwest can reach out across the Atlantic and develop bonds with a similar community in another nation and culture" (p. 37).

Short-Term Exchanges: A Flexible and Viable Solution for the 80s

One interesting and unexpected finding in Hansel and Groves' study (1980) was that students who went abroad only for the summer, as opposed to a full year, tended to show relatively greater increases in "adaptability" (p. 88). Other studies have confirmed significant increases in linguistic and culture skills as a result of short-term programs (Armstrong, 1982; Grittner, 1979), especially when homestays were combined with academic studies. Although the full-year program is still regarded as having the optimum linguistic, cultural, and personal impact, short-term programs are certainly more financially feasible and present a viable alternative for those students who find the cost of yearlong programs prohibitive. In fact, numerous short-term immersion experiences are being initiated by high schools across the nation. The shorter length of time also allows for more families in the community to participate and homestays are more easily arranged for a three- to four-week period. The potential for a large segment of the community to become involved in the preparation, hosting, projects, and follow-up activities is greatly enhanced.

New Rochelle High School in New York participates in a yearly short-term exchange with La Rochelle, France, and various cities in Venezuela. While in the foreign countries, students attend classes in the "linked" school and live with host families (Gaddy and Kelly, 1980). The high school principal, James R. Gaddy, involves the entire student body in the planning and coordinating of activities and special events. New Rochelle has a very large and diverse student population, and Gaddy sees this exchange as a unique opportunity "to integrate a study of ethnicity into their curriculum" (p. 114). A wide variety of classes and extracurricular clubs conscientiously prepare for the exchange. Social studies, English, and foreign language classes research the countries involved in order to permit the students to ask pertinent questions (p. 114). Other departments prepare exhibits and slide shows with which they will explain aspects of American society and culture to the visiting students. Many are involved in fund-raising activities, such as the annual "cultural evening," an attempt to bring to life a different culture through music, drama, and poetry. Gaddy feels that such exchange programs "breed an immeasurable respect for the contributions of all cultures in a way that cannot be achieved solely in the traditional classroom" (p. 114).

GAPP: A HIGHLY SUCCESSFUL SHORT-TERM EXCHANGE

Probably the most popular and currently best funded of the exchange programs for secondary students is the German American Partnership Program (GAPP). It has expanded to two hundred and fifty schools in thirty-three states in the United States. This unique and most successful program provides for an exchange between entire school classes of American and German high school students. Students, together with their teacher, visit each other's country for a maximum of four weeks. During that time, they attend daily classes at their partner school and reside with host families whose children will have the same experience during their visit to the United States at a later date.

GAPP is one of the lowest-cost high school student exchange programs in the country, and for good reason: (1) the costs are completely controlled by the travelling group; (2) GAPP charges no fee for its services; (3) financial assistance is made available by the government of the Federal Republic of Germany. The program's funding has been significantly increased by Germany, since its inception, in recognition of the importance that exchange programs can play in furthering understanding between countries. A four-day excursion to Berlin, for example, is financially underwritten by GAPP. GAPP publishes a brochure entitled *Practical Hints for a Successful Exchange* (1983), which is a must for anyone considering a GAPP exchange. GAPP is administered by the Goethe Institute and GAPP, Inc., a tax-exempt non-profit corporation in the State of New York, and, as indicated above, is subsidized by the German government.

Dr. Frank Grittner (1979), Supervisor of Foreign Language Education in the Wisconsin Department of Public Instruction, devised a sophisticated evaluation tool for GAPP participants and summarized the effects of an actual GAPP exchange on American students. He states that the program appears to be strongly conducive to (1) improving listening, speaking, and reading skills in German, (2) increasing the disposition among students toward better mastery of the German language, (3) developing highly positive attitudes toward the German people and their way of life, and (4) building a deeper awareness and general acceptance of other cultures and languages (p. 43).

Exchange Projects

Regular exchanges between partner schools are a gold mine for mutual projects that can be carried out in myriad areas. Several schools that have participated in these exchanges have developed particularly interesting topics and projects comparing various aspects of daily life (dating, school, food/meals) or have carried out interdisciplinary projects with science, art, political science, and history classes. These projects can easily be integrated into the foreign language classroom and allow the teacher and students alike to keep abreast of recent cultural developments not found in the textbooks.

One outstanding project that deserves mention is a bilingual booklet consisting of ninety-two pages that was prepared by a group of students from Kopernikus Schule (Ratingen-Lintorf, West Germany) who attended White Bear Lake Area High School in Minnesota from September 18 to October 18, 1985. This booklet (Meyer and Binsfeld-Rizkalla, 1985) discusses, from a German perspective, a wide range of aspects of American daily life. The topics include American behavior, weather, the code of honor of American students, McDonald's, homecoming, and many more. These articles were written by the students themselves and appear in both English and German, richly illustrated with cartoons, pictures, realia, caricatures, and newspaper articles. Authentic advertisements from both countries are included, for instance, which clearly point out various characteristics of both cultures. A good example of the usefulness of these materials is the chart of the cost of a college education in the United States in 1985–86 (p. 29). This simple chart can be effectively used in the foreign language classroom to point out the differences in public education between the countries or serve as a point of departure for discussion about the differences between state and private institutions in the United States. This booklet provides the participants with a lifelong souvenir of their family, school, and community in another country.

Exchange Programs: An Excellent Point of Articulation between Schools, Colleges, and Community

As was pointed out earlier in reference to the Indiana University Honors Program, the collaborative efforts of both high schools and colleges yield many benefits for both institutions. Several immersion programs abroad have also drawn on the support of ethnic organizations and the community in addition to the high schools and colleges. The Braunschweig (Germany)–Omaha high school/college exchange serves as a good example of mutual support and cooperation in the establishment of a study abroad program for high school and university students.

The program was initiated through the efforts of Ronald Roskens, the University of Nebraska-Omaha chancellor. He sought to establish international contacts and programs between the universities of Nebraska and Braunschweig. The German–American Society of Omaha wanted to organize a similar experience for high school students. In cooperation with the university and the Omaha public school system, it organized an annual exchange which subsequently joined the GAPP program, making this a local, regional, and national cooperative venture. This organizational collaboration brought about other unforeseen benefits, such as the establishment of scholarships funded by the German–American Society for students pursuing foreign language study. Many other study programs and homestays similarly owe their beginnings to individual efforts on the part of teachers and educators who have initiated contacts while abroad and then reaped the benefits for their students, institutions, and communities. Once the contact is made, it is also possible to alleviate considerably the administrative work by joining one of the established exchange programs mentioned above.

In order to make these types of exchanges available to a greater number of students and institutions, it has been suggested that consortia programs be established (Hull and Van Wart, 1982, p. 193). Thus secondary schools, colleges, communities, and organizations could join together in supporting study abroad programs. The responsibilities (recruitment, fund-raising, activities and projects, arranging homestays) and fiscal liabilities would be shared by all institutions concerned.

One of the many groups that promotes international exchange is an association of eight organizations called simply "The Consortium." These include AFS, Experiment in International Living, Friendship Force International, National Council for International Visitors, Partners of the Americas, People to People, Sister Cities International, and Youth for Understanding. A brief description of each of these organizations is provided by Staiger (1983), as well as addresses for those who wish to obtain further information.

Immersion Weekends, Camps and Workshops

What if finances or time simply do not make study abroad feasible? A variety of viable alternatives have been successful in motivating students to further pursue the study of foreign languages by offering them opportunities to put into practice language skills acquired in the classroom.

Bedford Public Schools in Massachusetts, in collaboration with M.I.T., carried out a successful total immersion weekend for high school and college students (Reizes and Kramsch, 1980). They sought and received funding from the national AATG to organize a three-day weekend of linguistic and socio-cultural activities: dancing, seminars, cooking, singing, eating, movies, skits, soccer, games, and a puppet show. The sponsors and the twenty participants alike applauded the program's success in developing a sense of *esprit de corps* between the high school and college students and in enhancing their understanding of German culture.

An expanded version of this type of program is provided by the foreign language camps at Virginia Tech that have operated since 1981. These camps provide a weeklong immersion experience for one hundred and fifty high school students of Spanish, French, and German (Shrum, 1985). The teams who teach the campers consist of a high school teacher, a native speaker, and a junior counselor. High school teachers wishing to improve their own skills in the target language, and to learn more about the target culture, have the opportunity to achieve these ends by working closely with a native speaker.

Bibliographies and Lists of Study Abroad Programs

It has been estimated that 750,000 United States students traveled, worked, or studied abroad in the first few years of this decade alone (Brown, 1983, p. 72). Correspondingly, we have seen the emergence of a plethora of study abroad programs. Several bibliographies of existing study programs have recently been published; these can aid in sifting through the volumes of programs to decide which best suits one's individual needs.

The Institute of International Education describes six hundred and ninety-nine programs in fifty-four countries (Cohen, 1977) and the Council on International Educational Exchange (CIEE) lists four hundred and seventy programs. The *Advisory List 1988,* produced and regularly updated by the Council on Standards for International Educational Travel, provides an extensive list and the most useful information about study abroad programs for secondary school students (see Appendix B).

Conclusion

The study abroad programs described above all have the same success story to report. In addition to the acquisition of linguistic skills in the target language, participants increased their understanding of peoples and cultures, showed significant personal growth (Hansel and Grove, 1980), developed new skills, and accelerated their learning (Hansel and Grove, 1984). Armstrong proved conclusively that a study abroad program motivates students to continue foreign language study into the advanced levels. Such studies and findings prove the importance of study abroad and encourage the creation of additional imaginative programs. Creative ventures, such as the Congress-Bundestag Exchange, funded and supported by the United States Congress and the West German Bundestag, should be developed with other countries. The indelible mark left on the young participants from such cross-cultural experiences can only help to strengthen ties and develop friendships between countries, as well as expand the students' own perspectives and awareness of other cultures.

Appendix A

Student-Developed Definitions of the Seventeen Personal Characteristics

Adaptability: Ability to deal flexibly with and adjust to new people, places, and situations, willingness to change behavior patterns and opinions when influenced by others.

Appreciation of own family: Belief in the value of the family as a social institution; appreciation for the care and support received from my natural family; feelings of care and concern for members of my family.

Awareness and appreciation of home country and culture: An understanding of the positive and negative aspects of my native country, and of its role in world affairs.

Awareness and appreciation of host country and culture: Considerable knowledge of the people and culture of my host country, and an understanding of that country's role in world affairs.

Awareness of opportunities: Recognition that a wide range of opportunities is open to me; motivation to respond positively to these opportunities.

Communication with others: Ability to understand and be understood by others; skill at interacting socially (such as speaking, listening and observation skills); willingness to accept and share with others.

Critical thinking: An inclination to be discriminating and skeptical of stereotypes; a tendency not to accept things as they appear on the surface.

Exchange of ideas: Need for participation in intellectual discussions, desire to stimulate thinking of other people.

Foreign language appreciation and ability: Ability to communicate with people in a second language and thus to take advantage of opportunities and alternatives resulting from bilingualism.

High standards for personal relationships: Need for deep, meaningful, and balanced relationships with a few people, rather than for superficial relationships with many people.

Independence — responsibility for self: Ability to exercise self-control and to be self-directed; capacity to avoid being a conformist and to resist peer pressure.

International awareness: An understanding that the world is one community; a capacity to empathize with people in other countries; an appreciation of the common needs and concerns of people of different cultures.

Non-materialism: Ability not to place high value on material things; concern for spiritual fulfillment.

Open-mindedness: A capacity to appreciate different attitudes, opinions, life-styles and values, and to accept people from different backgrounds.

Personal growth and maturity: An understanding of myself and of my strengths and weaknesses, and a determination to attempt to correct or compensate for my weaknesses.

Self-confidence: Feelings of self-worth and of being sure of myself and my relations with others; lack of self-consciousness.

Understanding other cultures: Interest in learning about other peoples and cultures; ability to accept and to appreciate their differences.

From: B. Hansel and N. Grove, "International Student Exchange Programs — Are the Educational Benefits Real?" In *NAASP Bulletin,* 1980, Volume 70, p. 86. (Used by permission.)

Personal Growth From an Intercultural Homestay

Chart comparing changes of AFS students with changes of non-traveled students.

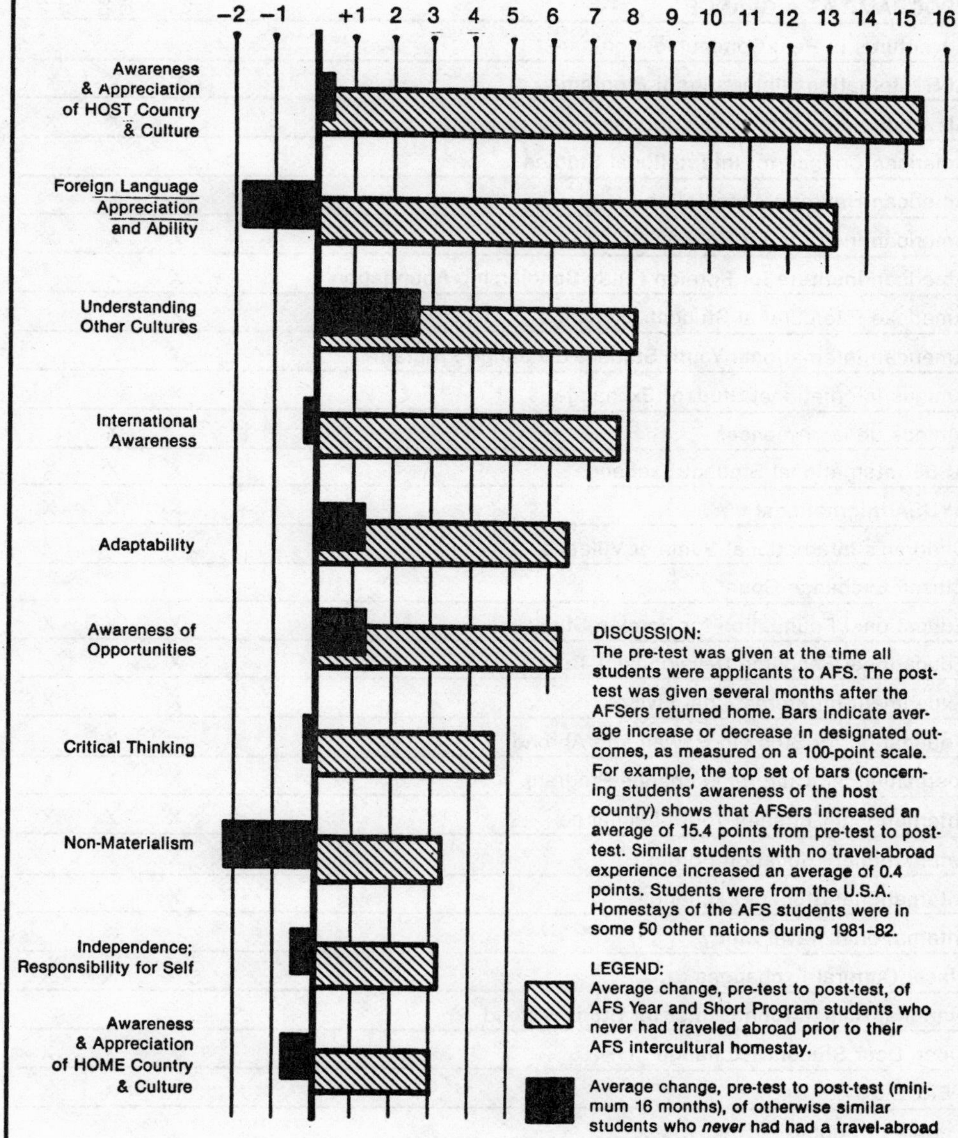
−2 −1 +1 2 3 4 5 6 7 8 9 10 11 12 13 14 15 16
Awareness & Appreciation of HOST Country & Culture
Foreign Language Appreciation and Ability
Understanding Other Cultures
International Awareness
Adaptability
Awareness of Opportunities
Critical Thinking
Non-Materialism
Independence; Responsibility for Self
Awareness & Appreciation of HOME Country & Culture

DISCUSSION:
The pre-test was given at the time all students were applicants to AFS. The post-test was given several months after the AFSers returned home. Bars indicate average increase or decrease in designated outcomes, as measured on a 100-point scale. For example, the top set of bars (concerning students' awareness of the host country) shows that AFSers increased an average of 15.4 points from pre-test to post-test. Similar students with no travel-abroad experience increased an average of 0.4 points. Students were from the U.S.A. Homestays of the AFS students were in some 50 other nations during 1981–82.

LEGEND:
Average change, pre-test to post-test, of AFS Year and Short Program students who never had traveled abroad prior to their AFS intercultural homestay.

Average change, pre-test to post-test (minimum 16 months), of otherwise similar students who *never* had had a travel-abroad experience.

Cornelius Lee Grove, 1985
Research Department, AFS International

PROGRAMS AT A GLANCE	Has USIA designation as Youth Exchange Visitor Program	Gives financial aid to participants on a need basis	Maintains own office in each country served
Adventures in Real Communication			
AFS International/Intercultural Program	X	X	X
Alexander Muss High School in Israel		X	X
American Council for International Studies			
American Heritage Association		X	
American Institute for Foreign Study	X	X	X
American Institute for Foreign Study Scholarship Foundation	X	X	
American Intercultural Student Exchange	X		
American International Youth Student Exchange Program	X	X	
Amicus International Student Exchange	X		
Amigos de las Americas		X	
ASSE International Student Exchange	X	X	X
AYUSA International	X	X	X
Children's International Summer Villages			
Citizen Exchange Council			
Educational Foundation for Foreign Study	X	X	X
Educational Resource Development Trust	X		
Experiment in International Living	X	X	X
Foundation for Study in Hawaii and Abroad		X	
Iberoamerican Cultural Exchange Program	X	X	X
International Christian Youth Exchange	X	X	X
International Education Forum	X		
International Student Exchange	X		
International Travel Study			
Nacel Cultural Exchanges		X	X
National Registration Center for Study Abroad			
Open Door Student Exchange	X	X	X
PEACE USA	X	X	X
People to People			
A Presidential Classroom for Young Americans			
School Exchange Service	X		
Spanish Heritage—Herencia Español	X	X	X
Student Travel Schools	X		X
Up with People		X	
World Experience, Teenage Student Exchange	X	X	X
Youth for Understanding International Exchange	X	X	X

Specializes in short-term non-home residence travel and travel/study program	Specializes in group travel programs	Provides 10-month (school year) home residence exchanges	Provides 5-month (semester) home residence exchanges	Provides short-term (6 weeks or less) home residence exchanges	Permits/encourages teachers to solicit groups for travel/study	Remunerates teachers by cash or travel benefits for participant recruitment	Provides or requires participants to provide medical/accident insurance	Provides manual of guidelines and instructions to participants	Provides manual of guidelines and instructions to host families	Provides clear policy guidelines to volunteer representatives	Conducts formal orientation and evaluation sessions for participants	Requires English proficiency for all inbound participants	Requires language proficiency for outbound participants	Has local representatives who contact participant, family & school during exchange
	X	X	X	X	X		X	X			X			X
		X	X	X			X	X	X	X	X	X		X
X	X						X	X	X		X			X
X	X			X	X		X	X						X
	X			X	X		X	X	X	X	X			X
X	X	X	X	X	X		X	X	X	X	X			X
		X		X			X	X	X	X	X			X
		X	X	X			X	X	X	X	X	X	X	X
		X	X		X		X	X	X	X	X	X		X
				X			X	X	X	X	X		X	X
		X		X	X		X	X	X	X	X			X
		X	X				X	X	X	X	X	X	X	X
X				X			X	X	X	X	X			X
X	X				X		X	X	X	X	X			
		X	X				X	X	X	X	X	X	X	X
X	X	X	X	X	X		X	X	X	X	X	X	X	X
				X			X	X	X		X	X		
		X	X	X			X	X	X	X	X	X		X
		X					X	X	X	X	X	X		X
		X	X				X	X	X	X	X		X	X
		X	X	X			X	X	X	X	X			X
X	X	X	X	X	X	X	X	X	X	X	X	X		X
				X			X	X	X	X	X	X	X	X
X	X			X	X	X	X							X
		X	X	X			X	X	X	X	X		X	X
		X		X			X	X	X	X	X	X		
X	X			X			X	X			X			
X	X						X	X			X			
	X		X	X			X	X	X	X	X			X
	X	X	X	X	X	X	X	X	X	X	X			X
		X		X			X	X	X	X	X			X
		X					X	X			X			
		X	X	X			X	X	X	X	X	X	X	X
		X	X	X			X	X	X	X	X	X		X

From: Council on Standards for International Educational Travel. *Advisory List of International Educational Travel and Exchange Programs,* 1988, pp. 48–49. (Used by permission.)

Appendix C

THE PROGRAM: SPONSOR AND FEATURES

1 2 3 The program has been conducted previously and has the support and endorsement of former participants.

1 2 3 The experience of the sponsor/operator is sufficient to indicate that program features will be provided as advertised.

1 2 3 The sponsor/operator maintains a security bond substantial enough to insure the financial liabilities to be incurred.

1 2 3 The transportation, accommodations and tours are arranged through reputable U.S. and/or foreign carriers and agents.

1 2 3 Provisions are made for attending to medical and other emergencies that may arise during the excursion.

1 2 3 A sufficient number of excursion leaders are provided to effectively accommodate the number of students being accepted for the program.

1 2 3 Assurances of cooperation are secured from the foreign governments, educational agencies, etc., involved with the program.

1 2 3 A formal program of study is included that offers the participants high school or college academic credit.

1 2 3 Academic credit being offered will be granted by an accredited U.S. educational institution.

1 2 3 All expenses and fees are clearly itemized in the promotional literature.

1 2 3 The literature clearly identifies those expenses that are not included in the fee and must be paid by the participants.

1 2 3 The schedule, itinerary and program format are clearly described in the promotional literature.

1 2 3 Overseas accommodations are identified and described in the literature.

1 2 3 All overseas travel arrangements are identified and described in the literature.

1 2 3 The format and content of the educational portions of the excursion are clearly described.

EXCURSION GOALS

1 2 3 There is a clearly defined statement of program goals presented in the promotional literature.

1 2 3 The program goals are consistent with the sponsor/operator's ability to provide them.

1 2 3 The nature of the scheduled activities and itinerary indicate that the program goals will be achieved.

1 2 3 The content and methods of the educational portion are consistent with stated program goals.

LEADERS AND INSTRUCTORS

1 2 3 The excursion leaders have been selected based on their experience and knowledge of the cultures and countries to be visited.

1 2 3 Excursion leaders include people of varied skills and talents, such as accredited instructors, professional tour guides and people from the host countries.

1 2 3 Excursion leaders and instructors are fluent in the native languages of the participants and the areas to be visited.

1 2 3 Instructors possess appropriate knowledge and experience to effectively conduct the educational portion of the program.

1 2 3 Instructors are capable of working effectively with Americans who are visiting foreign cultures and countries.

1 2 3 When academic credit is offered, the instructors possess the appropriate credentials and academic qualifications and are recognized by the institution granting the credit.

SELECTION OF PARTICIPANTS

1 2 3 The program has specific criteria for selecting participants; these include appropriate academic background and life experiences.

1 2 3   The promotional methods used are likely to attract participants whose interests and qualifications are compatible with the program.

1 2 3   Applicants are required to submit evidence that they satisfy the criteria for acceptance, such as personal data, references, and a statement of interests and goals for participating in the program.

1 2 3   For programs including an extended stay, participants are required to demonstrate or develop some proficiency in the language of the host culture.

1 2 3   The number of excursion leaders required to insure a safe and effective program determines the number of applicants accepted.

ORIENTATION

1 2 3   Participants are provided with printed materials that describe the itinerary, general travel and customs information, and other pertinent travel requirements and restrictions.

1 2 3   Specialized materials are provided, such as background readings, maps and a bibliography to prepare participants for the cultures and countries to be visited.

1 2 3   For the education portion of the excursion, participants are given a required reading list, books and other materials.

1 2 3   Other forms of orientation, such as pre-departure lectures, discussions and methods for investigating another culture are provided.

1 2 3   Instruction in the language of the host culture is provided as part of the pre-departure orientation.

1 2 3   Additional orientation and introductory sessions are planned for each new phase of the program, such as entering a new country.

EXCURSION ACTIVITIES

1 2 3   A wide variety of activities are planned that allow for broad exposure to the host culture(s), such as guided tours, opportunities to meet or live with people of the area and attend cultural events and popular entertainment.

1 2 3   Participants have the opportunity to pursue their personal interests to the extent that is feasible.

1 2 3   Time and suggestions are provided for informal and spontaneous contacts with people of the host areas.

1 2 3   The itinerary allows for contact with a broad spectrum of society, in addition to those whose interests and backgrounds are similar to the participants.

1 2 3   The excursion activities are designed to achieve the maximum cultural and educational benefit from the time spent and the people encountered.

CONCLUDING THE EXCURSION

1 2 3   Participants are given the opportunity to reflect on their experience, to analyze it, and to learn from it through group discussions, personal diaries, and the like.

1 2 3   Activities such as written reports, oral presentations, or evaluations are required to complete the educational portion of the program and earn academic credit if offered.

UTILIZING THE PARTICIPANTS

1 2 3   The participants are expected to share the benefits of their experience through presentations to school and community groups, written reports, news articles, or local radio or television interviews.

1 2 3   The sponsor/operator requests that the participants evaluate the program and make suggestions.

1 2 3   After returning, program participants are asked to assist with orientation sessions for other groups or to take leadership roles in future excursions.

From: R. E. Wicks, "Travel Study Guidelines," in *Social Education*, January 1986, pp. 35-36.

Appendix D

RESOURCES

Arendt, J. D.
Minnesota/Baden Württemberg Student Exchange Program
3709 48 Avenue So.
Minneapolis, Minnesota 55406
612-721-3237

Back-to-Back Program
c/o André Girod
Campus International
414 Plaza Drive, Suite 302
Westmont, Illinois 60559

Bavarian Youth Council (Bayerischer Jugendring)
Herzog-Heinrich-Strasse 7
Postfach 200603
8000 Munich, West Germany
(089) 51780

Congress-Bundestag Youth Exchange Program
3501 Newark Street, NW
Washington, D.C. 20016
202-966-6800

Council on Standards for International Educational Travel (*Advisory List*)
1906 Association Drive
Reston, Virginia 22091
703-860-5317

Fulbright-Gesellschaft e.V. German-American Cultural Heritage
Frankstrasse 26
D5000 Cologne 1, West Germany
(0221) 214091

GAPP, Inc. (*Practical Hints for a Successful GAPP Exchange*)
1014 Fifth Avenue
New York, New York 10028
212-744-8310

Meyer, R.
Kopernikus Schule (Ratingen-Lintorf) (92-page booklet)
Altenkamp 20
4030 Ratingen 4, West Germany
(2102) 34421

Pädagogischer Austauschdienst (PAD)
Nassestrasse 8
Postfach 2240
5300 Bonn 1, West Germany
(0228) 5011

Research Department
AFS International/Intercultural Programs
313 East 43rd Street
New York, New York 10017
(order *Publications in Print 1986: The AFS Research Department*)

References

Advisory list of international educational travel and exchange programs, 1988. Reston, Va.: Council on Standards for International Travel, 1987.

Armstrong, G. K. Language study abroad for high school students: Indiana's program for proficiency and recruitment. *Foreign Language Annals*, 1982, *15*, 365-70.

Barnett, H. G. *Innovation.* New York: McGraw-Hill, 1953.

Bendon, B. H. ACTFL in Arcachon: A program description revisited. *Foreign Language Annals*, 1970-71, *4*, 183-86.

Brière, J.-F. Cultural understanding through cross-cultural analysis. *The French Review*, 1986, *60*, 203-08.

Brown, A. M. U.S. students abroad. In H. Jenkins (Ed.), *Educating students from other nations.* San Francisco: Jessey-Bass, 1983.

Brown, R. W., Englekirk, J. E., French, D. H., Johnston, M. C., Lang, V. H., Marckwardt, A. H., Politzer, R. L., Sommerfeld, A., & Wheeler, B. W. Developing cultural understanding through foreign language study. In E. Reichmann (Ed.), *The teaching of German: Problems and methods.* Philadelphia: Carl Schurz Foundation, 1970.

Canfield, D. L. Evaluation of summer schools for American students and teachers of Spanish in Mexico and Spain. *Hispania*, 1974, *57*, 107-09.

Castallo, R. With a bit of planning, you can protect student travelers and your board. *The American School Board Journal*, 1985, *172*, 45.

Cohen, G. A. (Ed.). *U.S. college sponsored programs abroad: Academic year.* New York: Institute of International Education, 1972.

Conner, M. W. New curricular connections. In J. K. Phillips (Ed.), *The language connection: From the classroom to the world.* Skokie, Ill.: National Textbook Co., 1977.

Diller, E., & Markert, A. The telescope curriculum: An Oregon–Tübingen experiment in first year German. *Unterrichtspraxis*, 1983, *16*, 223-29.

Dodge, J. W. (Ed.). Other words, other worlds: Language in culture. In *Northeast Conference Reports.* Montpelier, VT: Capital City Press, 1972.

Global competence: Education for the future. Position paper of the Joint National Committee for Languages, page 6 (Point Number 5).

Frautschi, R. L., Modu, C., & Reed, Mariette. Additional French language experiences and the A. P. candidate. *The French Review*, 1976, *49*, 483-95.

Fry, G. W. The economic and political impact of study abroad. *Comparative Education Review*, 1984, *28*, 203-20.

Gaddy, J. R., & Kelly, L. International education exchange: A perspective. *The Clearing House*, 1980, *54*, 113-14.

Goldin, D. Overseas programs: Suggestions for a director. *Hispania*, 1984, *67*, 640-42.

Grittner, F. Results of GAPP exchanges. In *Practical hints for a successful GAPP exchange.* New York: Goethe House and GAPP, Inc., 1983, p. 43.

Hansel, B. Literature review: Studies of the impact of a travel-abroad experience. *Research Report 28.* AFS International, 1984.

Hansel, B. *The impact of a sojourn abroad: A study of secondary school students participating in a foreign exchange program.* Ph.D. dissertation, Syracuse University, 1985.

Hansel, B. The AFS impact study: Final report. *Research Report 33.* AFS International, 1986.

Hansel, B., & Grove, N. International student exchange programs—are the educational benefits real? *NASSP Bulletin*, 1980, *70*, 84-90.

Hansel, B., & Grove, N. Why an AFS experience accelerates learning and the growth of competence. *Research Report 25*. AFS International, 1984.

Hansel, B., & Grove, N. Learning by doing: What a high school student can learn from a homestay abroad. *The Journal of College Admissions*, No. 107, Spring, 1985.

Hartz, R. The "Mini-immersion"—a practical alternative. *Unterrichtspraxis*, 1986, *19*, 225–27.

Hendon, U. Introducing culture in the high school foreign language class. *Foreign Language Annals*, 1980, *13*, 191–199.

Hershberg, D., & Van Fleet, J. A. Work exchange program: Achieving more for less. *Modern Language Journal*, 1987, *70*, 21–27.

Hoeh, J. A., & Spuck, D. W. Effect of a three phase acculturation process on language skill development and social and personal attitudes of high school French students. *Foreign Language Annals*, 1975, *8*, 221–226.

Hull, W. F., IV. Cross-cultural experiential programming. *International Review of Education*, 1981, No. 1, p. 73.

Hull, W. F., IV, & Van Wart, M. R. Affordable and quality international programming for the 1980's. *Liberal Education*, 1982, *68*, 193–99.

Janes, J. K., & Scher, H. L. *Mixed messages: A report on the study of contemporary Germany in the United States*. German Marshall Fund of the United States, June, 1987.

Jacoby, D. R., & Veidt, F. P. Cincinnati–Donaueschingen: A middle school exchange program. Presentation at the 1984 annual AATG meeting in Chicago, Illinois, November 18, 1984.

Koester, J. A profile of foreign language majors who work, study, and travel abroad. *Modern Language Journal*, 1986, *70*, 21–27.

Lange, D. L., & Jorstad, H. L. A unique experience in French culture: A cultural materials work-in in Besancon. *The French Review*, 1978, *51*, 391–97.

Lulat, Y. G. M., & Cordaro, J. International students and study abroad programs: A select bibliography. *Comparative Education Review*, 1984, *28*, 300–39.

Martin, J. N. The impact of a homestay abroad on relationships at home. *Occasional Papers in Intercultural Learning*. New York: AFS International/Intercultural Programs, Inc., 1985.

Miller, I. This French/American exchange program puts the *joie* in the *joie d'étude*. *The American School Board Journal*, 1983, *170*, 36–37.

McCormack, W. Student exchange as an instrument of international understanding. *International Education and Cultural Exchange*, 1969, *5*, 27–31.

Morsink, D. Intensive language learning: Notes from a French C.E.S. *The French Review*, 1984, *58*, 191–201.

Naisbitt, J. *Megatrends*. New York: Warner Books, 1982.

Oberding, B., & Onofrietto, M. H. Schlumpftreffen II: Total immersion weekend New Jersey style. *Foreign Language Annals*, 1982, *15*, 355–58.

Reizes, S., & Kramsch, C. J. Mach mit: Deutsches Wochenende am Karlsfluss. *Unterrichtspraxis*, 1980, *13*, 222–25.

Shrum, J. L. Curricular teams: A new wrinkle in foreign language camps. *Foreign Language Annals*, 1985, *18*, 219–23.

Simon, P. Foreign language study: Political, economic, and social realities. *Foreign Language Annals*, 1980, *13*, 355–58.

Simon, P. *The tongue-tied American*. New York: Continuum, 1980.

Staiger, R. C. It's a small world, and it's yours through exchange programs. *Journal of Reading*, 1983, *27*, 124–28.

Wicks, R. E. Travel study guidelines. *Social Education*, January, 1986, 35–36.

Williamson, R. C. Taking advantage of the study abroad program: Before and after. *Foreign Language Annals*, 1978, *11*, 87–91.

Norman Stokle

Resident Director, Skidmore Programs in France

Linguistic and Cultural Immersion: Study Abroad for the College Student

Introduction

Let us go straight to the heart of the matter: only one in five candidates who take the Foreign Service Examination, including college graduates with a foreign language major, obtains the "3" rating ("Superior") which indicates near-native linguistic and cultural sophistication. It is our fundamental premise that study abroad, properly oriented, can sharply improve this ratio, bringing not only linguistic fluency but liberating students from the confines of their own culture and leading them to a deeper understanding of international perspectives. But what precisely do we mean when we speak of linguistic competence and cultural understanding? Edgerton (1979) asserts lucidly that someone who "knows" French not only understands, speaks, reads, and writes the language without conscious effort but, most important, "knows what native speakers of standard French mean by French words, what sorts of perceptions of self and of the surrounding world syntactical choices are used to signal, and what presuppositions and implications each of the available alternative ways of expressing 'the same thing' entails" (p. 23). And he makes a clear distinction between mere intellectual knowledge and intimate, visceral, emotional understanding.

We achieve true mastery of another language when we can assume the foreigners' set of norms as our own, function on their terms, and see, reason, and feel as they do as we recreate the multiple experiences of their daily life. We temporarily put behind us our own frames of reference to adopt theirs, including all the undesirable elements—blind spots, hang-ups, prejudices—their culture has passed down to them. We assume their collective psychology. Linguistic competence and cultural understanding are inseparable parts of a single whole; the one can only be attained through the other.

Criteria for Student Selection

This psycho-linguistic integration is the high aim we must set for our students. Anything less is tourism. But how can we reach these heady heights? The study abroad equation contains a plethora of variables, all of which, to a greater or lesser degree, determine the method of approach. Who are to go abroad? What is their age? their socio-economic background? their motivation for exploring the foreign culture? their previous foreign-language preparation and level of academic achievement? Where will they go abroad? With what kind of faculty support? And for how long? In the following paragraphs, I shall offer some suggestions based upon my own experience as a program director in France.

The selection of candidates for study abroad programs is usually based upon their foreign language skills and overall grade point average, two criteria which are designed to ensure a basic ability to survive in the foreign locale. Students meeting these requirements will only be rejected if they demonstrate some serious emotional imbalance or financial insolvency. What is regrettable about this selection procedure is that it discounts the most important criterion of all: the student's psychological receptivity to the foreign experience. A high grade point average and respectable foreign language skills displayed in a classroom are for naught if the student shares Rambo's sense of the world. Armed with the certainty of his own cultural superiority, he cannot admit the validity of mental or emotional structures other than those given to him by his own culture. Any difference he perceives between his own behavior or judgments and those of the foreigner will, in his eyes, be a deviation from common sense, hence stupid. His refusal to try experiences other than those with which he is already familiar deprives him of genuine contact with the host culture and reduces him to a ghetto existence with other like-minded Rambos. From my own observations, possibly a quarter of American students on study abroad programs belong in this category. Frankly, it would have been better had they stayed home.

On the other hand, many students seriously deficient in foreign language skills yet with an openness of mind and high motivation to learn can often quickly overcome their linguistic handicap, once in the foreign location, provided they are competently channeled by their program director. Low foreign language skills should not disqualify candidates from studying abroad. All candidates, however, should be required to undergo a "cultural receptivity test." This often includes video and/or cassette recordings of typical transactional situations and customs in the foreign location upon which the student is invited to comment. Topics can range from eating habits (a Frenchman dining on *langue de boeuf* or an Englishman eating fish and chips in the *News of the World*) to family relationships (forms of greeting), faculty-student contacts (in amphitheatre situations), public transport (ambiance in the Paris *métro*), merchandising procedures (unwrapped bread, exposed perishable food, open markets, the bagging of purchases by the client) and national festivities (Guy Fawkes Day, Bastille Day, Christmas). Students are not expected to display prior knowledge of these various cultural phenomena, but rather a receptivity toward them and a desire to reflect. Another exercise consists of showing foreign banknotes or postage stamps and asking what they reveal of the country's priorities and preoccupations. Yet another presents a picture of a Turkish toilet and asks why the device is still in common use throughout much of Europe.

Outreach Incitements

Once in the foreign locale, the students should be propelled, however reluctant they may be, into the swirl of life around them. This is a particularly difficult task for a director to perform, since it involves persuading the students to plunge headlong into the unknown, to explore what is for them uncharted territory. This exploration can be the cause of much anguish, as it must be pursued simultaneously on several different levels: the search for living accommodations, provision of meals, academic courses, and extra-curricular activities. New experiences, the successful outcome of which cannot be guaranteed, intimidate most people—and students even more than others, since they have been conditioned to define their intrinsic worth in terms of victories and defeats. The art of a good director is to select those outreach options and opportunities best suited to the ability levels and orientations of his students and which, although perhaps initially harrowing, afford them a better than even chance of success. For they must meet with success if they are to develop and sustain the kinds of contacts they desperately need in order to come to some deeper perception of the foreign culture. These options and opportunities will vary from one student to the next depending on their individual interests, temperament, and language ability. And the director's knowledge of what is available, where, when, and how, must be vast and continually up-dated. Directors on a one-year appointment cannot, by definition, be completely effective; they know too little and lack vital contacts.

The Ghetto Syndrome

Too many study abroad programs, geared to an annual change of director and, sometimes, of additional American faculty, take the easy way out: they abandon the challenge of cultural immersion altogether. In London, for example, a sizeable number of town houses have been transformed by American colleges and universities into cosy home-away-from-home ghettoes. The first floor is generally devoted to classroom activities, the second and sometimes the third to student dormitory accommodations, while the basement often serves as a communal kitchen and/or student lounge. If the house is large enough, it may also contain the director's living quarters. The basic, everyday needs—food, lodging, academic courses, leisure pursuits—are immediately at hand, all under the same roof. Any intellectually uncurious student has small incentive to look elsewhere. He is at one with his environment, which does its best to duplicate the norms of American life. To be sure, similar, if less comprehensive, American ghettoes exist in other countries too. Reid Hall, an elegant eighteenth-century mansion owned by Columbia University in the Montparnasse district of Paris, houses the offices of more than a dozen study abroad programs. The combined student population averages five hundred a year. It provides no student dormitory accommodation or catering service, only classrooms, program office space, library, and some leisure facilities. Altogether, it is a very pleasant environment. But inevitably, since its function is to cater to the American academic community in Paris, it inhibits the essential process of student integration into the French lifestream.

Undermining the Ghetto

Study abroad directors should steer their students away from American ghettoes of whatever kind, be they academic centers, bars, disco hang-outs, or apartments shared with fellow compatriots. This is easier said than done, since anyone determined to recreate America abroad, and especially in Western Europe, can always manage to do so. In France, where the process of Americanization has reached new peaks, perhaps the only ingredients still unobtainable are diet soft drinks and peanut-butter cupcakes! A tactic I have found effective is to shape as much of the student's daily life as possible before he or she has had time to fall into bad habits. This must be accomplished without heavy pressure, sometimes even surreptitiously, and with an eye to each individual's personal inclinations. And, above all, it must be done early.

The Homestay Experience

Under normal circumstances, junior-year abroad students should be placed with host families. No other arrangement affords a more intense cultural and linguistic immersion. The students find themselves with little alternative other than to converse in the foreign language and deal with the foreign mentality and customs head-on. The family is the source of their one ample meal a day. If they are not there to eat it, they face the prospect of hunger or financial loss or the family's displeasure—any one of which constitutes a solid deterrent to absence. As time goes by, the family becomes increasingly a source of emotional support and social contacts.

Of course, the trick is to find a family appropriate to each student. In purely objective terms, the perfect family or the perfect student does not exist. The success of the experience depends on the harmonic interplay between both parties. A "wonderful" family one year can be a "disastrous" family the next. The family has not changed, the student has—and with him or her the quality of the inter-relationship. The issue is not one of political affiliation, religious commitment, socio-economic background, pets inside the home, or even family size, age, or sexual distribution. It is one of compatible temperament and mutual interests, in that order. There are no other constant criteria.

To maximize the usefulness of the family in the integration process, it is preferable that the American student be the only foreigner in the household and that, in non-anglophone countries, the family be sufficiently inept in English to refrain from speaking it regularly at home. They should be ready to accept the student as a full member of their circle and incorporate him or her willingly into their daily life. The students, for their part, should receive careful instruction in behavior patterns within the typical French household before their integration into the family. Such instruction would cover local attitudes concerning the closing of doors, the switching off of lights, the use of the telephone, the taking of showers or baths, acceptable noise levels, daily greeting routines, table manners, etc. It would also apprise the students of their rights and responsibilities within the family household in such matters as the use of laundry facilities, the quality and quantity of meals, the sharing of family chores, access to keys, and having friends over. And, most importantly, it would teach them the importance of maintaining a frank and open dialogue with all family members, of readily stating their own point of view and being receptive to that of others, of taking intelligent initiatives, and of handling any criticism of the United States in a mature way. It is preferable that the principal expectations in regard to both family and student be clearly set out in a written document and signed by both parties.

Family selection is always a risky business. The director's assessment, based upon a forty-minute on-site interview, can never be any more than tentative. So many pieces of the puzzle may have escaped their view. All they can do is trust in their initial "gut" reaction and monitor the evolution of the student-family relationship at regular intervals.

Patterns of Learning Abroad

An easier task, because fraught with fewer imponderables, is deciding upon the organization of the students' academic program. A central fact to be borne in mind is that the whole foreign environment is a classroom in which the students can acquire and practice their culturo-linguistic skills. We must therefore expect them to spend a greater amount of time away from the formal classroom with desks and chalkboard than would be the case on their home campus. Their "stomping ground" should, of course, include museums, historical monuments, and cultural happenings, all intelligently prepared for by advance reading, discussions, and/or on-site commentaries. To understand the spiritual, intellectual, artistic, and social importance of Chartres Cathedral, for instance, it is one thing to gaze admiringly at the stained glass and iconography on one's own, and quite another to have them decoded by Malcolm Miller, the Cathedral's erudite and histrionic English-language lecturer. The first results in a glorious mystification, the second in a series of vital discoveries. But the stomping ground must also encompass such other cultural phenomena as the local urban and rural workplace: visits to factories, farms, trade unions, various levels of government (the local mayor's office, political party headquarters) and administration (Social Security, police, etc.), educational institutions (primary and secondary school classrooms while pupils are in session), and local mass media outlets (newspapers, radio and television stations). Some of these visits will have to be undertaken as a group, but as many as possible should be done by the students individually or working in pairs. The stress must always be on direct contact and discussion with the on-site personnel.

All of the above-mentioned activities can be structured within the students' academic program through courses in the history of art, European history, civilization, politics, business, and language, and can involve the regular presentation of reports, *exposés*, essays, term papers, and the like. The number and form of activities undertaken by any individual student will be governed to some degree by his or her course choices. But whatever they may be, it is essential that the activities concerned be accomplished with great attention to detail, evidence of on-site interviews, and perceptive analytical comment.

Course Choices: "In-House" or Foreign-Institutional?

All of which brings us logically to the question of faculty recruitment. Who will do the teaching? To what extent will there be reliance on program-generated "in-house" courses or participation in those offered by local university-level institutions? Since our intention must be to reduce the duplication of home campus learning patterns to an absolute minimum, professors, no matter how brilliant, should not be imported from an American campus to teach their favorite specialty. Moreover, in determining the range of courses to be offered, preference should be given to those possessing an inherently larger capacity to make use of the extra-classroom environment. In Paris, for example, courses in French Literature are less desirable than those in Art History or Contemporary French Society. On the other hand, seminars in French theater—say, on Molière—do allow for a study of the plays both as literature and as dramatic creations through access to the city's theaters. Back-stage visits to the Comédie-Française, l'Odéon, or la Cartoucherie and discussions with leading actors and directors of the classical and modern repertories, not to mention certain dramatists (who are more reachable than one might at first imagine), can bring unique enrichment to such seminars.

"In-house" courses offer the advantage of greater control, an important factor when faced with testy or mistrustful administrations on the home campus. The Program hires the instructor, decides upon the general parameters of the course content, the number and timing of contact hours, student evaluation procedures, and, to a greater or lesser degree, the number and variety of extra-classroom activities. Periodic adjustments to course content and basic texts can be easily arranged. Mediocre instructors can be replaced easily and good ones encouraged to stay through a variety of incentives: pecuniary, contractual, and the allure of an invitation to experience life on the American campus. A regular and more personal contact between Program director and hired faculty on the one hand and faculty and students on the other makes for the prompt elaboration of respective needs and the defusing of potential problems. Provided there are at least eight to ten students in any given class, "in-house" courses are less expensive to the Program than similar courses offered at French institutions.

The basic foreign language course, mandatory for all program participants, demonstrates the "in-house" advantage within the French context. The *Cours pour Etrangers* departments in French universities are not simply devoid of French students (as one must naturally expect), they are notoriously traditionalistic in their approach to the teaching of the language. The acquisition of grammatical knowledge and the subsequent application of that knowledge in the analysis of literary texts are such overriding preoccupations that they tend to preclude the acquisition of language skills within the context of broader cultural realities. A more effective way to promote speedy culturo-linguistic immersion within a classroom situation is to develop an "in-house" course using an imaginative socio-cultural text and a "communicative" approach. The CREDIF's *Archipel* method (three volumes/three levels) must be considered close to ideal in this regard.

The obvious weakness of "in-house" courses, confined as they are to program participants, is that they perpetuate the narrow ghetto environment and, as such, dilute the foreign experience. So, it is important that our students also frequent the local university institutions as much as possible and enroll in courses followed primarily by the foreign nationals themselves. This sounds like a daunting challenge—and no doubt it is, especially when advanced foreign language skills are required in addition to a sophisticated level of academic preparation. Yet, over the last twenty years, we have witnessed just such a movement from the *Cours pour Etrangers* into the heartland of the French university system. Most French universities—both Parisian and provincial—have now opened their classrooms to American programs through exchange agreements of one kind or another. The prestigious Institut d'Etudes Politiques even provides special examination arrangements in certain of its courses to accommodate the American academic timetable.

Survival Techniques Within the Foreign University

The more loosely structured approach to learning within the French university system, as indeed in European universities in general, places a much heavier burden of responsibility upon the students themselves to acquire knowledge in the discipline they have chosen to study. The more distant — and sometimes anonymous — professor-student relationship can also be disconcerting to Americans accustomed to a much more informal classroom situation characterized by the free exchange of ideas. To ensure the survival of their students in such an environment, many American programs have developed a tutorial support system, engaging professors from the same universities frequented by their students to assist the latter in understanding the principal elements of their lectures. The arrangement's success has certainly contributed to the increased involvement of American programs in the French university system.

But care must be taken to avoid placing American students in academically untenable situations within the foreign university. French or British students of history, for instance, have normally studied that subject for seven or eight years prior to entering university. Their knowledge and frames of reference are already vast, permitting them to explore very limited time periods in great detail and to place the events in their broader historical context. Most American students lack this background and cannot hope to compete with their European counterparts in discussing the detailed flow of European history. Courses in Business, Fine Arts, and the Performing Arts, however, lie more within our students' reach and can be followed in a spirit of confident equality.

Another academic area not to be overlooked is Anglo-American literature. At first glance, this might seem like carrying coal to Newcastle, but the experience of a number of my students at the University of Paris IV in this area has proven particularly rewarding. In D.E.U.G.-level courses (the first two years), they have learned the French approach to close literary analysis and battled with French interpretations of such works as *The Scarlet Letter* and *Hamlet*. On their part, they have brought to their classes both a relative mastery of the English language and an American cultural point of view in their discussion of the course texts. Their superior English language skills have brought them an additional bonus: attention, solicitations, and friendship from their French classmates. Similar benefits have been reaped in English Department *Thème et Version* courses. A *thème* (translation into a foreign language) for a French student is a *version* (translation into one's native language) for the American, and vice-versa. All in all, the English Departments of French universities open the door to a happy symbiosis which our students find particularly valuable in their struggle toward linguistic and cultural immersion.

Local Community Activities

Beyond the academic program lies a wealth of "immersion" opportunities in the cultural, recreational, and artisanal activities sponsored by the local community. Even in the most provincial of French cities, the Maison des Jeunes et de la Culture organizes group activities in soccer, tennis, the martial arts, badminton, cycling, swimming, pottery, painting, amateur theater, and music. The list is usually quite exhaustive and the registration costs low because subsidized by the local government. The mayor's office can supply full information and hand-out materials or tell you where they are available. To help our students make their initial contact with these local organizations, I have found it useful to employ French student *moniteurs* with upbeat personalities. The ice is more speedily broken and intimidation levels kept manageable. These same French *moniteurs,* if well-chosen, are worth their weight in gold on excursions and during the orientation segment of the program. Their presence helps to ensure the use of the foreign language as the exclusive means of communication and the constant access of our American students to a vast assortment of cultural information.

Excursions and Cultural Visits

Flexibility should be the key word, however, in our approach to excursions and other field experiences. Some excursions are valid for all students because of the overwhelming historical or cultural importance of the sites to be visited. One thinks of Chartres Cathedral and the Château de Versailles in France, Toledo and Santiago de Compostela in Spain, Canterbury and Shakespeare's Stratford in England. Other locations can be determined by individual student choice from a sizeable list of possibilities furnished by the program director. I encourage my art history students in France, for instance, to visit Monet's house at Giverny or retread the steps of Van Gogh at Arles. Political science majors, on the other hand, are better off taking in a parliamentary debate at the National Assembly or visiting the Senate or a local prefecture, while History majors are pointed in the direction of the Carnac megaliths, the flamboyant Gothic "Merveille" at Le Mont Saint Michel or the pock-marked landscape of Verdun. In this way, students can deepen their understanding of those areas which are of most interest to them and do it at their own pace. The same principle governs outings to concerts, plays, and other theatrical and cultural events. Required reports ensure that the excursions, whether collective or individual, are undertaken with seriousness of purpose.

For field trips involving overnight accommodations, I encourage my students to avoid hotels in favor of the usually less costly *maisons familiales de vacances* and seminar centers—many of them historic monuments in their own right—which are strewn across the length and breadth of France. These centers provide basic lodging facilities and meals in a friendly communal setting, allowing our students the opportunity to make easy contact with typical French families rather than with foreign tourists.

The Internship Experience

The ultimate step in culturo-linguistic immersion, in my opinion, is the internship experience in the foreign workplace. Many directors and students are reluctant to involve themselves in such a potentially complex undertaking because:

- work opportunities for foreign nationals are not readily available overseas—they are the result of hard soliciting;
- temporary work permits can be difficult or expensive to obtain for Americans overseas;
- many students lack the skills or the assurance to attempt an internship experience abroad and prefer to work back home where wages are higher and more easily negotiated;
- many employers consider the training experience offered as a sufficient reward in itself for services rendered and resist paying salaries;
- most employers with positions to offer prefer to engage the student on a full-time five-day-a-week basis. This means the student must prolong his stay—and possibly the American program directors' (!)—beyond the academic session into the summer months.

All of these obstacles need not deter the student who has set his or her heart on doing an internship. In France, work permits, valid for four months, can be secured by any American student who has participated in a program in France during the previous academic session. The Council on International Educational Exchange (C.I.E.E.) in Paris assists the French government in identifying legitimate candidates for such permits. It processes applications and provides a job-search service. It does not, however, guarantee employment.

Nor can such guarantees be given by program directors. All the latter can do is open a few promising doors and push their better students through them. In Paris, my students and I have managed between us to open many doors in a broad range of fields from professional theater and radio and television to banking, insurance, art curatorship and sales, accounting, school teaching (primary and secondary), and archeological excavation. Internships have lasted from four to six weeks and been undertaken for degree credit (rarely for financial remuneration). Apart from the valuable insights our students have received into the French workplace with regard to organization, production techniques, labor relations, and company-client and after-sales services, they have also developed links which have proven of long-term value. One student who worked in the newsroom at *Radio 7* in Paris is now employed by ABC News in New York. Another who spent two months with a small Parisian theater company is now a professional actress in Montreal. Yet another who spent six weeks in the B.N.P.'s Overseas Commerce Department on the Boulevard des Italiens now works in a similar department of a leading Manhattan bank.

The most flexible and perhaps most enriching internship experience in terms of linguistic and cultural immersion is school teaching. This is because the key to understanding any group of people — their values, priorities, aspirations, fears, hang-ups — is through observing how they shape and condition their young. And where better to do that than inside the classrooms of their schools? Opportunities for American students to teach their own language and culture abound in France and at all instructional levels. The local *Inspecteur d'académie* or his supervisor of English-language programs is the logical person to contact for access to the public school system. Private schools can be contacted directly. The customary workload is four hours per week, and they can usually be timed to accommodate the rest of the student's academic program. Under the direct supervision of one or more English-language instructors at the school, the student provides instruction in oral American English centered around topics of cultural interest or everyday transactional occurrences. Guidance in pedagogical methodology may sometimes be provided by the French supervising faculty member. If not, the task must be assumed by the program director or delegate, for it is too important to be ignored. This first-hand contact with French pupils, coupled with the obligation to teach their own language and culture — probably for the first time — forces our American students into a heightened awareness of and receptivity to linguistic and cultural differences which perhaps they would not otherwise have felt.

All internships overseas, whatever their field of activity may be, require careful planning and regular monitoring if they are to be beneficial to both parties, employer and employed, and sufficiently enriching in professional or academic terms to justify college credit. Faced with unimaginative or lethargic management personnel, program directors must be ready to take initiatives to help them understand the importance of a rounded and structured experience for the students concerned; insufficient preparation or supervision can result in an unfocused and highly frustrating experience of little use to anyone. It can also result in a closed door to future student applicants.

The Problem of Adjustment

The progress of all students in the immersion process, whatever their academic orientation, temperament, or apparent well-being, should be monitored regularly through brief individual sessions with the program director, supplemented whenever possible by director-instructor and director-family contacts. Cultural withdrawal can happen to any student at any time, not merely during the first weeks of the foreign experience. This phenomenon, however, seems most prevalent after the first and the fourth month. The symptoms can vary from homesickness and resistance to speaking the foreign language to increased interest in American ghetto hang-outs, the skipping of classes, repeated negative judgments concerning the foreign nationals and their lifestyle, or even the desire to withdraw completely from the world outside.

In France, a frequent cause of cultural withdrawal stems from the complaint that "the French are too difficult to get to know." This simply means that their approach to social contact and friendship differs from that of the typical American. For, unlike Americans, they are unwilling to make friendly gestures indiscriminately or to demonstrate an immediate interest, however superficial, in the well-being of the "other." Highly protective of their private inner lives, they are very selective about who will gain admission and are used to dealing with negativism and hostility. Our students must therefore call upon all the perseverance they can muster and a level of social aggressivity and projection of self that does not come naturally to them. Their range of expressed emotional response must be considerably broadened, as must their ability to expose their ideas and desires with energy and candor. In a word, they must learn to think, feel, and act like the French or run the risk of being judged colorless and devoid of inner life.

It is a major function of the program directors to bring their students to a clear understanding of these attitudinal realities and to help them adopt the appropriate behavior patterns. They should also indicate new doors to open and new avenues to explore and propel their students back into the cultural fray, while taking care to ensure that they do not live the experience in their students' place.

Cultural and linguistic immersion in the foreign country is no picnic. It is a difficult challenge which can reduce unsuspecting students to confusion, frustration, and despair. But, undertaken with imagination and a courageous openness of mind, it can be the most enriching journey of a lifetime. Armed with their wider perceptions of the world and of themselves, they will put their former uncritical certainties behind them and gain in wisdom and humanity—no meager reward for one year abroad!

References

Edgerton, Mills F. On knowing a foreign language. *Association of Departments of Foreign Languages Bulletin*, 1979, *11(1)*, 22–26.

Barbara Lotito
University of Connecticut at Hartford
Mireya Pérez-Erdélyi
College of New Rochelle

Learning Culture through Local Resources: A Hispanic Model

> All the world's a stage
> And all the men and women merely players:
> They have their exits and their entrances;
> And one man in his time plays many parts.
> William Shakespeare

Introduction

Learning another language is not much different from an actor learning a part. Consequently, language teachers are really directors, leading students through the process of rehearsing lines to be used in some future real-life drama. The recent emphasis on establishing proficiency goals for their students has led many foreign language teachers to provide opportunities for students to develop *both* linguistic and cultural proficiency. These astute directors realize that students need to rehearse nonverbal language as well as words and structures. Many have also become aware of their students' need to understand what it's like to *be* Italian, French, Japanese, Mexican, German, or Puerto Rican, so they can play their role with empathy, accuracy, and ease. Creative foreign language teachers at all levels have begun to devise ways to integrate cultural understanding into the teaching of the target language. Many have come to view local resources as indispensable in their students' process of achieving this understanding. Our purpose here is to present a paradigm within which language students "learn" culture via the systematic incorporation of local resources into the curriculum. But before proceeding any further, let us first define the central terms to be used in this discussion: "culture-learning," "cultural information," "cultural awareness," "cultural proficiency" and "local resources."

Culture-learning refers to how students learn cultural information in the process of becoming culturally proficient. It occurs at both an intellectual and an experiential level. *Cultural information* is the sum total of culture specific data that students are expected to know about a given culture in order to function comfortably with natives of that culture. It includes verbal and nonverbal language, cultural values, assumptions, norms, beliefs, and behaviors. It also includes historical, anthropological, and sociological facts about the target culture, as well as the artistic expression reflective of the collective experience of that culture over time. *Cultural awareness* can be defined as the internal, affective process of knowing oneself as a product of the culture(s) in which one has been raised and understanding how that self relates to others from different cultural backgrounds. *Cultural proficiency* refers to those observable, measurable skills and behaviors that students are expected to demonstrate as a result of culture learning.

Figure 1 presents an overview of "culture learning," the way in which students learn, process, and incorporate cultural information in order to demonstrate measurable skills and behaviors. Emphasis in language-teaching circles has been on how the input is *taught* to students. A shift in focus to how students *learn* culture allows us to examine more carefully *both* the external input ("cultural information") and the internal process ("cultural awareness") that result in the final output: students' "cultural proficiency." *Local resources,* finally, are those people, places, things, and events that offer access to cultural information. The way such local resources are used and integrated into the culture-learning process can have a dramatic impact on expanding students' cultural awareness as they work to achieve cultural proficiency.

Obstacles to the Integration of Local Resources in Culture Learning

It is our contention that, until recently, local resources have been neglected, overlooked, and under-utilized in the teaching of foreign languages and cultures. Even though the foreign language teaching profession, as a whole, has sought a new direction every few years, "always with renewed enthusiasm as though 'the way' to second language teaching had finally been discovered" (Fantini, 1977, p. 47), most such efforts have bypassed the key role that culture-learning can play in the development of proficiency. Most foreign language teachers have, at some time in their career, puzzled over the enormous gap between how second languages are taught and how we, ourselves, learned to be comfortable speaking another language and interacting with natives of culture(s) where that language is spoken. Many of these same teachers sense the need to supplement the artificial, contrived scripts of textbook dialogues and standardized "realia." Why, then, is it only recently that real-life target cultural resources that abound next door or, at least, within easy travelling distance, have begun to expand the language

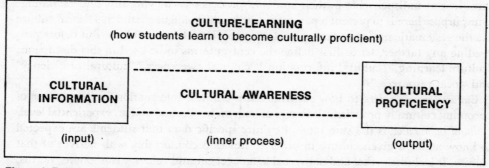

Figure 1. Relationship of culture-learning, cultural information, cultural awareness, and cultural proficiency.

classroom environment? In designing a foreign language curriculum that stresses culture-learning via the integration of local resources, we discover four major barriers that have hindered teachers in their efforts to provide students with this type of educational experience:

- the bias in the United States towards traditional as opposed to experiential education;
- the pervasive attitude of the mainstream culture that views as "un-American" both speaking a foreign language and those individuals who insist on maintaining their native language and culture;
- the emphasis in foreign language teaching on the verbal mode of expression, even though 65% of communication is nonverbal (Birdwhistell, 1970, p. 213);
- the lack of training of foreign language teachers in cultural information, cultural awareness, and in approaches that facilitate culture-learning.

A closer look at these four obstacles reveals their close relationship to the culture-learning model described above. Figure 2 illustrates this relationship. Let us now examine each of the obstacles in question.

PREDOMINANCE OF TRADITIONAL LEARNING OVER EXPERIENTIAL LEARNING

There has been a movement in the last fifty years "to define, understand and produce something called 'experiential education'" (Gochenour, 1977, p. 29). It contrasts with traditional education, which emphasizes conceptualization and intellectualization (left hemisphere activities), by encouraging a more holistic, relational, process-mode of learning typical of right hemisphere activities. As Gochenour points out, despite pressure from both students and educators, most education still remains left-brain oriented (p. 32). Foreign language teaching has primarily followed the traditional model, based on the hypothesis that language is predominantly a left-brain function. This same approach has been most often applied to the teaching of culture. Figure 3 provides a look at some of the differences between the two models that Fantini offers us.

While foreign language teachers may view what they encourage students to do in

CULTURE-LEARNING MODEL	OBSTACLES TO INCORPORATING LOCAL RESOURCES IN THE FOREIGN LANGUAGE CURRICULUM
Culture-learning	Bias toward traditional as opposed to experiential education
Cultural awareness	Attitude of mainstream culture that views foreign languages and foreign language speakers as "un-American"
Cultural proficiency	Emphasis in foreign language teaching on *verbal* over nonverbal language
Cultural information	Lack of training of the foreign language teacher in the target culture and in ways to facilitate culture-learning

Figure 2. Relationship between culture-learning and obstacles to incorporating cultural resources into the foreign language curriculum

EXPERIENTIAL EDUCATION STRESSES:	TRADITIONAL EDUCATION STRESSES:
Getting involved and doing.	Watching and listening.
Learning from classmates and on your own.	Expecting teacher to have all the answers.
Learner and teacher sharing responsibility for learning.	Teacher being responsible for the learning.
Sharing decision making.	Decision making by teacher only.
Learning *how* to learn.	Learning facts or skills.
Identifying problems and solutions.	Memorizing and acquiring information.
Recognizing importance of learners' experience and knowledge.	Minimizing learners' experience and knowledge.
Guiding and assisting in learning on one's own.	Telling, prescribing and ordering.
Understanding learners' motivation for what needs to be learned.	Reinforcing *others'* ideas of what needs to be learned.
Applying practical, immediate approaches.	Building repertoires of information for future reference.

Figure 3. Differences between traditional and experiential education. From "Experiential Education" in Alvino Fantini (Ed.), *Cross-cultural Orientation: A Guide for Leaders and Educators* (Brattleboro: VT: The Experiment in International Living, 1984).

the foreign language classroom as experiential, it can only be truly termed as such if it meets two basic criteria:

• Students learn by doing.
• Students become aware of the meaning of a particular experience through their reflection on it.

Although such recent reality-based developments in the field of foreign language teaching as the functional-notional approach and proficiency testing seem more experientially oriented, the basic tenets of experiential education are still, as yet, not fully integrated into the foreign language curriculum. This is particularly true in the case of cultural study. As Galloway (1987) concludes, in criticizing the ill-fated ACTFL guidelines for cultural proficiency:

> The cultural guidelines reflect no . . . hierarchical skills arrangement. Further, while intrinsic to the language proficiency guidelines are demands for spontaneity, flexibility, and the ability to handle the unpredictability of real-life language use, the cultural guidelines do not reflect a complementary emphasis. Specifically, they fail to take into account two critical questions: how does a learner come to know and/or know about the target culture in addition to learning how to behave appropriately in it; and how does the individual process cultural information on his own (p. 70).

Galloway further emphasizes the importance of "devising goals, implementing strategies, and linking the two for the presentation of culture" (p. 70). Yet, even this more enlightened view of how students need to achieve cultural fluency rests on traditional educational principles that are teacher-centered, involving the *teacher's presentation* of culture, rather than the *student's experience* of it.

Our position in this discussion agrees with that of Allen (1985) who states that what is needed is a focus on an evolutionary process that centers on the students' own awareness of cultural phenomena and how they interact with it ("cultural awareness," in our terminology). She affirms that "a new conception of cultural proficiency must replace [that] now in existence" (p. 149).

In spite of the profession's traditional shortcomings in this area, hope has appeared on the horizon, stemming from an interdisciplinary field commonly referred to as cross-cultural communication. Its strategies reflect the latest developments in the fields of anthropology, sociolinguistics, psychology, communications, sciences, and, to a lesser extent, foreign language teaching. Its practitioners are many and varied and its scope broad, focusing on the whole gamut of interpersonal skills necessary to communicate effectively across linguistic and cultural boundaries. It is based on the principles of experiential learning and is student-centered in its techniques. The teacher serves as a facilitator of specific experiences through which students grow in their awareness of themselves as products of cultural conditioning as well as in their understanding of cultural relativity. Gaston (1985) defines four stages in the process of developing cultural awareness within an experiential framework. In the first phase of the process ("recognition"), we see ourselves and others as products of cultural conditioning. From there, we proceed to the second stage in which we either accept or reject our own or another's culture as a valid way to organize reality. In the next phase, we must decide whether to allow ourselves to act biculturally or, instead, to revert to a rigid, ethnocentric posture. The fourth and last stage in this process is that of transcendence, an attitude of respect toward all cultures even though we may be critical of aspects of a particular culture (pp. 3–5). Many foreign language teachers at all levels have come to realize the importance of leading their students through these stages of cultural awareness if they are to develop cultural proficiency. The consistent integration of cultural information experienced through local cultural resources and processed through discussion and reflection is one key to achieving this goal.

THE MAINSTREAM VIEW OF LANGUAGE MINORITIES AND FOREIGN LANGUAGES

The tendency to undervalue native speakers of other languages as national resources is the second major obstacle to the inclusion of local resources into the foreign language teaching process in this country. This xenophobic attitude is exacerbated by recent incursions of foreign-owned companies and foreign-built goods into the American domestic market. Those who exhibit their foreignness by speaking the native language and/or maintaining aspects of their culture are targets for the "America, love it or leave it" elements. Recent movements to make English the official language of this country demonstrate the extent to which this collective paranoia has invaded the national psyche. People who choose to speak a language other than English inevitably encounter one or more of the following myths that Zentella (1986) describes as "inflaming the passions of linguistic chauvinism" in this country (p. 33):

- Some languages are better than others.
- English is the best language in the world.
- Americans should speak English at all times.
- People who speak two or more languages do not master any of them.
- Bilingualism causes political upheaval.

Students of foreign languages are thus affected by the mainstream's cultural bias toward monolingualism and monoculturalism. In addition to their different learning styles and personal experiences with foreign languages and cultures, students also bring themselves as products of cultural conditioning to the language classroom. While their teacher encourages language and culture-learning in the classroom, their parents may counteract that enthusiasm with their xenophobic views at home. After viewing a film such as *El Norte* in class, students may hear ethnic jokes and slurs outside the classroom and view ethnic stereotypes on television and in the movies. And we wonder why many students are not motivated to learn foreign languages.

The effective utilization of local resources in the culture-learning model described above is thus contingent upon the reshaping of student attitudes toward linguistic and cultural pluralism in the United States. Simply presenting students with cultural information is not enough. An experiential learning approach that focuses on guiding students through the various stages of *cultural awareness* must become a top priority. Interestingly, it is the experience of the authors that once this process is engaged for students of foreign languages, the learning of oral skills is itself greatly facilitated.

THE BIAS TOWARD VERBAL LANGUAGE TRAINING

The third major obstacle to the consistent integration of local resources in language learning is the foreign language teacher's love affair with verbal language despite the fact that over two-thirds of meaning in any dialogue is conveyed by *nonverbal* clues. As Morain (1978) mentions, ". . . teachers in our highly literate society are oriented toward the verbal channel of expression. They tend to see the word as the central carrier of meaning. At an intuitive level, they recognize the importance of prosodic elements (pitch, loudness, rhythm, stress, resonance, and pauses), because these add emotional dimension to the spoken word. They are less inclined, however, to accord importance to what Edward Hall (1959) terms 'the silent language'" (p. 3). Morain further divides these nonverbal modes of communication into three categories:

1 *Body language:* movements, postures, gestures, facial expressions, eye contact, touching (kinesics), and distancing (proxemics);

2 *Object language:* the way signs, designs, realia, artifacts, clothing, and personal adornment are used to communicate with others;

3 *Environmental language:* the way one's surroundings, including color, lighting, architecture, space, direction, and use of nature, communicate with those who live in a given environment.

These three categories govern the way we perceive ourselves and others. They reflect culturally determined behaviors and norms. They are, however, by no means inclusive of all aspects of culture that affect communication, nor do all members of a given culture behave in the same way in the same set of circumstances. In order to avoid replacing old stereotypes with new ones, students need exposure to a wide range of experiences with the target culture that allow them to observe how native speakers communicate in nonverbal ways.

A systematic reliance on local resources brings the world of nonverbal communication to foreign language students. Textbooks and the teacher are not enough: the former, as we have seen elsewhere in this volume, tend to distort cultural realities through overgeneralizations, inaccuracies, omissions, and other failures; the classroom teacher, even if highly qualified and motivated, can only offer students a severely limited contact with cultural reality. A thoughtful, guided experiential learning tour through the real-life world of local resources offers students the opportunity to observe and experience both verbal and nonverbal communication activities, as well as their own reactions to these human dramas. As students expand their perspectives, they grow in cultural awareness and, eventually, begin to enjoy a measure of authentic cultural proficiency.

FOREIGN LANGUAGE TEACHERS AND THE "TEACHING OF CULTURE"

The fourth obstacle to regular, effective contact between language students and real-life cultural resources is often, unfortunately, the foreign language teacher. Many teachers lack an understanding of what constitutes culture-learning, and even teachers who demonstrate a high level of cultural proficiency are frequently unsure of the accuracy of their knowledge, especially since most of their understanding may have come through their own personal experiences and *not* through systematic study. Others may operate from their own subconscious prejudices and stereotypes, or, if aware of them, may lack the resources to work through their own process of cultural awareness. Most foreign language teachers tend to view themselves as inadequately trained in ways to integrate the variety of culture-teaching strategies with which they may be familiar into a bona fide study of culture that does more than merely supplement language learning (Crawford-Lange, 1984, p. 141).

The attitude of the students themselves is not always conducive to a productive culture-learning experience. The recipients of all our erstwhile efforts to expand their cultural awareness may, at first, view reality-based cultural experiences as "days off" or "frills." Their attitude is not surprising, since it reflects the prevailing perspective of parents, school administrators, and textbooks that language learning is the task at hand. Students may also feel uncomfortable at first with experiential learning techniques that encourage them to be introspective and responsible for not only *what* they learn but *how* they learn it. Again, this is not a surprising response from students who have spent most of their educational lifetimes in traditional classrooms. Once students understand the process of cultural awareness and how the cultural experiences in which they participate actually make learning exciting, they often become enthusiastic allies. As students become aware of the stereotypic views they have unconsciously absorbed and see themselves as products of cultural conditioning, they tend to become more open to new experiences that place them in control of their own learning and cultural awareness process. The resulting benefit, as mentioned earlier, is that language teaching often becomes easier and more efficient. Students motivated by the direct correlation between what they are learning and the real world in which they live become avid learners.

While the pedagogical paradigm described in the second half of this study is designed to develop cultural awareness in students of any foreign language, regardless of the ethnic community involved, students of Spanish present their teachers with a special opportunity with regard to the incorporation of local resources into the language/culture curriculum. Since Hispanics currently comprise nearly ten percent of the total population of the United States and have become the largest and fastest growing non-English-speaking minority in the country, many students opt to learn Spanish as an adjunct skill in preparing for careers in fields in which they will work directly with native Spanish speakers living in their area. Others seek to understand better the language and culture of their neighbors, even though they may not foresee using Spanish in a professional context. The need for cultural understanding between Hispanics and non-Hispanics has increased dramatically at every level, from the board room to the *barrio*. A culture-learning model that relies on local resources to introduce students to the colorful mosaic of Hispanics living in this country provides a strategy for achieving such intercultural sensitivity.

In the next section, we offer language teachers specific guidelines they can use immediately to incorporate local resources into their curriculum.

Experiencing the Target Culture Through the Involvement of Local Resources

DEVELOPING CULTURAL AWARENESS IN STUDENTS

How can we sensitize our students to issues of relevance to the target culture, to the people themselves, their history, social characteristics, values, and lifestyles? This is the first question we encounter as we attempt to develop a culture-learning curriculum that integrates local resources. The answer lies in designing a process in which students begin to view themselves within their relationship to their own culture. Before being able to understand the reality of natives from the target culture, students must first become aware of their own cultural background and their preconceived ideas about the target culture. The following exercises provide a careful sequencing of experiential techniques that expand students' cultural awareness as they progress toward cultural proficiency.

Exercise 1: "Who Am I?"
Objective: To develop self-awareness of student's own cultural background.

Preparation: Divide class into groups of four or five students, making the groups as diverse as possible (male/female, black/white, etc.).

Procedure: Each group selects a spokesperson who will ask group members the questions listed below, and then later summarize their answers to report to the class.
- What is your name?
- Where do you come from?
- Where do your parents and grandparents come from?
- Why are you in this course?
- What is your experience with other cultures (travel, interest, personal relationships)?
- What do you want to learn in this course about the target culture?

Exercise 2: "Preconceptions."
Objective: To discover concepts students have about members of the target culture.

Preparation: Have world maps in class showing regions where the target culture is dominant.

Procedure: Ask the students to fill out a sheet listing both positive and negative traits they associate with people from the target culture. Small groups then discuss characteristics they associate with the target culture, focusing first on positive traits, then negative ones, while a member of each group records the various responses. As each group recorder reads each list of characteristics, the teacher writes these on the board under the appropriate heading of "positive" or "negative" and then asks the following questions of the students:
- How many of you have met people from the target culture (who, when, where, how)?
- If you do not know members of the target group, where did you obtain your information (family, school, television, movies, books, etc.)?
- How accurate, in your opinion, is the information received from these sources?

What does the teacher do if there is no target culture in his or her area, or if the students have never met anyone from the target group? You might adopt the strategy proposed by Savoie (1987) in his "France Today" course: "The opening lecture centers on stereotyping: what it is, why it occurs, its dangers, where our cultural concepts originate (books, films, soldiers returning home, etc.), and some of the concepts the French have of the United States and of Americans [. . .] In the second class period, students list the concepts they have of France and of the French" (p. 55). The students' awareness of themselves as products of their own culture is heightened as they become acquainted with stereotypic views people from the target culture hold about Americans. From this perspective, they can analyze and understand their own stereotypic views regarding those from other cultures. They are then better prepared to learn relevant historical data regarding the development of the target culture through the following exercise.

Exercise 3: "Background Essentials."

Objective: To learn historical and geographical information about the target area.

Preparation: Have maps and/or charts available to present data on the history and geography of area(s) where members of the target culture live and, where applicable, on the periods of immigration of groups from these areas to the United States.

Procedure: After the presentation of information, students discuss reasons for specific historical events as well as the role of geography in shaping the development of the target culture. Contrasting this data with similar data relevant to the development of the U.S. is particularly helpful to the students' understanding of cultural relativity. Immigration of the target group to the U.S. can also be discussed. Where relevant, students may be interested in interviewing members of their own family or circle of friends about their personal experiences regarding immigration. After the presentation of the data, students answer the following questions, working in small groups with one student recording the responses to share with the entire class:

- What one historical fact concerning the target culture impressed you the most? In what way?
- How does the geography of areas where members of the target culture live compare with that of your area? What advantages and disadvantages do you associate with each geographical reality?
- How does the history of your family and/or community compare with that of the target culture during these specific periods (teacher suggests several key historical eras)?

OTHER PEOPLE AS RESOURCES: GUESTS FROM THE TARGET CULTURE

We often overlook, as cultural resources, colleagues and students in other classes who are from other cultural backgrounds and may serve as guest speakers to discuss a specific aspect of the target culture. Students may also interview such individuals outside of class and report on this experience to their classmates. Even more exciting for students is the experience of inviting to the class a representative of the target culture who lives in the local community. The Latino Poetry Series at the College of New Rochelle (N.Y.) provides both students and faculty the opportunity to meet artists who represent the various Hispanic groups (Puerto Rican, Mexican-American, etc.). Their thematics touch on the reality of their respective group's experience in the United States. From their unique vantage point they are able to present to students a different perspective on the problems and aspirations of their people. Of course, the fact that they are writers and, in many cases, college professors as well, is a powerful refutation of negative stereotypes that students may hold. The exercises that follow are designed to help the students prepare to host visitors from the target culture.

Exercise 4: "Playing Host."

Objective: To increase students' awareness of culturally sensitive ways to greet, welcome, and entertain a guest from the target culture.

Preparation: Students practice polite forms, rehearse verbal and nonverbal greetings, and prepare the room and refreshments to help the guest feel welcome. Students prepare culturally sensitive questions to be asked of the visitor and arrange to record the whole event on videotape or audiotape.

Procedure: Students greet the guest in a manner appropriate to the target culture. During the visit they ask questions, offer refreshments, show appreciation, and take leave of the guest in a culturally sensitive way. Students then write to thank the guest in the target language according to cultural norms. Soon after the visit, students answer the following questionnaire:

1 What impressed you about the visitor?

2 What did you learn about the target culture?

3 How did you feel when you had to greet the visitor?

4 Did your feelings toward the visitor change after the talk? In what way?

5 What did you experience when you asked the visitor your questions?

Students then discuss their answers in small groups, with one student recording the responses; each group spokesperson reports responses to the entire class. Subsequently, if the visit has been videotaped, the students view selected parts of the tape, focusing on:

- the visitor's gestures and body movements;
- the visitor's facial expressions;
- proxemics (distance between people) during moments of interaction between students and visitor (greetings, serving and eating refreshments, farewells);
- language usage.

The students then discuss in small groups their observations, with a group recorder reporting culturally different behaviors noted by the students. Finally, students re-enact segments of the tape in culturally correct ways and then discuss how they felt while adopting the target culture's behavior and movement patterns.

TAKING THE CLASSROOM INTO THE LOCAL TARGET CULTURE COMMUNITY

Once the students have progressed in their personal process of cultural awareness and gained access to cultural information through representatives of the target culture (supplemented by media representation—magazines, newspapers, films—of cultural values, attitudes, behaviors, and beliefs), they are prepared to become immersed in the local cultural community. An ethnic neighborhood is perhaps the most powerful local resource available to teachers seeking to expand their students' cultural awareness and develop their cultural proficiency. The successful visit is the result of careful planning and preparation so that both students and the community are enriched by the experience. It is especially important to inform students of what they will be seeing and doing so that they may interact with people living in the community in a culturally sensitive way, based on acceptance and respect for the ethnic culture.

There are two basic types of class visits to the local ethnic community. The first focuses on a single cultural event; for example, a concert, play, movie, celebration, etc. The second is a more general experience during which students are immersed in the daily life patterns of the target community.

Exercise 5: "Attending a Cultural Event in the Ethnic Neighborhood."

Objective: To expose students to a specific manifestation of the target culture through their attendance at a cultural event, as well as to have them observe both verbal and nonverbal modes of communication used by representatives of the target culture in attendance.

Preparation: Distribute to students as much background information on the chosen event as possible, together with a list of tasks for students to carry out during their attendance and report on afterwards. Include specifics on nonverbal communication, descriptions of people in attendance and their behavior, their dress, the ways in which they greet friends, etc. Also, provide specific questions for students to answer regarding their own feelings while at the event.

Procedure: Instruct students to write down their observations soon after the event, but not during it, so as to be unobtrusive observers as well as totally focused on what is happening. In the next class period, after the students discuss in small groups their observations and feelings, the teacher synthesizes this information on the board as reported by the secretary for each group.

The actual contact between students and the local cultural community deserves even more careful planning and preparation. At this point students become active participants; they speak the target language as well as hear it spoken as they interact with members of the culture. The anxiety and fear that may accompany the students' first venture into the real world of the target language and culture are very much like the opening night "jitters" common to even the most experienced actors. Rehearsals are essential prior to the big event.

As in the case of the preceding exercises, specific guidelines are useful in helping students derive maximum benefit from their intercultural experience. Born (1976) suggests assigning students specific tasks to accomplish while visiting the local community. These may range from buying food in an open market to asking the price of an item offered for sale in a jewelry store. While the assigning of such tasks may seem inconsequential, it is a crucial step in the students' progress toward attaining cultural (as well as linguistic) fluency. The task becomes the catalyst for the giant step from observer to actor. Jerald (1983) stresses the need for students to be able to control both the linguistic and the cultural aspects relevant to the task they will be performing. Thus, the in-class preparation phase assumes a most important role in this experience. The astute teacher-director provides students with an opportunity to rehearse their questions, to role play interactive situations, and to use appropriate ways to begin and end a conversation. The following exercises are designed to guide students successfully through a direct contact situation in an ethnic neighborhood.

Exercise 6: "Through the Looking-Glass."

Objective: To offer students the opportunity to observe directly people, places, and modes of communication on a visit to an ethnic neighborhood, and to speak to one person from the community during the visit.

Preparation: The teacher must first study the area in question, make contact with community leaders, and arrange a meeting with them. He or she then visits the area and meets the contacts, asking them to help plan the visit and setting dates for meetings with the students. Background materials and guidelines must then be prepared and distributed to the students. Inform students of practical aspects of the visit (what to wear, what to bring, money they will need, and the itinerary of the visit). Then, hand out and review guidelines for the visit with the students. Finally, assign tasks for students to carry out during the visit and have them rehearse appropriate verbal and nonverbal language needed to carry out their speaking mission.

Procedure: The guidelines that follow serve as a suggested model for a visit to an ethnic neighborhood.

A Visit to the Barrio

OBJECTIVES OF THE VISIT

1 To foster a reasonably unbiased attitude toward Hispanics and promote sensitivity to them as individuals;
2 To learn about ourselves by paying attention to our feelings and our reactions to different lifestyles;
3 To observe cross-cultural interactions.

ADVICE TO STUDENTS

1 Try to observe objectively, without making value judgments.
2 Experience Hispanics as individuals with needs and hopes rather than just as members of a particular group.
3 Stay open to what you are experiencing through all your senses — taste, smell, sight, hearing, and touch. If you walk with other students, conversation with them may hinder your ability to observe, and it may color your impressions.
4 Be honest in observing your personal reactions and impressions of what you experience; try not to "censor" your feelings but, rather, accept them as valid.
5 See the visit as a way of comparing and contrasting:
   • your pre-visit view of *el barrio* with what you actually observe and experience during the visit;
   • advantages and disadvantages of living in *el barrio* with those of living in your own neighborhood;
   • the initial impressions you receive from observing exterior living conditions with the inner reality of the people and places you meet during the visit;
   • problems that you perceive facing people in *el barrio* and solutions being used or considered to resolve them.
6 In order to get the most out of the visit, choose one of the following categories to observe:
   People: men, women, children, adolescents, senior citizens, social classes, types of activities;
   Places: housing, schools, stores, places of worship, community agencies, restaurants, recreational areas;
   Communication: spoken language(s), nonverbal communication, graffiti, commercial messages, written communication, artistic expression, cross-cultural communication.
7 You are to speak to *at least* one person from the community to request some information. Some possibilities might be:
   • Ask directions to the nearest drugstore or public telephone.
   • Ask someone the time.
   • Ask for an item in a supermarket or food shop.

PRE-VISIT ACTIVITY

Immediately before you leave for the visit, have the students complete the following sentences quickly, with the first thought that enters their mind:

1 My main objective during the visit is to _____.
2 Hispanics in *el barrio* are, for the most part _____.
3 I (do/do not) know a lot about Hispanics in this area because _____.
4 Today I am looking forward to _____.
5 I am afraid (of, to, that) _____.
6 The Spanish I will hear today will probably be _____.
7 I may not be able to _____.
8 The Hispanics I will meet will probably _____.
9 The women I will observe are most likely _____.
10 The men I will observe are most likely _____.
11 I may feel uncomfortable because _____.
12 The most important aspect of today's experience for me is_____.

POST-VISIT ACTIVITY

After the visit it is most important to discuss the students' impressions, and to have them share their observations on the particular category they were assigned. Again, ask the students to complete the following statements with the first thought that enters their mind:

1 This visit has helped me to _____.
2 I discovered that Hispanics in *el barrio* are, for the most part_____.
3 I can find out more about Hispanics in this area if I _____.
4 Today I was most impressed by _____.
5 I was afraid (of, to, that) _____.
6 The Spanish I heard today was _____.
7 I was not able to _____.
8 The Hispanics I met were _____.
9 The women I observed were _____.
10 The men I observed were_____.
11 I felt uncomfortable _____.
12 The most important aspect of today's experience for me was_____.

Then divide the class into small groups according to the category they chose and have them select a spokesperson who will report the observations of their group to the class. Encourage general discussion of the impressions recorded. Students tend to feel freer in expressing their true reactions to this experience if their anonymity is respected. One way to accomplish this is simply not to collect these exercises but, rather, to view them as an important personal experience for each student.

Adaptation

The use of local resources outlined in this chapter lends itself very readily to adaptation by the instructor to any student level. Goldstein (1986), for instance, has devised a very thorough guide for the seventh and eighth grade teacher who wishes to know what step-by-step preparations are necessary to have successful field trips in the ethnic community. The visit to the ethnic community is a highpoint of any course, and one

of the most effective means we have of putting the student in the place of the other—
which is the goal of cultural awareness.

Fantini (1984, p. 117) explains how going beyond the classroom imposes changes
on all of us who are taking those first steps in devising a model of culture-learning based
on students' experiences through local resources:

- You may have to be willing to adapt or alter your lesson plan and move away from
  the confines of your textbook.
- You, as the teacher, may feel a loss of some authority by giving students the freedom
  to become more independent learners and to explore the community on their own.
- You will have less control over the language structures, pronunciation, and idioms
  presented. Students will experience the language in all its diversity from many
  speakers, in many ways, and in varying situations; you must be able and willing
  to help students learn from all of these.

Fantini's point is well taken, especially with regard to linguistic diversity—the different
types of target language which students engaged in experiential learning may encounter.
While textbooks present students with "standard" dialects that are scarcely spoken
anywhere besides language laboratories, *real* people speak *real* language. They make
grammatical errors, they hesitate, they put their thoughts into reverse and begin again.
They also speak different dialects, use forms other than *tú* and *usted* (e.g., *vos*) in direct
address, and pronounce certain sounds differently. They may even, at times, drop some
sounds, add others, and, heaven forbid, use anglicisms such as *le.week-end* and *el info!*

Conclusion

In the preceding pages we have presented a culture-learning model that funnels
cultural information through the process of cultural awareness in order to develop cultural
proficiency. Crucial to this learning model is the deliberate, systematic integration into
the foreign language classroom of local resources—people, things, places, and events—
that reflect the target culture. To effect this integration, curricula at every level must
be revised to provide a role for experiential education in which students become the
center of the learning experience. Local resources should be viewed as valuable assets
to the language and culture curriculum and integrated on a consistent, planned basis.
We have much to learn in this area from our colleagues in cross-cultural communication, linguistics, anthropology, sociology, and history—it is time to form interdisciplinary
alliances throughout the educational system. And we need, above all, to support the
development of teacher-training programs which prepare classroom teachers to organize
experiential forms of cultural education. When all is said and done, the buck stops there.

References

Allen, W. Toward cultural proficiency. In A. C. Omaggio (Ed.), *Proficiency, curriculum, articulation:
The ties that bind.* Rowley, MA: Newbury House Publishers, 1985.

Arizpe, V., & Aguirre, B. E. Mexican, Puerto Rican, and Cuban ethnic groups in first-year
college-level Spanish textbooks. *Modern Language Journal,* 1987, *70,* 125–37.

Banning, B., & Yerick, W. SIN in the language lab. *Hispania,* 1987, *70,* 187–88.

Batchelder, D. Preparation for cross-cultural experience. In D. Batchelder, & E. G. Warner (Eds.),
Beyond experience: The experiential approach to cross-cultural education. Brattleboro, VT: The Experiment Press, 1977.

Birdwhistell, R. J. *Kinesics and context: Essays on body-motion communication.* Philadelphia: University of Pennsylvania Press, 1970.

Born, W. C. Suggestions for classroom implementation. *Northeast Reports,* 1976, 133–36.

Brown, J. L. ¡Diga! Telephone protocols and strategies in the intermediate Spanish conversation course. *Hispania,* 1986, *69,* 413–17.

Casse, P. *Training for the cross-cultural mind.* Washington: SIETAR, 1980.

Chase, Cida S. An Hispanic tale for the second language elementary classroom. *Hispania,* 1986, *69,* 395–98.

Condon, J. C., & Youset, F. Out of house and home. In E. C. Smith, & L. F. Luce (Eds.), *Toward internationalism: Readings in cross-cultural communication.* Rowley, MA: Newbury House, 1979.

Crawford-Lange, L. M., & Lange, D. L. Doing the unthinkable in the second language classroom: A process for integration of language and culture. In T. V. Higgs (Ed.), *Teaching for proficiency, the organizing principle.* Lincolnwood, IL: National Textbook Co., 1984.

Díaz, W. A. *Los hispanos: problemas y oportunidades.* New York: Ford Foundation, 1984.

Fantini, A. E. Focus on process: An examination of the learning and teaching of communicative competence. In D. Batchelder, & E. G. Warner (Eds.), *Beyond experience: The experiential approach to cross-cultural education.* Brattleboro, VT: The Experiment Press, 1977.

Fantini, A. E. *Cross-cultural orientation: A guide for leaders and educators.* Brattleboro, VT: The Experiment Press, 1984.

Fantini, A. E. (Ed.). *Beyond the language classroom.* Brattleboro, VT: The Experiment Press, 1985.

Fernández, J. B. Teaching Hispanic literature of the United States. *Hispania,* 1987, *70,* 395–99.

Galloway, V. From defining to developing proficiency: A look at the decisions. In H. Burns, & M. Canale (Eds.), *Defining and developing proficiency: Guidelines, implementations, and concepts.* Lincolnwood, IL: National Textbook Co., 1987.

Gaston, Jan. *Cultural awareness techniques.* Brattleboro, VT: Pro Lingua Associates, 1985.

Gochenour, T. Is experiential learning something fundamentally different? In D. Batchelder, & E. G. Warner (Eds.), *Beyond experience: The experiential approach to cross-cultural education.* Brattleboro, VT: The Experiment Press, 1977.

Goldstein, N. W. Vamos al Barrio: Presenting Spanish in its primary context through field trips. *Foreign Language Annals,* 1986, *19,* 209–17.

Griffin, R. J. Using current magazines as a resource for teaching culture. *Hispania,* 1987, *70,* 400–02.

Hall, E. T. *The silent language.* New York: Fawcett, 1959.

Hall, E. T. *Beyond culture.* Garden City, NY: Anchor Press/Doubleday, 1976.

Hall, E. T. Proxemics in a cross-cultural context: Germans, English and French. In E. C. Smith, & L. F. Luce (Eds.), *Toward internationalism: Readings in cross-cultural communication.* Rowley, MA: Newbury House, 1979.

Hanvey, R. G. *An attainable global perspective.* New York: Center for Global Perspectives in Education, 1976.

Janeway, A. The experiential approach to cross-cultural education. In D. Batchelder, & E. G. Warner (Eds.), *Beyond experience: The experiential approach to cross-cultural education.* Brattleboro, VT: The Experiment Press, 1977.

Jerald, M., & Clark, R. C. *Experiential language teaching techniques.* Brattleboro, VT: Pro Lingua Associates, 1983.

Lafayette, R. C. *Teaching culture: Strategies and techniques.* In *Language and education: Theory and practice,* No. 11. Washington, D.C.: Center for Applied Linguistics, 1978.

Lerner, D. An American researcher in Paris: Interviewing Frenchmen. In E. C. Smith, & L. F. Luce (Eds.), *Toward internationalism: Readings in cross-cultural communication.* Rowley, MA: Newbury House, 1979.

Littlewood, N. *Foreign and second language learning.* London: Cambridge University Press, 1984.

Loew, H. Z. Tuning in: Popular culture in the second-language classroom. *Foreign Language Annals,* 1979, *12(4),* 271–74.

Lotito, B. *Entre nosotros: Communicating with the Hispanic client.* New York: Newbury House/Harper & Row, 1988.

Morain, G. *Kinesics and cross-cultural understanding.* Arlington, VA: Center for Applied Linguistics, 1978.

Nine Curt, C. J. *Non-verbal communication in Puerto Rico.* Cambridge, MA: National Assessment and Dissemination Center, 1978.

Nine Curt, C. J. *Intercultural interaction in the Hispanic-Anglo ESL classroom from a non-verbal perspective.* Puerto Rico: University of Puerto Rico, 1983.

Normand, G. Culture and commerce in France: An anthropological/sociological approach. *Foreign Language Annals,* 1986, *19(4),* 311–13.

Pérez-Erdélyi, M., & Kupferschmid, G. S. *Carreras: casos en la comunidad.* Boston: Houghton Mifflin, 1985.

Resnick, M. C. *Interact in Spanish.* (Instructor's edition.) Rowley, MA: Newbury House, 1984.

Richmond, E. B. Utilizing proverbs as a focal point to cultural awareness and communicative competence: Illustrations from Africa. *Foreign Language Annals,* 1987, *20,* 213–16.

Sacco, S. J. The intercultural communication course: A response to the Carter Commission's call for increased citizen education in international affairs. *Foreign Language Annals,* 1987, *20,* 239–43.

Sadow, S. A. Experiential techniques that promote cross-cultural awareness. *Foreign Language Annals,* 1987, *20,* 25–30.

Saville-Troike, M. *A guide to culture in the classroom.* Rosslyn, VA: National Clearinghouse for Bilingual Education, 1978.

Savoie, N. R. A French culture course for non-language majors. *ADFL Bulletin,* 1987; *18,* 55–59.

Scott, J. R. *Understanding Spanish-speaking cultures.* Hayward, CA: Alameda County School Department, 1976.

Shapiro, H. Suggestions for improving film discussions. In D. Batchelder, & E. G. Warner (Eds.), *Beyond experience: The experiential approach to cross-cultural education.* Brattleboro, VT: The Experiment Press, 1977.

Shensul, J. J., González Borrero, M., & Garcia, R. Applying ethnography in educational change. *Anthropology and Education,* 1985, *16,* 149–64.

Simon, Paul. *The tongue-tied American: Confronting the foreign language crisis.* New York: Continuum, 1980.

Snyder, B. *Encuentros culturales: Cross-cultural mini-dramas.* Seelye, H. N. (consulting ed.). Lincolnwood, IL: National Textbook Co., 1984.

Teasley, M. M. German language study at the Dwight D. Eisenhower Library. *Foreign Language Annals,* 1987, *20,* 39–41.

Valencia, A. A. *Bilingual-bicultural education for the Spanish-English bilingual.* New Mexico: New Mexico Highlands University, 1972.

Zanger, V. V. *Exploración cultural.* Rowley, MA: Newbury House, 1985.

Zentella, A. C. Language minorities and the national commitment to foreign language competency: Resolving the contradiction. *ADFL Bulletin,* 1986, *17,* 32–42.

1987 RECIPIENTS OF THE BOARD OF DIRECTORS AWARD FOR EXCELLENCE IN LANGUAGE STUDY

Many secondary schools offer achievement awards to their outstanding students, and the Board of Directors of the Northeast Conference on the Teaching of Foreign Languages feels that more language students should be among those recognized. The following list represents the Awards for Excellence in Language Study presented in 1987. Any school wishing to recognize student achievement by awarding a Board of Directors Award for Excellence in Language Study should contact the Northeast Conference Awards Committee, Box 623, Middlebury, VT 05753, and request a nomination form.

ARKANSAS
Fort Smith: **Northside HS**, Martin Harmon (F).
West Memphis: **West Memphis SHS**, Margaret Campbell (F).
Conway: **Conway HS**, T. Andrew Mobley (F).
CALIFORNIA
Burlingame: **Mercy HS**, Linda Banchini (I), Cristina Collas (S).
Lancaster: **Antelope Valley College**, Lora Shoffstall (S).
Spreckels: **Spreckels S**, Alex Mendez (F), Diana Allen (S).
CONNECTICUT
Cheshire: **Cheshire HS**, Daniel Terrill (S), Kevin Wetmore (G), Alison Rydzewski (L), Peir Eckersley (F).
Colchester: **Bacon Academy**, Dominique Coiro (F).
Glastonbury: **Glastonbury HS**, Beth Ann Valdati (R), Laura Butler (F), Lori Michaelson (S). **Academy S**, Allison Monaco (S), Gwen Wilmes (F). **Gideon Wells**, Sarah Ellovich (F), Becky Asikainen (G), Gretchen Peterson (R). **Buttonball Lane**, Mellissa Roy (S). **Hopewell**, Jennifer Drignat (S). **Hebron Ave.**, Renee Voisine-Kocher (S). Eastbury S, Susan Strickland (S). **Naubuc**, Kim Overcast (S).
Guilford: **Guilford HS**, Debbie Thurberg (F), Cheryl DellaPietra (S).
Meriden: **Maloney HS**, Stella Bauco (I), Eric Daley (L).
Newtown: **Newtown HS**, Daryl Miller (F), Marianne Jackson (S), Robert Constant (L).
North Haven: **North Haven HS**, Miquel Garcia (S), Fiorella Sacchetti (I).
Norwalk: **Ponus Ridge MS**, Bessy Sidiropoulos (S), Jennifer Vaughn (F). **West Rocks MS**, Larry Lazarides (S), Robert Entwistle (F). **Nathan Hale MS**, Amy Couzelis (F), Diana Kasdan (S). **Norwalk HS**, Chris Suhoza (S), Kenneth Craw (L), Kathy Nino (I), Kacia Komarowska (G), Lisa Billings (F). **Boston MS**, Mariaelena Malizia (F), Christine Nikolis (S). **South Norwalk: Brien McMahon HS**, Max Gaurdado (S for Hispanos), Mary Cutrufello (S), Debra Gottlieb (L), Richard Gemza (I), Heidi Derdiarian (G), Mary Cutrufello (F).
Old Saybrook: **Old Saybrook SHS**, Katie Mortali (F), Wendy Poyer (S), Marianne Mathers (L). **Main Street S**, Marie Cassidy (F), Chris Milardo (S).
Redding: **Joel Barlow HS**, John Vermilyae (F).
Stratford: **Bunnell HS**, Lara Manzione (F).
West Hartford: **Conard HS**, Linnea Alvord (S), Christine Coch (F), Lucia Perruccio (I), Douglas O. Reale (G), John Bartosz (L), Kevin Bradley (Chinese), Michael Piper (R). **King Philip MS**, Jesse Hochman (S), Joel Rosenberg (F). **Sedgwick MS**, Jane Barbaro (F), Todd M. Gustafson (S). **Hall HS**, Meredith Gordon (S), Matthew Walsh (F), Monika Lahiri (G), Kimberly Fine (I), Saritte Ruran (R), Matthew Eisenfeld (L), Charles Smith (L).
West Haven: **Notre Dametts**, Marc Anthony Solli (F), Greg Catalano (S), Ralph DeMarzo (I).
Wethersfield: **Silas Deane MS**, Lauren Gold (F), Catherine O'Connor (S). **Wethersfield HS**, Giuseppina Gionfriddo (F), Michael York (S).
Wilton: **Wilton HS**, Meredith Prichard (S), William Hutfilz (G), Christina Cahalan (L), Lisa Rosenthal (R), Julie Tevis (F).

DELAWARE
Claymont: **Archmere Academy**, Christian Ryan (I), Marie Walsh (G), Yvette Hart (S), Karen Feeney (F).
Dover: **Holy Cross HS**, Michelle DeMartin (F).
DISTRICT OF COLUMBIA
Washington: **St. Anselm's Abbey S**, Thomas Hyukjin Lee (L), Thomas Hyukjin Lee (F). **Theodore Roosevelt SHS**, Mary White (S), David Ruffin (F).
FLORIDA
Miami: **Miami Christian C**, Shawn Beightol (G).
St. Petersburg: **St. Petersburg HS**, Alexandre De Maio (F).
INDIANA
Knoxville: **Nell McGowen JHS**, Terri Bennett (S).
Mason City: **Mason City HS**, Alex Wolbrink (S).
ILLINOIS
Evanston: **Evanston Township HS**, Olivia Lerner (G), Lory Price (Hebrew), Eric Rysner (F), Bennett Johnson (L), Julie Gluck (S).
Kankakee: **Bishop McNamara HS**, Francisco Jones (S).
Libertyville: **Libertyville HS**, Karl Geoffrey Feld (G), Robert Padera (S), Andrew Franta (F).
Mendota: **Mendota HS**, Lisa Sawin (S).
Ottawa: **Marquette HS**, Jennifer Caruso (F).
Park Ridge: **Maine Township HS East**, Irene Cohen (F), Martin Rave (G), Adriana Lopez (S), Anna Maria Consiglio (I).
Rock Island: **Rock Island HS**, Amy Hegg (G), Patricia Sanders (F), Amanda Ferrell (S).
Springfield: **Sacred Heart Academy**, Lucille Gotanco (F).
Urbana: **Urbana JHS**, Barney Alexander Joyce (G).
KANSAS
Wichita: **Wichita Collegiate S**, Stephen Lai (G).
LOUISIANA
New Orleans: **St. Mary's Academy**, Susan Reine (F). **Xavier Prep**, Marla Robertson (F).
MAINE
Boothbay Harbor: **Boothbay Reg HS**, Jennifer Hale (F).
Kennebunk: **Kennebunk HS**, James Michael Pierce (S), Rebecca Elizabeth Browning (F), Melissa Lee Turkington (L).
Portland: **Univ. of Southern Maine**, Aynslie Hanna (Greek), Rosemary Miller (L), Jay E. Kuhlmann (G), Julianna Nielsen (F).
Waldoboro: **Medomak Valley HS**, Rebecca Benner (F), Kimberly S. Campbell (S).
MARYLAND
Baltimore: **Notre Dame Prep S.**, Michele Co (F). **Overlea SHS**, Tracey Tressler (F), Christie Petza (S). **Roland PK Country MS**, Ellen Chang (S), Christina Culotta (F), Motty Rice (L). **Roland PK Country Upper S**, Mariana Szklo (F), Caroline Beck (R), Michelle McMacken (S).
Bethesda: **Walt Whitman HS**, Andrew Tagliabue (J & S), Sybil Cineas (S), Jehan Velji (F), Barbara Beenhakker (G), Evan Sherbrooke (L).
Burtonsville: **Paint Branch HS**, Michael Nies (L), Roy Zimmerman (S), Stephany Wenzel (G).
Columbia: **Oakland Mills HS**, Lisha Werba (F).
Damascus: **Damascus HS**, Amy Martin (G), Sanjay Sanghui (S), Claire Boccia (F).

Ellicott City: **Mt. Hebron HS**, Karen Yee (S), Tom Kim (G), Valerie Henson (F).
Frederick: **Hood C**, Laura McGonagle (S), Jill S. Thompson (F).
Garrison: **Garrison Forest S**, Kalah Freeman (F).
Monkton: **Hereford MS**, Brett B. Baier (F).
Parkville: **Parkville HS**, Allen Fleischmann (S).
Potomac: **Winston Churchill HS**, Stephanie Daneberg (S), Michelle Kao (F), Natalie White (L), Can Uran (G).
Salisbury: **James M. Bennett SHS**, Frances Haberstroh (S), Anne Brush (L).
Towson: **Notre Dame Prep S**, Mikella Gallagher (S).
Upper Marlboro: **Queen Anne S**, Joanne Asuncion (F).
Westminster: **Westminster HS**, Kenneth Fischer (S).
MASSACHUSETTS
Attleboro: **Attleboro HS**, Cheryl Gariepy (F), David Leroux (G), Tracey McCann (L).
Bridgewater: **Bridgewater-Raynham Reg HS**, Jennifer M. Booth (L), Jeffrey Cabral (S), Richard White (F).
Byfield: **Trinton Reg HS**, Laura Nastasia (F), Felicia Smith (S).
Deerfield: **Eaglebrook S**, Eric K. Klaussmann (S), Samuel W. Byram (F).
Groton: **Groton-Dunstable Reg Secondary S**, Abby Herrly (L). **The Lawrence Academy**, Ketnna Knuff (S).
Haverhill: **Haverhill HS**, Patrick Hunt (G), Angela Moll (L), Jason Mazza (I), Mark Kalashian (S), Sara Quimby (F).
Hingham: **Hingham HS**, Kathy Mahoney (F), Molly Pitcher (L), Amy Travis (S).
Hudson: **Hudson Catholic HS**, Ellen Martin (S), Christina Stanley (F).
Lawrence: **Lawrence HS**, Marcella Iacono (I), James Wilson (S).
Milton: **Milton HS**, Julie Voveris (F), Maureen Malaney (S).
Needham: **Needham HS**, Nicholas Sterling (L), Katie Henderson (S), Nicholas Sterling (F).
North Dartmouth: **Southeastern Mass. Univ**, Denise La-Flamme (F).
Quincy: **Quincy HS**, Michele Palardy (L).
Randolph: **Randolph HS**, Joanne Pokaski (S), Jennifer Michaud (F).
Sudbury: **Lincoln-Sudbury Reg HS**, Christina Brink (S), Cecily Morgan (L), Sharm Colligan (F), Lukas Barr (G).
Walpole: **Walpole HS**, Pamela Baker (S), Ted Marschke (F), Pamela Baker (F).
Wellesley: **Wellesley HS**, Christine Nuwayser (F), Chris Libertino (S), Christopher Chin (G), Charles Batchelder (L).
West Springfield: **West Springfield SHS**, Christina Lyn Grimaldi (F), Judith Anne Pacitti (G), John Domenic Breda (I), Martha Elizabeth Norris (L), Alfred Charles Rehor (S).
Winchester: **Winchester HS**, Dawn Whelan (S), Lisa Spencer (G), Katrina Nelson (F).
Wrentham: **King Philip Reg HS**, Todd Tomkinson (F), Christy Yatsuhashi (G), Heather Strohl (S).
MICHIGAN
Detroit: **Cass Technical HS**, Christine Pitcole (L), Rochelle Bowen (S), Heidi Schultz (F).
Farmington Hills: **Mercy HS**, Annalisa Raymundo (S).
Fraser: **Fraser HS**, Kim Pollock (F), Jennifer Ann Buyle (S).
Gladwin: **Gladwin HS**, Jean Balconi (S).
Houghton: **Michigan Technological Univ**, Melissa L. Albrecht (G).
Sault Saint Marie: **Sault Saint Marie Area HS**, Georgia Kotsiopoulou (F).
MISSISSIPPI
Biloxi: **Biloxi HS**, Edythe Byrd (S).
MISSOURI
Independence: **Van Horn HS**, Tammie Packnett (G).
NEW HAMPSHIRE
Hanover: **Hanover HS**, Kari van Wrinkle (G), Tina Yen (F), Pamela Bogart (L).
NEW JERSEY
Annadale: **North Hunterdon HS**, Susan Ludwigson (L), Michelle Lipka (F).

Atco: **Edgewood SHS**, Cathy Gately (F).
Bayville: **Central Reg HS**, Shirley Ruzo (F), Renee Borio (S).
Berkeley Heights: **Governor Livingston Reg HS**, Michelle Harmon (S), Asya Rabinovich (F).
Bloomfield: **Bloomfield HS**, Claudio Urriago (I).
Bound Brook: **Bound Brook HS**, Dyanne Ostlind (L & S & F).
Chatham: **Chatham Boro HS**, James Grosjean (G), Peggy Ann Goetz (F), Lisa Thompson (S).
Cinnaminson: **Cinnaminson HS**, Maria Santonastasi (F), William Oppelt (G), Jennifer Bleiholder (S).
Clark: **Arthur L. Johnson Reg HS**, Lori Ann Philipone (I), Jennifer Carrea (S).
Demarest: **Northern Valley Reg HS**, Wendy Brauner (S), Erica Fox (F), Angela Rodin (I).
Denville: **Morris Knolls HS**, Craig McGiffin (F), John Berg (G), Catherine Reese (S).
East Brunswick: **East Brunswick HS**, Robert Tiberi (I), Helen Yoon (L), Rajiv Kinkhabwala (S).
Edison: **John P. Stevens HS**, Brian Henke (F), Matthew Schweber (S), Melissa Newman (G). **Edison HS**, Gail Schwartzbard (F), Susan Proleika (S).
Elmwood Park: **Elmwood Park Mem HS**, Arlene Sethi (S), Salvatore Falletta (I), Linda Perna (F).
Fair Lawn: **Fair Lawn SHS**, Shari Livneh (F).
Freehold: **Freehold Township HS**, Eric Schaer (F), Priscilla Non (S), Christopher Stopyra (L).
Hillsdale: **Pascack Valley HS**, Stacey Lewis (F), Kim Baumbach (S), Lori Morse (G).
Holmdel: **Holmdel HS**, Erica Daniels (F), Celeste Tambaro (S). **St. John Vianney HS**, Andrea Caruso (F), Therese Wicelinski (G), Susan Van Bergen (S).
Iselin: **John F. Kennedy Mem HS**, Frank Carbon (S), Adrian Schmidt (G), Mario Chiavuzzo (F).
Kenilworth: **David Brearly Reg HS**, Susan Buchner (S), Marie Cugno (I).
Lakehurst: **Manchester Township HS**, Philip Prain (S), Teresa Mariano (F).
Linden: **Linden HS**, Debra Pohl (S), William Garone (F), Robert Jenco (G). **McManus MS**, Merari Velazquez (S), Michelle Nowak (G), Cathy Marques (F). **Soehl MS**, Antoine Peck (F), Stephen Szabo (G), Maria Arca (S).
Lyndhurst: **Lyndhurst HS**, Robin Rose Napotano (S), Maria S. Farela (F), Kellie Marie Hart (I), Janice Lee Scillieri (G).
Maplewood: **Columbia HS**, Margo Novak (L), Edna Neivert (G), Pamela Huberman (F), Tiziana Vescio (I), Trusha Palkhiwala (S). **Maplewood MS**, Heather Grossman (F), Deborah Schaaf (S).
Medford: **Shwnee HS**, Sam Fineman (L).
Millburn: **Millburn SHS**, Daren Chapin (G), Melanie Marin (F), Catherine James (S).
Montclair: **Immaculate Conception HS**, Paulette Raney (S). **Montclair HS**, Elizabeth Ford (S), Sonja Cole (F), Carla DeLuise (I), Mora Melican (L), Linda Ulrich (G).
Montvale: **Pascack Hills HS**, Victor Bongard (S), Meg McDonald (F), Michael Barsa (G).
Morristown: **Villa Walsh Academy**, Karen A. Saliter (S), Kathleen Ann Herzog (F).
Metuchen: **Metuchen HS**, Donna Roche (F), Jennifer Manheim (S).
New Brunswick: **New Brunswick HS**, Debbie Walther (S), Joanne Telemdschinow (F).
North Arlington: **Queen of Peace HS**, Indira Perez (F), Karen Petrecca (S), Catherine Viscomi (I).
North Brunswick: **North Brunswick Twp HS**, Anna Lisa Cavotta (I & S), Marina Svetlov (F & L).
Oakland: **Indian Hills HS**, Tracey Monteferrario (S).
Oradell: **Bergan Catholic HS**, Nantha K. Suppiah (F), Nicholas T. Pecorelli (I), Kevin P. Barrett (S). **River Dell HS**, Ann Dabrowski (S).
Palisades Park: **Palisades Park J/SHS**, Hae Kyung Lee (F), Carolyn Dagogliano (L), Stefania Bruni (I).
Park Ridge: **Park Ridge HS**, Melanie Hoeschle (F), James McClane (S), Christina Alphonso (G).
Paramus: **Paramus HS**, Stuart Schweidel (L), Irene Burgas (I), Russell Lipkin (Hebrew), Joan Dolder (G), Tracy Waldman (F), Jill Persico (S).

Parsippany: Parsippany Hills HS, Dorothy Lin (G), Edmond Wong (F), Jonathan Kornreich (S), Caterina Poccia (I).

Princeton: St. Joseph's Prep Seminary, James Reho (S).

Princeton Junction: West Junction-Plainsboro HS, Linda Sun (G), Sean DiGiovanna (F), Jeannette LaFors (S).

Riverside: Riverside HS, Stephanie Sparks (F)

Rockaway: Morris Hills HS, Robin Schulz (G), Donna Russo (S), Tracy Chop (F).

Rumson: Rumson-Fair Haven Reg HS, Corey Oser (F), Jennifer Milmore (S).

Somerset: Franklin HS, Conrad Guardiola (F), Daisy Vega (S), Maren Linett (I), Maren Linett (L).

Somerset: Rutgers Prep S, Cynthia Nacson (F), Ryan Lore (S).

South Orange: Mary Lawn of the Oranges, Maria Viola (S & L), Tzetasi Waters (F). **South Orange MS,** Abigal Joseph (S), Melissa Jongco (F).

Springfield: Jonathan Dayton Reg HS, Susan Lynskey (F), Rita Lombardi (I).

Succasunna: Roxbury HS, Bill Dabelstein (G), Joanne Pinter (F), Denise Dennis (S).

Summit: Oak Knoll S, Sarah Lynch (F), Monica Pelosi (S). **Oratory Prep S,** Robert Merkle (S), Martin Benegas-Lynch (F), Robert Salm (Greek). **Summit JHS,** Steven Pearson (L), Steven Roman (S), Marty Nagle (G), Jennifer Placke (F).

Tinton Falls: Monmouth Reg HS, W. Larry Parker (S), Darcy Terpening (G), Alyssa Wilk (L).

Toms River: Monsignor Donovan HS, Claudia D'Andrea (S), **Toms River HS North,** Christine Thompson (S), Lyndsey Moore (F), **Toms River HS South,** Michael Ilnseher (G), Debra Vandermeer (F), Penni Patton (S).

Trenton: Ewing HS, Jill Edwards (F), Kimberly Borland (S). **Hamilton HS West,** Michelle Gels (G), Christine Allen (I). **Mc Corristin Catholic HS,** Peter Mattis (S) Lisa Krulikowski (F), Joseph Povio (I), Deborah Cleary (L).

Union City: Holy Rosary Academy, Nancy Salvatore (I), Ileana Hernandez (F), Yevette Tierney (S).

Vineland: Vineland HS, Tracey Gressman (F), Mathew Coombs (G), Lorena Iori (I), Thomas Eckbold (L), Magdaly Casillas (S).

Wayne: De Paul HS, Michael Bryne (S).

West Orange: West Orange HS, Brian Reich (S), Mark Policarpio (I), Kim Grossmann (F).

Wood-Ridge: Wood-Ridge HS, David Brian Clayton (L).

NEW YORK

Accord: Rondout Valley HS, Marcie Davis (F)

Conklin: Susquehanna Valley SHS, Kathleen O'Donnell (S). **Susquehanna Valley HS,** Kristina Scalone (F).

Delhi: Delaware Academy and Central S, Robert Warren Barrett Jr. (G).

Elmont: Elmont Memorial HS, Kris Bronars (S), Tamara Calixte (F).

Farmingdale: Farmingdale SHS, Louis Abate (I), Calleen Boyle (S), Eric Piasta (G).

Flushing: John Bowne HS, Juanita Espindza (S), Domenica Carrier (F), Sobbi Freshteh (I).

Franklin Square: Valley Stream North HS, Carmela Leone (I & S), Melissa Dennis (F).

Garden City Park: Mineola HS, Suzanne Glassman (S), Deborah Schnabel (F).

Greene: Greene Central S, Susan Price (S)

Greenlawn: Harborfields HS, Rachel Wifall (G), Nicola Vitkovich (S), Jennifer Fink (F).

Henrietta: James E. Sperry HS, Dawn Pixley (F), Katy Wolitzky (S). **Charles H. Roth HS,** Melanie Quick (F), Kimberly Knittel (S), Jeff Scheuer (L).

Kings Park: William T. Rogers JHS, Craige Luckowicz (F), Ellen Hanley (S). **Kings Park SHS,** Tom Mills (F), Beth Coletti (S).

Livingston Manor: Livingston Manor Central S, Debra Lenkiewicz (S).

Mexico: Mexico MS, Brian Burrows (G). **Mexico HS,** Patty Mondrick (G). **Mexico Academy & Central S,** Jamie Shelmandine (S).

New Rochelle: The Ursuline S, Dawn Dowgiallo (S).

Niskayuna: Niskayuna HS, Andrew Hershon (F), Jordan Katine (G), Christopher Brownsey (L), Paul Bennice (S).

Orangeburg: Tappen Zee HS, Peter Chipman (G), Elizabeth Hayes (S), Manjula Jindal (F).

Pelham: Pelham Mem HS, Elizabeth Fisher (S), Richard Greco (I), Carolyn Pasquantonio (F).

Rochester: Brighton HS, Mychelle Featherstone (G), Holly Bolane (L), Kathryn Fleischer (F), Shari Perlstein (S), Anna Primrose (R).

Rockville Centre: South Side HS, Anna Lancman (F), Michelle Delin (S).

Roslyn: Roslyn HS, Laura Minionis (F), Mark Schattner (S).

Seneca Falls: Mynderse Academy, Kimberly Troisi (S), Stacey Alessio (F).

Snyder: Amherst Central HS, Leticia Gracia (F), Andrew A. Goodwin (G), Sean E. Martin (L), Mary Valentic (S).

Staten Island: St. John Villa Academy, Yolanda Napolitano (I), Sherrie Moona (S).

Valley Stream: Central HS, Linda Gruenthaler (G), Ruth Ellen Vecchio (S), Alice DeSimpliciis (I), James McDermott (F).

Wantagh: Wantagh HS, Douglas Emanuel (S), Jodi Mager (F).

Watervliet: Watervliet HS, Donna Drescher (S), Sarah Lewis (F), Teri Van Leuvan (R), Teri Van Leuvan (G).

West Henrietta: Rush-Henrietta JHS, Loren McBean (F), Thomas Hughes (S).

Yonkers: Saunders Trades & Technical HS, Michele Maffei (I), John Evanko (S).

OHIO

Bellaire: Bellaire HS, Lisa Blazak (S), Jennifer Fisher (F).

Cincinnati: Univ. of Cincinnati, Lainey Kahlstron (Swedish).

Martins Ferry: Martins Ferry HS, Jill Wilson (F).

Toledo: Whitmer HS, Timothy J. Wolf (S), Jean Kim (F).

PENNSYLVANIA

Abington: Abington SHS, Rachel Hogg (S), Michele L'insalata (I), Valerie Yoder (G), Edward Fitzgerald (L), Young-Hee Kim (F).

Aliquippa: Hopewell HS, Regina Hart (F), Corrine Gardner (L), Amanda Rhines (G).

Ambler: Wissahickon SHS, Roberta Susan Petusky (S), Raymond Middleton (Chinese), Lynn Frank (F), Scott Keller (G), Heidi Lutz (L).

Camp Hill: Cedar Cliff HS, Peter Kim (S), Maria Kyriakopoulos (F), Jeffrey A. Bowen (G).

Emporium: Cameron County HS, Laurie Carnovale (G).

Fairless Hills: Pennsbury HS, Darren Carroll (G), Stephanie Segal (S), Christopher Heisen (F).

Flourtown: Mt. St. Joseph Academy, Christine Paul (F), Kathleen Dinda (L), Susan Knasiak (S).

Freeland: MMI Prep S, Farhat Quli (S).

Jenkintown: Jenkintown HS, Jennifer Unterberger (F), Sherry Longstreth (S).

Latrobe: Greater Latrobe SHS, William Ober (G), Lori Reagan (S), Robert Raymond (F).

Lewistown: Chief Logan HS, Scott Casnel (G).

Merion: Merion Mercy Academy, Jodi Capriotti (S).

Newtown Square: Marple Newtown SHS, Kara Raezer (F), Robert Capaldi (S), April Harshaw (G).

Newville: Big Spring HS, Shari Ludf (S), Chrystal Cook (F).

Philadelphia: George Washington HS, Holly Ellencrig (F), Yuri Zalzman (G & Hebrew), Marc Wolf (S). **St. Joseph's Univ,** Joanne Madden (G), Alberto Lago (S), Margaret A. Roberts (F).

Reading: Albright C, Mark Barnhart (G), Barbara Gibbon (S).

State College: State College Area SHS, Kristin Tressler (R), Marguerite Eisenstein (F), Caroline G. March (G).

Stoneboro: Lakeview HS, Shari Shelton (F, S), Brian Reiser (L).

Tyrone: Tyrone Area HS, Terry Lee Branstetter, Jr. (F), Nicole Sultage (L).

Warminster: Archbishop Wood HS for Girls, Laurie B. Spadaro (G), Kristen Shapren (F), Denise D'Aulerio (S).

West Chester: East HS, Tracy Pollard (F). **Henderson HS,** Michael Walsh (G), Sandra Eberle (L), Cheryl Reed (S), Sabrina Yeh (F).

West Lawn: Wilson HS, Tracey Rachlin (F), Sonal Daphtary (S), Carol Berger (G).
Willow Grove: Upper Moreland HS, Christopher Tygh (S), Joshua Hoff (F), Bryan Brendleg (G).
Wyncote: Cheltenham HS, Joshua Goode (S), Joy Stretton (L), Talley Logan (F).

RHODE ISLAND
Cranston: Cranston HS East, Timothy M. Eagon (S), Liz H. Boloyan (F), Kathy N. Brusco (I), Michael L. Forcier (L).
Kingston: Univ. of Rhode Island, John Giovanelli (I).
Newport: Salve Regina C, Margaret Sabetti (S).
Pawtucket: St. Raphael Academy, Joseph Leonardo (F), Lynn Calabro (S). **Tolman SHS,** Grace De Abreu (F), Ana Pais (Portuguese), Paula Wilden Hain (S).
Providence: Classical HS, Miguelangel S'anchez (S), Jennifer Allen (L), Heidi Petrucci (I), David Gehrenbeck (F). **La Salle Academy,** Jeffery Guilbert (F), Thomas Angelone (I).
Wakefield: South Kingston HS, Chelsea Carlson (L), Lara Johnson (S), Joan Shao (F), Michael Friselia (I).
Warwick: Toll Gate HS, Lisa Baute (F), Eric Amelio (I), Jennifer Mills (S).

SOUTH CAROLINA
Spartanburg: Spartanburg HS, Kelly Petosky (S). **Dorman HS,** Deana Hartley (S).

SOUTH DAKOTA
Sioux Falls: North American Baptist Seminary, Cynthia Hodgen (Hebrew), Jeanne Semrad (Greek).

TENNESSEE
Memphis: St. Agnes Academy, Alicia Klyman (F).

UTAH
Hurricane: Hurricane HS, Phillip Snow (G).

VERMONT
Bennington: Mt. Anthony Union HS, Tammy Mclellan (F), Laura Greene (S).
Brattleboro: Brattleboro Union HS, Kathy Koller (G), Heidi Glick (F), Anna George (S).
Essex Junction: Essex Junction Educational Center, Wendi Haugh (F & L).

VIRGINIA
Arlington: Bishop Denis J. O'Connell HS, Melissa Temeles (S), Kelly E. Hollister (G), Elizabeth Duffy (F), Andrew Keyes (L). **Wakefield HS,** Lara Robillard (F). **Yorktown HS,** Jennifer Green (S), Anne Matsuura (F), Betsy Kent (G).
Charlottesville: Albemarle HS, Carrie Weber (F), Shawn Grammer (G), Melissa Hutchinson (S), Thomas J. Hollingsworth (L).
Radford: Belle Heth Elem S, Liberty Ann Boor (F).
Richmond: Douglas S. Freeman HS, Janet Jenness (F), Anne Michelle Mowery (G), Ruth Holsinger (L), Jean Brush (S). **Manchester HS,** Elizabeth L. Peterson (S), Meredith E. Taylor (F), Christin L. Craggs (G), Tanja A. Husmann (L).

WEST VIRGINIA
Fairmont: Fairmont SHS, Rochelle Ribel (L), Jennifer Romino (S), Jacqueline Francis (F).

WISCONSIN
Appleton: Xavier HS, Grant Walter (S), Paul Tetting (G).
Waukesha: Butler MS, Eric Larson (G).

WYOMING
Casper: Natrona County HS, Randy Hanson (G), John Leman (S), Merlisa Bitzenhofer (L), Kerri Richard (F).

Northeast Conference Officers and Directors Since 1954

Andersson, Theodore [Yale U.]* U. of Texas, Director 1954-56.

Andrews, Oliver, Jr., U. of Connecticut, Director 1971-74.

Arndt, Richard, Columbia U., Director 1961.

Arsenault, Philip E., Montgomery County (MD.) Public Schools, Local Chairman 1967, 1970; Director 1971, 1973-74; Vice Chairman 1975; Conference Chairman 1976.

Atkins, Jeannette, Staples (Westport, CT) HS, Director 1962-65.

Baird, Janet, U. of Maryland, Local Chairman 1974.

Baker, Robert M., Middlebury C., Director 1987-90.

Bashour, Dora, [Hunter C.], Secretary 1963-1964; Recording Secretary 1965-68.

Baslaw, Annette S., [Teachers C.], Hunter C., Local Chairman 1973.

Bayerschmidt, Carl F., Columbia U., Conference Chairman 1961.

Bennett, Ruth, Queens C., Local Chairman 1975-76.

Bertin, Gerald A., Rutgers U., Local Chairman 1960.

Berwald, Jean-Pierre, U. of Massachusetts, Director 1980-83.

Bird, Thomas E., Queens C., Editor 1967-68; Director 1969.

Bishop, G. Reginald, Jr., Rutgers U., Editor 1960, 1965; Director 1961-62, 1965, 1968; Vice Chairman 1966; Conference Chairman 1967.

Bishop, Thomas, W., New York U., Local Chairman 1965.

Born, Warren C., [ACTFL], Editor 1974-79.

Bostroem, Kyra, Westover School, Director 1961.

Bottiglia, William F., MIT, Editor 1957, 1962-63; Director 1964.

Bourque, Jane M., [Stratford (CT) Public Schools] Mt. Vernon (NY) Public Schools, Director 1974-75; Vice Chairman 1976; Conference Chairman 1977.

Brée, Germaine, [New York U., U. of Wisconsin] Wake Forest U., Conference Chairman 1955. Editor 1955.

Brod, Richard I., MLA, Consultant to the Chairman, 1983, Director 1985-88.

Brooks, Nelson†, [Yale U.], Director 1954-57, 1960-61; Vice Chairman 1959.

Brown, Christine L., [West Hartford (CT) Public Schools] Glastonbury (CT) Public Schools, Director 1982-85, Vice Chairman 1986, Conference Chairman 1987.

Byrnes, Heidi, Georgetown U., Director 1985-88.

Cadoux, Remunda† [Hunter C.], Vice Chairman 1969; Conference Chairman 1970.

Campbell, Hugh, [Roxbury Latin School] Rocky Hill Country Day School, Director 1966-67.

Churchill, J. Frederick, Hofstra U., Director 1966-67; Local Chairman 1971-72.

Ciotti, Marianne C., [Vermont State Department of Education, Boston U.] Barre (VT) Public Schools, Director 1967.

Cincinnato, Paul D., Farmingdale (NY) Public Schools, Director 1974-77; Vice Chairman 1978, Conference Chairman 1979.

Cintas, Pierre F., [Dalhousie U.], Penn. St. U.-Ogontz, Director 1976-79.

Cipriani, Anita A., Hunter C. Elem. Sch., Director 1986-89.

Clark, John L.D., [CAL] DLI, Director 1976-1978, Vice Chairman 1979, Conference Chairman 1980.

Clark, Richard P., Newton (MA) HS, Director 1967.

Clemens, Brenda Frazier, [Rutgers U., U. of Connecticut] Howard U., Director 1972-1975.

Cobb, Martha, Howard U., Director 1976-77; Recording Secretary 1978.

Covey, Delvin L., [Montclair State C.] Spring Arbor C., Director 1964-65.

Crawford, Dorothy B., Philadelphia HS for Girls, Conference Chairman 1956.

Dahme, Lena F., Hunter C., Local Chairman 1958; Director 1959.

Darcey, John M., West Hartford (CT) Public Schools, Director 1978-81. Vice Chairman 1982, Conference Chairman 1983, Editor 1987.

Del Olmo, Filomena Peloro, [Hackensack (NJ) Public Schools] Fairleigh Dickinson U., Director 1960-63.

De Napoli, Anthony J., Wantagh (NY) Public Schools, Local Co-chairman 1980-82, 87, Director 1982-85.

Di Donato, Robert, MIT, Consultant to the Chairman 1986.

Díaz, José M., Hunter Coll HS, Director 1988-91.

Didsbury, Robert, Weston (CT) JHS, Director 1966-69.

Dodge, James, W., Middlebury C., Editor 1971-73; Secretary-Treasurer 1974-89.

Dostert, Leon E.†, [Georgetown U.] Occidental C., Conference Chairman 1959.

Dufau, Micheline, U. of Massachusetts, Director 1976-79.

Dye, Joan C., Hunter C., Local Co-chairman 1978.

Eaton, Annette, Howard U., Director 1967-70.

Eddy, Frederick D.†, [U. of Colorado], Editor 1959; Director 1960.

Eddy, Peter A., [CAL/ERIC], CIA, Director 1977-78.

Edgerton, Mills F., Jr., Bucknell U., Editor 1969; Director 1970; Vice Chairman 1971; Conference Chairman 1972.

Elling, Barbara E., SUNY at Stony Brook, Director 1980-83.

Feindler, Joan L., Easton Williston (NY) Public Schools, Director 1969-71; Vice Chairman 1972; Conference Chairman 1973.

Flaxman, Seymour, [New York U.] City C. of New York, Editor 1961; Director 1962.

Freeman, Stephen A., [Middlebury C.], Director 1957-60.

Fulton, Renee J., New York City Board of Education, Director 1955.

Gaarder, A. Bruce, USOE, Director 1971-74.

Galloway, Vicki B., ACTFL, Consultant to the Chairman 1985.

Geary, Edward J., [Harvard U.] Bowdoin C., Conference Chairman 1962.

Geno, Thomas H., U. of Vermont, Director 1975-76; Vice Chairman 1977; Conference Chairman 1978, Recording Secretary 1979, Editor 1980-81.

Gilman, Margaret†, Bryn Mawr C., Editor 1956.

Glaude, Paul M., N.Y. State Department of Education, Director 1963-66.

Golden, Herbert H., Boston U., Director 1962.

Grew, James H., [Phillips Acad.], Director 1966-69.

Hartie, Robert W., Queens C., Local Chairman 1966.

Harrison, John S., Baltimore County (MD) Public Schools, Local Co-Chairman 1979, 1983; Director 1983-86. Recording Secretary 1988.

Harris-Schenz, Beverly, U of Pittsburgh, Director 1988-91.

Hayden, Hilary, O.S.B., St. Anselm's Abbey School, Vice Chairman 1970; Conference Chairman 1971.

Hayes, Alfred S.†, CAL, Vice Chairman 1963; Conference Chairman 1964.

Hernandez, Juana A., Hood C., Director 1978-81.

Holzmann, Albert W., Rutgers U., Director 1960.

Jalbert, Emile H. [Thayer Acad.] Berkshire Comm. C., Local Chairman 1962.

Jarvis, Gilbert A., Ohio State U., Editor 1984.

Jebe, Suzanne, [Guilford (CT) HS], Minn. Dept. of Ed., Director 1975-76; Recording Secretary 1977.

Johnston, Marjorie C. [USOE], Local Chairman 1964.

Jones, George W., Jr., Norfolk (VA) Public Schools, Director 1977-80.

Kahn, Timothy M., S. Burlington (VT) HS, Director 1979-82.

Keesee, Elizabeth, USOE, Director 1966-70.

Kellenberger, Hunter†, [Brown U.], Conference Chairman 1954; Editor 1954.

Kennedy, Dora F., Prince George's County (MD) Public Schools, Director 1985-88.

Kesler, Robert, Phillips Exeter Acad., Director 1957.

Kibbe, Doris E., Montclair State C., Director 1968-69.
Kramsch, Claire J., MIT, Director 1984-87.
La Follette, James E., Georgetown, U., Local chairman 1959.
La Fontaine, Hernan, New York City Board of Education, Director 1972.
Lenz, Harold, Queens C., Local Chairman 1961.
Lepke, Helen S., [Kent State U.] Clarion U. of Pennsylvania, Director 1981-1984; Vice Chairman 1985; Conference Chairman 1986.
Lester, Kenneth A., Connecticut State Dept. of Education, Recording Secretary 1982.
Levy, Harry†, [Hunter C.] Fordham U., Editor 1958; Director 1959-61; Conference Chairman 1963.
Levy, Stephen L., [New York City Board of Education] Roslyn (NY) Public Schools, Local Chairman 1978, 80-82, 87, 88, Director 1980-83; Vice Chairman 1984; Conference Chairman 1985.
Lieberman, Samuel, Queens C., Director 1966-69.
Liskin-Gasparro, Judith E., [ETS] Middlebury C., Recording Secretary 1984; Director 1986-89.
Lipton, Gladys C., [New York City Board of Education], Anne Arundel County (MD) Public Schools, Director 1973-76.
Lloyd, Paul M., U. of Pennsylvania, Local Chairman 1963.
Locke, William N.†, MIT, Conference Chairman 1957; Director 1958-59.
MacAllister, Archibald T.†, [Princeton U.] Director 1955-57; 1959-61.
Masciantonio, Rudolph, School District of Philadelphia, Director 1969-71.
Mead, Robert G., Jr., U. of Connecticut, Director 1955; Editor 1966; Vice Chairman 1967; Conference Chairman 1968, Editor 1982-83.
Mesnard, André, Barnard C., Director 1954-55.
Micozzi, Arthur L., Baltimore County (MD) Public Schools, Local Committee Chairman, 1977, 79, 83, 86; Director 1979-82.
Mirsky, Jerome G., [Jericho (NY) SHS], Shoreham-Wading River (NY) HS, Director 1970-73; Vice Chairman 1974; Conference Chairman 1975.
Nelson, Robert J., [U. of Pennsylvania] U. of Illinois, Director 1965-68.
Neuse, Werner, [Middlebury C.], Director 1954-56.
Nionakis, John P., Hingham (MA) Public Schools, Director 1984-87, Vice Chairman 1988, Conference Chairman 1989.
Obstfeld, Roland, Northport (NY) HS, Recording Secretary 1976.
Omaggio, Alice C., U. of Illinois, Editor 1985.
Owens, Doris Barry, West Hartford (CT) Public Schools, Recording Secretary 1983.
Pane, Remigio U., Rutgers U., Conference Chairman 1960.
Paquette, André, [Middlebury C.] Laconia (NH) Public Schools, Director 1963-66; Vice Chairman 1968; Conference Chairman 1969.
Parks, Carolyn, [U. of Maryland] French Int'l. S., Recording Secretary 1981.
Perkins, Jean, Swarthmore C., Treasurer 1963-64; Conference Chairman 1966.
Petrosino, Vince J., Baltimore (MD) City Sch., Local Chairman 1986.
Phillips, June K., [Indiana U. of Pennsylvania] Tennessee Foreign Language Institute, Director 1979-82, Vice Chairman 1983; Conference Chairman 1984, Consultant to the Chairman 1986, 89.
Prochoroff, Marina, [MLA Materials Center], Director 1962-64.
Ramirez, Mario L., School District of Philadelphia, Director 1974.

Reilly, John H., Queens C., Local Chairman 1968-69; Director 1970.
Renjilian-Burgy, Joy, Wellesley C., Director 1987-90.
Riley, Kerry, U. of Maryland, Consultant to the Chairman 1986.
Riordan, Kathleen M., Springfield (MA) Public Schools, Director 1988-91.
Rochefort, Frances A., Cranston (RI) Public Schools, Director 1986-89.
Russo, Gloria M., [U. of Virginia], Director 1983-86.
Sandstrom, Eleanor L., School District of Philadelphia, Director 1975-78.
Selvi, Arthur M., Central Connecticut State C., Director 1954.
Senn, Alfred, U. of Pennsylvania, Director 1956.
Serafino, Robert, New Haven (CT) Public Schools, Director 1969-73.
Sheppard, Douglas C., [SUNY at Buffalo] Arizona State U., Director 1968-71.
Shilaeff, Ariadne, Wheaton C., Director 1978-80.
Shuster, George N.†, [U. of Notre Dame], Conference Chairman 1958.
Simches, Seymour O., Tufts U., Director 1962-65; Vice Chairman 1965.
Sims, Edna N., U. of D.C., Director 1981-84.
Singerman, Alan J., Davidson C., Editor 1988.
Sister Margaret Pauline, Emmanuel C., Director 1957, 1965-68; Recording Secretary 1969-1975.
Sister Margaret Therese, Trinity C., Director 1959-60.
Sister Mary Pierre, Georgian Court C., Director 1961-64.
Sousa-Welch, Helen Candi, West Hartford (CT) Public Schools, Director 1987-90.
Sparks, Kimberly, Middlebury C., Director 1969-72.
Starr, Wilmarth H., [U. of Maine] New York U., Director 1960-63, 1966; Vice Chairman 1964; Conference Chairman 1965.
Steer, Alfred G., Jr., Columbia U., Director 1961.
Stein, Jack M.†, [Harvard U.], Director 1962.
Stracener, Rebecca J., Edison (NJ) Public Schools, Director 1984-87.
Tamarkin, Toby, Manchester (CT) Comm. C., Director 1977-80, Vice Chairman 1981, Conference Chairman 1982, Recording Secretary 1987.
Thompson, Mary P., [Glastonbury (CT) Public Schools], Director 1957-62.
Trivelli, Remo J., U. of Rhode Island, Director 1981-84.
Tursi, Joseph, [SUNY at Stony Brook], Editor 1970; Director 1971-72; Vice Chairman 1973; Conference Chairman 1974.
Valette, Rebecca, Boston C., Director 1972-75.
Vasquez-Amaral, Jose, Rutgers U., Director 1960.
Walker, Richard H., Bronxville (NY) HS, Director 1954.
Walsh, Donald D.†, [MLA], Director 1954; Secretary-Treasurer 1965-73.
Warner, Pearl M., New York City Public Schools, Recording Secretary 1985.
White, Emile Margaret, [District of Columbia Public Schools], Director 1955-58.
Williamson, Richard C., Bates C., Director 1983-86. Vice Chairman 1987, Conference Chairman 1988.
Wing, Barbara H., U. of New Hampshire, Editor 1986.
Woodford, Protase E., Educational Testing Service, Director 1982-85.
Yakobson, Helen B., George Washington U., Director 1959-60.
Zimmer-Loew, Helene, [N.Y. State Education Dept.] AATG, Director 1977-79; Vice Chairman 1980; Conference Chairman 1981.